MAURICE HAYES

♦

MINORITY VERDICT

Experiences *of a* Catholic Public Servant

THE
BLACKSTAFF
PRESS

First published in 1995 by
The Blackstaff Press Limited
3 Galway Park, Dundonald, Belfast BT16 0AN, Northern Ireland

© Maurice Hayes, 1995
Typeset by Paragon Typesetters, Queensferry, Clwyd

Printed in Ireland by ColourBooks Limited

A CIP catalogue record for this book
is available from the British Library

ISBN 0-85640-548-5

CONTENTS

for Joan

Confusion is not an ignoble condition
from *Translations*
BRIAN FRIEL

INTRODUCTION

THIS IS A BOOK I AM NOT SURE I should be writing at all. There is a natural reluctance among civil servants to expose the inner workings of the machinery of government. There is, too, a professional reticence which allows the limelight to be taken by ministers, the statements to be made by politicians. There is a convention that senior civil servants should not write while in office, or for some time after, of their dealings with ministers or with sensitive issues that might affect the public or specific private interests. This can be interpreted as a conspiracy to obfuscate the public, but there is an honourable and sensible reason for it too. Ministers should be able to rely on their advisers. An element of trust, built up over years, assures politicians that in their off-guard moments there was not somebody scribbling notes in the corner and waiting to tell all. And in taking counsel and making up their minds, ministers should not have the added fear that their doubts and uncertainties may be exposed, that their havering between option A and option B or other failures to take advice may be brought up to embarrass them or to prove the omniscience of the civil servant concerned.

And yet the business of government is public business, carried on by human beings. Much depends on human relationships, on who was in a certain position at a particular time, on how he or she reacted to the pressures of circumstances, on how the various actors were culturally determined by tradition, upbringing, education, allegiance or ideology, and on how they reacted to each other.

1

It is important, in a democracy, that the citizen should be aware of the processes involved in running the business of the state. It is necessary also to demystify much of what goes on. The idea of the divine right of kings has long since gone, but there remains a residue of awe and mystery about affairs of state which are thought to be too complex and serious for the ordinary person to comprehend. There are, of course, issues from time to time where secrecy is required but these are few and far between, and are intended to protect society from its enemies rather than politicians and civil servants from embarrassment. I think it is right to draw aside the veil to the extent of allowing serious students of government a glimpse of what goes on, so as to improve their understanding of the processes.

At another level, I can, I hope, hold a mirror up to some of the important events in the recent history of Northern Ireland. No mirror is ever entirely true, no reflection flawless. The quality and trueness of the mirror itself will have an effect, so too will the angle at which it is held, the location and posture of the observer, and the amount of light already available from external sources to illumine the scene. Nevertheless, one person's observations, taken in some sort of context and added to all the other views that are available, may add perspective or depth or detail to an emerging picture. I happen to have been around at a few of the important turning points: the closing years of the old local government system, the civil rights period, the Community Relations Commission, internment, the power-sharing Executive, the Ulster Workers' Council stoppage, the Constitutional Convention and others. In all of these I had a seat more or less near the centre of the action. I was able to observe the participants under more or fewer degrees of stress, and I offer my observations as a help towards understanding some aspects of a very complex period in our history.

I write from memory. I have not had access to papers and I did not keep a diary except for one short period, as I shall explain. I did not keep a diary because people, from time to time, told me the most amazing things in confidence, which I was unwilling to commit to paper. Also I believed that it would not be conducive to the trust that should exist between ministers and civil servants for one party or the other to be running home to write it all down, often in remembered rancour, and sometimes with a degree of hindsight. Neither Richard

Crossman nor Barbara Castle, nor Alan Clark either, can have done much for the collegiality of cabinet government, and many of their colleagues must have wondered what damning observation was being committed to paper to make them look small and the diarist prescient.

The one time I kept a diary was during the Constitutional Convention in 1975 when I acted as an adviser to the chairman. I entered on this as a short-term engagement – six months in the first instance. It looked like an episode that would have a beginning and an end, and with any luck a middle too. It would either work in producing a viable model of government, or it would not. In either case it would be of interest to students of government and to future historians. I also saw it as something outside the ordinary civil service procedures, and I saw my relationships with members as temporary and transient, and not at all like those between ministers and civil servants. In any case, I did not intend to publish the diary, or to use it in the meantime for any purpose. It was to be a source for future historians when the other papers from the convention became available, a document to put flesh and blood on the official records.

I have not used the diary for the present work. In this, for the period of the Constitutional Convention, as for the rest of my working life, I have relied on my memory. Of course, memory can be fallible. But I do have a good ear for conversation and a fairly retentive memory, and I am prepared to rely on both for the accuracy of what I have recorded. What memory lacks, sometimes, is perspective. There is a danger that the order in which events unfolded might be lost, or that several episodes might get compacted into one. In order to avoid this, I have checked my memory where possible against other published sources, and in particular against the Deutsch and Magowan *Chronologies* and against the invaluable *Northern Ireland: A Political Directory* of Billy Flackes and Sydney Elliott.

In Northern Ireland over the past forty years, I have experienced devolved and nearly autonomous regional government, breakdown, direct rule, a devolved power-sharing Executive, direct rule mark 2, attempts at rolling devolution, several attempts to find a constitutional settlement, turbulence, conflict, strife, and a modicum of good administration which kept the place going. This period also saw the decline and fall of local government, the transfer of powers to nonelected boards, the centralisation of power and decision making, and the emasculation of locally elected bodies. We moved across the spectrum from a regional parliament dominated by a single party, when the cry was for 'one man one vote' to a situation when no man's vote in Northern Ireland – and no woman's either – had the slightest effect on the outcome of policy decisions that affected them, and when the only people with electoral leverage who could influence those decisions were the voters in Leeds or Barnsley or Westminster or Norfolk or Bath or wherever the secretary of state for Northern Ireland and his junior ministers happened to hold their parliamentary seats. It was a period too when Europe, scarcely conceived of as an influence at first, loomed larger and larger in the administrative mind, and much of the action shifted beyond London to Brussels and Strasbourg. It was a period too which started in the optimism of postwar Keynesianism and ended in the pessimism of monetarism in the eighties and the fashion for minimalist government in the nineties.

The period from the middle fifties to the early seventies was generally a period of optimism. Not only in Northern Ireland or even in the United Kingdom, it was a time when the planner was in the ascendant, when the answer to a problem was to nationalise it and create an agency. It was the era of the tower block, of the new motorway, the new university, the new town, and the era when slums were cleared and vast areas of land were taken into public ownership. It was a time for regional planning and the direction of industry. It was the age of rapid expansion of public sector employment and the power of the public service trade unions.

Northern Ireland shared much of this optimism and this activity. Schools were built and houses, and new man-made fibre industries replaced the old mills. Things did seem to be getting better in the sixties. The old animosities seemed to be succumbing to the new functionalism. Then, almost out of a blue sky, came the civil rights movement to break the back of local government and ultimately of Stormont.

I do not myself subscribe wholly to the 'fifty years of Stormont misrule' thesis – preferring to regard that period as half a century of lost opportunities, or even, in some senses, of not very much rule at all. For the striking feature that differentiates the periods before and after the Second World War is the pervasive presence of government in the latter period. A.J.P. Taylor once remarked, 'Until 1914 a sensible and law-abiding Englishman could pass through life and hardly notice the existence of the state beyond the post office and the policeman.' The same was true in Ulster, by and large, up to 1939. The state was the rate collector, the policeman on punitive raids against after-hours drinkers or noxious weeds, the customs man on the border, and not much else. There was of course the 'buroo' which was important to many, and income tax, which affected a few, but beyond that not much. The two communities inhabited virtually separate economic and social systems in which they kindled memories of past outrage, attack and dispossession.

Terence O'Neill, in an acerbic aside in his otherwise fairly anodyne memoirs, refers to the public perception of his predecessor Lord Brookeborough, who took a six months' antipodean journey every year (on a shipping line of which he was a director), as a busy man relaxing away from his desk. 'What they didn't know,' said Terence, 'was that there wasn't a desk.' This remark catches, unwittingly, much of the flavour of that period. Brookeborough, I believe, was the quintessential anarchist in that he did not really believe in government. Running the country was something that could be fitted into a few half-days midweek while running an estate in Fermanagh. And anyway it was mostly about security and keeping the B Specials up to the mark, and the party faithful happy and quiescent.

Indeed it can be argued that it was the very adoption of economic and social planning by O'Neill and the use of the planner's tools of quantification, estimation, demographic forecasting and outcome measurement that exposed the conflicts latent in the society and began to impose strains which its members could not bear. Inequality could be fudged or ignored (as can poverty or social disadvantage or poor housing) so long as it was not quantified. When the masses start to read, the establishment is in trouble – when they start to count, the game is up.

I entered local government in 1955 at a time when it had been almost unchanged in powers and functions for over a century, and I left in 1972 when it had almost collapsed in a welter of recrimination about discrimination and jobbery. I think I can claim some credit for first describing the functions of the new district councils set up in

1973 as 'bins, bogs and burials'. I transferred to a civil service that had been through a change of regime, civil strife and disturbance, but still retained enough self-confidence to believe in the possibility of change through social engineering.

In a working life that stretched back to the antediluvian regime of Brookeborough, through the reformist tendencies of Terence O'Neill, to Chichester-Clark and Faulkner and, following direct rule, to every secretary of state from Whitelaw to Mayhew, I have seen and worked through an era of new-town expansionism, through civil rights agitation, through internment, Bloody Sunday, Bloody Friday, bloody every day, politically motivated stoppages, hunger strikes, political talks, talks about talks and the failure of talks, through the terrorisation and intimidation of whole communities, evictions and segregations, bombs, bullets and mayhem, through the collapse of the manufacturing base, economic stagnation and the inexorable rise of unemployment.

What I have also seen are the efforts of ordinary people in communities trying to maintain dignity, to preserve the fabric of social life, to rear their children and to live with their neighbours in harmony. I have also seen and worked with dedicated people right across the public service whose concern has been to keep services running, to provide for the basic needs of the community. These people have tended to put their heads down, to get on with the job. Even then, at the delivery end, to be a fireman or a bus driver or an ambulance man or simply a workman repairing a house in a hostile area required its own level of quiet courage and dedication. Some writers on conflict argue that the question is not why things do not get better in Northern Ireland, but why haven't they got worse. That they have not done so is in large measure because of the very many ordinary people who have kept society from disintegrating simply by doing their jobs.

There is another book to be written about political attitudes within the civil service. My own impression was of a group who tried to be nonpolitical – even when this was a very political thing to do. There was, I think, a tendency to see politics as a dirty business best left to the politicians and to stress the professional ethics of the civil servant as the servant of the government of the day in the best British tradition. But the government of the day was also the government of yesterday and tomorrow and the day after, and was unlikely to change. Indeed, given the nature of things, the possibility of change was seen as heretical if not totally subversive of the normal order. My impression of the Stormont days is generally, and with a few exceptions, of officials trying to restrain ministers, where this was necessary, from the wilder excesses of partisan policies and trying to preserve an administration that would deliver services fairly to all sections of the community, which was a very good reason for sticking, where possible, to the concept of 'parity' that would ensure equivalence in social services with other parts of the United Kingdom.

I think that the great test of the professionalism of the Northern Ireland Civil Service came in the transfer of power when Stormont was prorogued and again when the Executive was set up. There is an argument, primarily founded in conspiracy theory, that individual civil servants regressed to unionist type at the time of the Ulster Workers' Council stoppage, which I do not accept as necessarily true, and to which Bob Fisk's illuminating account in *The Point of No Return* lends little support. Since then, under direct rule, the civil service has tended to keep its head down and let the great political debates about security and systems of government roll on overhead.

I entered the civil service when there were few or no Catholics in senior positions. In my career, I moved from a situation where jobs were just not on offer, and you did not waste your own and other people's time applying for them. There is a double myth dating back to the foundation of Northern Ireland: a unionist myth that Catholics rejected the state and refused to participate, and a Catholic myth that it was they who were rejected and oppressed by the unionist state. The trouble is that both myths are, in part, true. Be that as it may, at the time I was growing up, employment in the Northern Ireland Civil Service was not an attractive prospect for a Catholic graduate, and the local government service was fairly circumscribed too. The position eased slightly in the late sixties, as described in Paddy Shea's delightful and perceptive memoir *Voices and the Sound of Drums*. There was a change of attitude, but very little real change in practical terms, after direct rule.

I found myself very often the only, and sometimes the first, Catholic at my rank as I progressed through the civil service. I must say that I never found any sense of antipathy, any element of rejection, or any indication that I was not a full playing member of the team. We were all in the same boat when it came to files that were said to bear the legend 'UK eyes only', but, oddly enough perhaps, I generally found it easier to get on with 'the Brits' than some of my colleagues from a unionist background, but then nobody had shoved me aside from the levers of power, and I did not carry the baggage of having served, apparently unquestioningly, a regime that was now being blamed for the trouble we were in. There is in the civil service a great sense of collegiality. It might be hard to get in, but once in, so far as I could see, no distinctions were made. I saw all the papers I would have expected to see, and some others I need not have seen, I was able to take full part in discussing sensitive issues, and I believe that on many occasions my views were welcomed as providing an alternative insight or as an antidote to the received wisdom.

I would like to think that I fought my weight. I was conscious of being challenged in many of the posts I held, but never of being over-whelmed. Neither did I find it necessary to trim my own views or to curtail the expression of them. I believe that an administration should mirror the diversity of the community it serves, especially in a multicultural society, and that the debate inside at the policy-making level should reflect the complexity of the discussions outside, and the cares, fears, needs and apprehensions of people of all classes and shades of opinion.

I was lucky to be senior enough, and at this stage self-confident enough, to hold my own in a group whose shared values, developed over the years, were quite different from mine in several important respects. This was a matter not primarily of religion or politics, but of the friendships people had formed at school, the games they played, where they went on holiday, the papers they read, the ordinary staple of daily converse. I could see how a woman could feel discouraged and threatened upon entering the locker-room atmosphere of an all-male society; it is one aspect, I suppose, of the 'glass ceiling', the invisible barrier to women's promotion and advancement.

This book is not intended as an autobiography, but as a comment-ary on some administrative systems when they were under stress, and on the behaviour of the personalities who manned them. I do not deal with my family life or generally with my outside interests, which were mainly in the arts, theatre and reading. There is still, however, the danger, latent in autobiography, of the doubtful imperialism of the first-person singular. I am aware that some of the situations I describe might begin to sound like a one-man band. In most cases, I was acting as a member of a team, the work was the product of communal effort as was the achievement, if any.

I was not, I am afraid, a very conventional civil servant. Perhaps I came to the game too late for that.

1

SMALL TOWN BOY

I WAS BORN IN 1927 IN KILLOUGH, a fishing village on the County
Down coast about thirty miles south-east of Belfast, and I lived
there until I was ten. My experiences of early childhood there I
have already described in *Sweet Killough, Let Go Your Anchor*. My
father, a clerk in the office of the Clerk of Petty Sessions in
Downpatrick whose boss doubled as the dole officer and the part-
time town clerk, was a native of County Waterford. He had arrived
in Killough via a short period as a bank clerk, marriage to my mother
in Dublin in 1916, and service in the Middle East and India in the
British Army in the concluding years of the First World War, or as
we called it the Great War. My mother was a native of Listowel in
Kerry who had married my father whilst she was working in a hotel
in Dublin. When he went off to war, she remained working in
Dublin until the hotel was destroyed in the fighting that followed the
Easter Rising. Unable to get a train to Kerry, she travelled north to
take refuge with her sister who was managing a pub in Killough, and
there she made her home. Her first child was born there and her
sister was widowed shortly after when her husband's ship was mined
in Lough Swilly. The sisters remained together in Killough until my
father returned, late, from the war; my mother took over the pub and
my father got a temporary clerical job in Downpatrick. I grew up in
Killough as one of a family of six, the second or third youngest,
depending on how you count twins, of whom I was one.

When I was ten we moved to Downpatrick where my father was

by now town clerk and my mother had bought a small hotel, where we lived. This she was to run until she died, and we all pitched in to help. I often think that the only work for which I was really trained, and for which I served my time, was hotel work. It was an interesting place to grow up in, with people always coming to the house with news and gossip. What the hotel business gave you was an interest in people as individuals, a respect for them as customers, and a view of mankind at its best when people were enjoying themselves, and at its worst when they were most demanding and impossible. It was a great training, now that I reflect on it, for a career in the public service.

I remember an interview I did on television in the early seventies: David Bleakley was talking to me on a religious programme about my work in community relations. He introduced me, slightly pompously and sententiously, as 'man of peace' and asked me to what I attributed my success as a peacemaker. Unfortunately the live programme came on just after the national news which was dominated by pictures of Belfast in flames as the Irish Republican Army, the IRA, launched yet another bombing campaign. It was not a great advertisement for the success of my peacekeeping efforts. Slightly at a loss for words, I said that I attributed it almost entirely to having had the good fortune to be brought up in a pub. David, a strict teetotaller, did not pursue the point, but I think there is a lot in it.

Downpatrick was a good place to grow up. The town had seen better days, and some of the buildings reflected the glory and commercial importance of the place in the eighteenth and early nineteenth centuries when Lecale, the surrounding barony, had been a rich grain-growing area and Downpatrick a thriving port. The town still cherished its links with Saint Patrick, and an earlier connection with the Red Branch Knights as the Fort of Cealtair, and clung to vestiges of the Normans and John de Courcey in the twelfth century who built Inch Abbey and the Mount, and to Edward Southwell, an improving landlord in the eighteenth century who left the schools and the almshouses in the Mall. We grew up in English Street, a street of gracious and well-proportioned Georgian houses leading from the Italianate red-brick town hall at the bottom, with its highly undependable clock, up past the Down Hunt Club and the courthouse to the Mall, with the old militia barracks on one side and the

Southwell School on the other, to the cathedral of the Holy Trinity and Saint Patrick's grave crowning the Hill of Down.

Downpatrick was the hub of a wheel, the centre of a circle which comprised the peninsula of Lecale, which was largely Catholic, and an area on the other side of the Quoile river, which was largely Protestant. Lecale had been settled by the Normans in the twelfth century as a northern extension of the Pale, serviced by sea and cut off from the hinterland. It was largely a farming area, mainly Catholic, and it had retained a tradition of tranquillity and good-neigh-bourliness that had protected it (as had its comparative isolation) from much of the rancour and strife that characterised those parts of Ulster that had been planted by English and Scottish settlers in the sixteenth and seventeenth centuries.

The town was at the centre of two other population flows. An analysis of family names shows that to the east in Lecale the com-monest names are Norman or Gaelic while, over the Quoile Bridge, to the north the names are predominantly Scottish, and to the south largely English in origin. These differences were reflected in religion too, Catholic, Presbyterian and Church of Ireland.

The result was a rich mix of traditions and cultures in a town redolent of history, and clinging to the past as offering more to boast about than the present, but characterised in the main by an air of tolerance of difference and a willingness to get along together with-out too much friction or open display.

I was educated by the de la Salle Brothers in a secondary school that had opened in 1934 (in a sectarian response, it must be said, to the opening of the county school, Down High, a few years before). St Patrick's, which I attended, was popularly known as the Red High, after the colour of the blazers and to distinguish it from the other school which, for the same reasons, was called the Green High.

The de la Salle order was a French foundation, and although the brothers were usually Irish, they had mostly been all over the world. The school retained some of the French ambience of the founder, and the brothers provided from their experience glimpses of other and more exotic cultures. The fees were very low as the brothers and the lay teachers worked for very little and thereby subsidised the education of the pupils. This was before the days of universal free secondary education. There were a few county council scholarships but, for whatever reason, not many of these seemed to go to Catholics. However, the classes were small, there were some stimulating teachers, and we got a good basic education in the humanities.

Wartime was an exciting period, both at home and at school. In the town there was the influx of soldiers, first British, then American, and the excitement of local people we knew going off to the war, and the sorrow when they did not return. This was mainly a period of blackout and black market, of the attempt to make ends meet and, in the case of my mother, to keep a business running. On the one hand business was booming because of the troops, on the other it was very difficult to get supplies. I became adept at trading in various black markets and in smuggling supplies in from the country area or occasionally across the border on trips to Dundalk or Dublin. This has left me scarred by deep feelings of guilt every time I cross an international frontier without having smuggled something, especially if I have escaped being searched. I am afraid that open frontiers disorient me, even though there is now nothing that I wish to smuggle, and very little point in smuggling anyhow.

My first employment of a clerical nature was helping a small shopkeeper a couple of hours a week to keep his books in order. This involved an entirely new concept in double-entry book-keeping, perhaps even triple-entry. He kept three sets of books: one for the food control to show that he was selling enormous quantities of rationed goods, one for the tax man to show that he sold practically nothing at all, and a third set for himself to show how he was really doing. It was not the worst preparation for the Public Accounts Committee.

My first contact with the public service, apart from devilling for my father, was as a messenger in the Air Raid Precautions service, the ARP. My mother was not very keen on the idea, and advised strongly against my wearing my lapel badge, which had a crown on it, at school. I am afraid that I was motivated more by the prospect of getting a free-issue torch and endless batteries, which were then in short supply, than by any ideal of public service. The main call to arms came after the April 1941 blitz on Belfast, when we were engaged for days in looking after refugees from Belfast and getting them billeted in houses round the area. Country people were amazingly generous and hospitable in taking in these urban refugees, some of whom stayed through the winter and longer. There was the odd upsetting moment when a householder (usually in one of the larger houses) rudely asked the religion of the evacuees before they would take them in. We took some sadistic pleasure in informing them that they did not have a choice, and in then depositing on them the largest, dirtiest and most disruptive family on our list.

It was at this time that I went with my father to the burial of some unnamed and unrecognised sailors whose bodies had been washed up at St John's Point near Killough. My father had some official responsibility to arrange the burial, which was in the cathedral graveyard. As far as I can remember, only the Protestant clergyman attended. What I do remember clearly is that the council workmen, decent men all, who had brought the bodies reverently to burial, set the coffins down outside the door of the cathedral, because Catholics could not go inside to take part in a Protestant service. They were finally persuaded to bring the bodies inside, which they did fearfully and then scuttled out to the comparative safety of the churchyard. My father brought me in with him to join in prayers for the dead. I was often grateful to him for that lesson in Christian charity.

I was at university at Queen's in Belfast from 1944 until 1948. At that time, few of the local students would have aspired to go further afield for a university education. Very few boys from St Patrick's had ever gone to university, there were few scholarships and I was very conscious of moving into an unknown and slightly menacing world, one where I was more likely to be discriminated against and done down than otherwise. It was an interesting enough time at Queen's, with ex-servicemen beginning to come back from the war, but there was not a great deal of mixing. I spent the first three years as a clerical student based in St Malachy's College, emerging only for lectures and the odd game, and that imposed its own restrictions. There was not much intellectual excitement about either. Queen's was a dull and earnest place where people went to get a qualification and to keep their heads down and get out as quickly as possible. It offered very much a continuation of the secondary school curriculum and there were very few exciting teachers.

I took an honours course in English, which at least got me into the library and the stacks, with access to special collections of more interesting books. One of the most stimulating lecturers was

J.I.M. Stewart, later to gain fame as a writer of detective stories under the name Michael Innes. He caused offence in the faculty by suggesting that Queen's should mark the centenary of its foundation in 1845 by purchasing for the library at least a few of the books that had been published in the intervening years. It is perhaps a mark of the narrowness of the curriculum that I was introduced seriously to Joyce and Yeats by an Egyptian student who arrived at the end of the war. Professors generally sought a quiet life by having very few honours students and hardly any postgraduates. There were two honours students in my year in English (which was a compulsory course at pass level for graduation), none the year before and only one the year after. In 1971 Queen's gave me an honorary doctorate for my work in community relations, the only honour I ever coveted, and in my dotage as Ombudsman I returned to study for a master's in Law. I became a member of the University Senate in 1993.

After university, I moved straight into a teaching job in my old school, without very much thought, I am afraid, as head of English, and also, for the first couple of years, teaching Irish. This brought me my first contact with the rituals attendant on public or quasi-public employment at the time. Before the Ministry of Education would sanction my appointment, and before I could be paid a salary, I was required to sign an oath of allegiance to the Queen and her government in Northern Ireland. Most Catholic teachers satisfied this requirement, and squared their consciences that the oath was being taken under duress, by taking the form to a Catholic justice of the peace like E.K. McGrady. He would wander off to the back of his shop and fiddle around at other things while the paper was being signed, and return rather guiltily to append his name. With all the pomposity and brashness of a young graduate I would have no truck with this. I searched out a Protestant JP and made my declaration. Then, rather preciously, I told him that I had made the declaration in good faith at the time, and that if I ever felt impelled to withdraw my allegiance, I would come and tell him. He looked at me with mounting horror and said he did not think that would be necessary, that it was no part of his function and that, in such a case, he would be better not knowing. We had a pleasant discussion about the novels he remembered from his Edwardian schooldays, and the proprieties had been attended to.

I left teaching in 1955 to succeed my father as town clerk, and it is at this point that the present book takes up my story. The only other relevant biographical details are my marriage to Joan in 1967 and the birth of five children between 1968 and 1976; both marriage and children provided me with a very happy and stable family life. We lived in Strangford from 1967 until 1976, which accounts for the location of some of the events recorded during that period. Strangford is a beautiful village situated on the narrows where the lough drains out to the sea. It was homely and warm and welcoming, with great neighbours, and it was a sorrow when a combination of logistics and the oil sheikhs' assault on petrol prices drove us back to Downpatrick, where I have lived since. I was never tempted to move to Belfast, closer to my work. I did not want to live over the shop. I dreaded the closed society that centred on suburbia dominated by civil servants and professionals or by the Catholic middle class. I preferred to meet real people on the streets and in the countryside, to be near the sea and the river and sport and recreation. The children were growing up in a settled community with a good tradition of openness and tolerance, and I thought it was worth a twenty-mile journey each way every day to enjoy all that.

For most of my working life, I have spent almost as much time on outside interests as on work. Mostly these have been enriching experiences and they have enabled me to meet many interesting and stimulating people. From an early stage, I became very interested in the Irish language and in Gaelic games, which have both remained sources of pleasure and enjoyment for me. I tend to get involved in local voluntary organisations and in bodies associated with the arts. My preference is to try to make a contribution for a time and then to move on to something else. This, I believe, refreshes both me and the body concerned. I have been associated with the Arts Council of Northern Ireland in many guises, and particularly in the fields of traditional arts and community arts, with local studies and the foundation of a museum in Downpatrick, and with broadcasting. I was a member of the Broadcasting Council in the late sixties when local broadcasters needed all the help and encouragement they could get to stand up to the censoring tendencies of the Stormont establishment, who wished to suppress coverage of the civil rights protests, or wanted to blame it all on the media. Incidentally, I had an aborted career as a sports journalist when at Queen's. A nice man in the BBC called Kenneth Best decided in 1945 that the BBC should begin to cover Gaelic games, and he asked me to contribute a short notice about each Sunday's games, to be broadcast on the preceding Friday. I submitted the first piece on a match between Antrim and Laois, only to get an embarrassed letter saying that he had been instructed that the BBC could not make any reference to games that were played on a Sunday. Where that left golf, I am not sure. I have maintained my connection with the BBC both as a member of the General Advisory Council and as an occasional contributor.

My entry to my career in the public service, which is what this book is about, came unexpectedly. I must be the only person to have been interviewed for a job at a wake, a procedure that would now outrage the Fair Employment Commission, but there it is.

2
RITES OF PASSAGE

M Y FATHER DIED IN 1955 AFTER a short illness. He had been town clerk of Downpatrick for twenty-one years, and as was the custom of the time, there was a wake in the house for two days before the funeral. And a wake meant just that: a vigil with the body that extended through the night. It was not, however, a ghoulish affair. Friends and neighbours came to sit with the family and to offer sympathy. There was tea and cakes and drink and chat, and prayers too from time to time. I have always thought of a wake as a civilised way of easing the passing for the bereaved. At worst it was a distraction that helped to fill in the time and to occupy the minds of relatives between death and burial. Generally it was more than that, the outflowing of the respect and love of a community, a sense of support and understanding which made the loss easier to bear, and a social occasion on which past kindnesses were remembered and bonds of friendship were renewed and strengthened. I think those people have lost a lot who have moved to the bourgeois respectability and blandness of the funeral parlour and the clinical impersonality of the bereavement counselling session.

As a mark of respect, all the town councillors sat up through the last night of my father's wake, and I sat with them. The conversation ranged widely from football to racing to public affairs, to great issues of life and death and back again to the mundane municipal affairs of houses and sewers and bins and burials. In retrospect it has struck me that I was in a way being interviewed, or at least measured, for a job in which up to that time I had not been very interested. This was partly because it was my father's job and he was fit and well, partly because it was the last thing on my mind in the circumstances of his death, partly because I did not regard myself as particularly qualified for it, and also because I had just accepted, but not yet taken up, a post as Inspector of Schools in the south of Ireland.

At that time appointments were made by vote of the whole council. No unionist-controlled council would appoint a Catholic to senior office, and only Catholics would be appointed by nationalist councils (of which there were only a handful). Indeed the nationalist councils tended to be even more restrictive since they would seldom, if ever, appoint an outsider.

Next day at the funeral a very old friend of my father's, Tom McDonald, town clerk of Lisburn, one of the great men of local government, asked me if I was interested in the job. I told him I had not thought about it, and was likely to go for the inspectorate. He abused me for leaving my mother (who would not get a pension), Northern Ireland, and the town. He then accosted the chairman of the council, then E.K. McGrady (an uncle of the present MP, Eddie McGrady) and persuaded him of my suitability. On being asked whether such an appointment would be approved by the Ministry of Development, as was then required, he said to leave that to him.

The question of ministerial approval was a very real one. Statutory regulations prescribed that applicants for appointment as town clerk should be barristers, solicitors or accountants of seven years' standing, or have appropriate service in local government, or, exceptionally, have 'such other qualification and experience as the Ministry may deem suitable'.

Over the next couple of months the post was advertised and it was conveyed to me by sundry nods and winks that my candidacy would be welcomed. In the meantime I stalled on the inspectorship – much to the annoyance of the Appointments Commission and the aggravation of the Department of Education in Dublin. I gave up on this job even before the town clerk appointment was made, partly because of family circumstances, partly out of a sense of commitment to the North, and mainly because, having become accustomed to the higher level of investment in education and school buildings in Northern Ireland at the time, I did not fancy being engaged in guerrilla warfare

with clerical managers over the state of schools in the south and west of Ireland.

I was advised, however, that I should canvass the councillors. This was the practice of the time, and far from being banned it was actually expected. Even with a reasonably fair wind, I found it a wholly distasteful process. Some people said they would vote for me anyhow. Others, equally politely and very honestly, said they would not. In the end, I was appointed without a further interview, not unanimously but with a substantial majority which crossed party lines. A month later I took up office, but not without making yet another declaration of allegiance, this time without pomposity and with a great deal of levity, at the counter in E.K. McGrady's grocer's shop.

The practice of canvassing which was prevalent at the time was both degrading and potentially an abuse. It applied not just to senior posts, but right down the line to junior nursing and clerical posts and teaching assistants. You could tell the location of county councillors' houses, if not by the better state of the roads leading to them, by the string of cars driving round at weekends and on the clear evenings when teaching appointments were being made. I don't know that there was much in the way of actual corruption, of jobs being bought and bribes taken. It was more an improper exercise of power, the sense of status that an often unlettered, if not illiterate, county councillor enjoyed when a young teacher or graduate had to come cap in hand and virtually beg for a job. I knew a couple of councillors who dined well as a result of canvassing, and many others who regarded it as an insufferable burden.

In the event, Tom McDonald did his work, and the ministry, in the person of Joseph E. Shuttleworth, deemed me suitable.

Tom McDonald was a larger-than-life character who ran Lisburn and the Town Clerk's Association for a generation. Stories about him abound. He had a direct manner, an endless store of expletives, and a gift for the telling phrase. One story about him which reflects the political temper of the time, as well as Tom's irascibility, the greater subservience of the electors and the widespread unwillingness to challenge authority however unreasonable, concerns a local government election held just after the Second World War. Two men in dungarees were filling up nomination forms as the town clerk came past.

'What are you doing here?' he asked.

Touching their caps, they said meekly: 'We're going for election, Mr McDonald.'

'Nonsense. The council is for the solid businessmen of the town, not for the likes of you.'

And the story records, perhaps apocryphally, that they laid down their pens and left.

I was not sorry to leave teaching, but neither was I sorry to have taught. The lasting benefits I gained were the practice it gave me in communicating complex concepts, the confidence to stand up before a group and expound. I think all managers are teachers, trainers, developers of people around them, and teaching was a great preparation for this.

I was thrown in at the deep end in local government. I was forced to learn quickly and from scratch. It was great experience. The first task was to prepare the accounts for the previous year, which were now overdue. In order to do so I had to understand the reason for every payment and the statutory authority under which it was made. It was a crash course in local government finance. I told the man in the ministry, who had been sending increasingly impatient reminders, that it would take me a little time, but that I would submit the abstract at the end of the month. On the last day of the month I bore the accounts proudly to Stormont and laid them on his desk, only to be told, 'You're not the last.' I could have hit him.

I was in fact warmly welcomed and assisted in the ministry, mainly, I suppose because of my father's record, and I made many friends. One very considerate assistant secretary, J.K. O'Neill, took me round and introduced me to people that I would be working with over the years.

At that time there were 73 local authorities in Northern Ireland, ranging from Belfast with over 400,000 inhabitants, to Ballycastle and Keady with less than 2,000. There were three layers or orders of authority, all established under Victorian legislation, and based on boundaries that in many cases predated the nineteenth century. Only the county boroughs – Belfast and Londonderry – were all-purpose authorities; the rural councils had a restricted range of public health and environmental functions, and while urban authorities had no functions in health, welfare or education, they generally managed a varied range of functions in their own areas. The six county councils had been set up mainly as roads authorities and to deal with some wider functions such as harbours, infirmaries and lunatic asylums. These were elected too, but they were in spirit and style a continuation of the grand jury system which had existed since Elizabethan times mainly for the administration of justice, but with no pretence of democracy.

Having led a relatively quiet and sheltered life for half a century, and having lost hospitals and lunatic asylums to the new hospitals authority, the county councils had become the main vehicle for driving forward the most important elements of the welfare state in planning, education, community health and social services. The two county boroughs regarded themselves as several cuts above anyone else, and as having more in common with the larger English local authorities than with any of their counterparts in Northern Ireland. Belfast, in particular, despised the ministries of the Northern Ireland government at Stormont with which it dealt. The city was the product of late Victorian commercialism rather than the custodian of venerated civic values extending over centuries, it was brash rather than urbane; nevertheless, in comparison with Stormont, Belfast regarded itself as the older and senior partner.

This ragbag of authorities with overlapping jurisdictions led to confusion, to ill-feeling and to inefficiency. There was very little contact and virtually no co-operation between the different orders of councils, either individually or in groups. One aspect of the division into urban and rural councils was that market towns were separated from their natural hinterlands. Another factor, peculiar to Northern Ireland, was the fact that towns and their hinterlands often differed sharply in political allegiance. In many cases, if the urban centre was unionist, the rural area might have a substantial nationalist population, and vice versa. Very often the town had sought urban status in order to escape from bondage, as was the case with Kilkeel, a unionist enclave in a largely nationalist area, and with Downpatrick in the other way. One effect of this was to lessen the likelihood, indeed the possibility, of co-operation between the town and adjacent rural district.

Politics in local government could be quite accommodating at the personal level, but was generally confrontational on public or symbolic issues. Majorities were winners: they took the spoils and held the field. Councils were 'won' or 'lost', positions were so well entrenched, heads so well counted that change rarely took place. Offices were not shared, committees, where these existed, were dominated by majorities, minorities knew their place and took the crumbs with as much grace as possible, with a ritual protest at the annual meeting for the benefit of the local press, but not much more. One veteran nationalist councillor, finding himself in hospital for a minor ailment, joked to the nurse when she removed the bedpan, 'I've been on the council for twenty years and that's the first motion I've ever had carried.'

Public goods were part of the spoils and were distributed accordingly. This was particularly true of jobs, especially in administration and at the professional and technical levels. There were very few cases of a council appointing an officer who did not 'dig with the right foot' or who was not drawn from the supporters of the majority party. There was a celebrated case in Belfast in 1942 when the town clerk of Barrow-in-Furness was appointed town clerk of Belfast. He was encouraged to withdraw after a public row when it was discovered that his wife was a Catholic. Notwithstanding the usual manner of allocating jobs, there were many very able men (no women) in local government offices. At a time when scholarships were few, secondary education was limited, and university places were rarely available to the less well-off, local government was an outlet for bright school leavers who could join at fifteen and progress through the ranks. Not everyone was first class: there were many duds and placemen and timeservers, but some of them were very capable and dedicated men indeed.

Housing was a main preoccupation in urban and rural districts (county councils did not have housing powers). Houses were a scarce commodity, much prized in the shortage after the war. Only the public authorities were in a position to respond, and given the housing drive of successive UK governments, housing became almost the most important function of district councils.

In Northern Ireland, apart from the tradition of patronage and the desire to reward one's followers in the distribution of public goods, there was another complication. Under the local government franchise, the vote was restricted to rated occupiers and their spouses, to business occupiers and their wives (who might thus have a second vote), and to the nominees of companies occupying large premises (who might have several more). This had been the position in Britain too before the Second World War, but the changes there had not been reflected in Northern Ireland. These arrangements stood out as increasingly anomalous in a climate where the vote was seen to be an entitlement of citizenship on reaching the qualifying age. The effect of all this was to make housing even more overtly political. No longer was the argument only about the distribution of public goods. In building a house, or allowing one to be built, a council created two votes, and it was important that these should not be used to upset the balance of power. Whether, as in some councils, the winning party took all and houses were built to let only to its supporters or, as in some cases in rural districts, each councillor took a share of the spoils with freedom to dispose of them as he wished within his own electoral area provided he did not interfere in another, housing became a potent weapon in the armoury of the electoral strategist.

It is common, in these days of unionist revisionism, to look back on the postwar period as a sort of golden age for local democracy, with councillors close to, and accountable to, an interested and involved electorate. In fact, once it had been settled which side had won control of a council, and that control was likely to last for years, the prevailing spirit was apathy. In rural areas, only about one third of seats were contested, and the average turnout in those was about 30 per cent. Some seats were uncontested for years and were held as a sort of personal fief by individuals. In county councils, contested elections were even more of a rarity. Apart from which, there was in both rural and county councils a power to co-opt three non-elected members. This was generally used by the majority group to consolidate its position. In Down County Council it produced the ludicrous situation in which the chairman of the council was himself a co-opted member, and the two most powerful committees were chaired by men who had not faced the electorate for years. This did not stop them protesting vigorously at the loss of local democracy involved in any proposal to change the powers of county councils.

Some commentators recently have tended to present this as a simple age of municipal innocence before people became corrupted by politics. John Oliver, in particular, in giving the view from the bridge in the Ministry of Development in the 1960s paints a picture that deserves to rank for romanticism with de Valera's 'comely maidens dancing at the crossroads' in the rest of Ireland. It requires a considerable intellectual leap, and some modicum of explanation, to move from the utopia so described to the riots at the end of the decade.

In urban districts there was rather more activity. The division of towns into wards and segregated housing, or failure to build houses, virtually predetermined the results of elections. In towns like Downpatrick where there were no wards, the electoral system was such that a party that captured over 50 per cent of the votes could, if it wished, take all the seats. To avoid this there was often agreement in small towns to share out the seats without going to the bother of an election. The trouble with this was that it cut out the electorate too. It had the effect of stifling debate on contentious political issues.

Even then, some thirty or forty years later, there was an additional stimulus to separation and to discrimination in the events of the early and middle 1920s. Old habits die hard. The Northern Ireland state had been set up in a hostile political environment, and it was under attack from within and without. This induced a suspicious and defensive frame of mind which soon hardened into a laager mentality among the unionists, who felt that every possible vantage point had to be guarded for ever. There had been fear on the one hand, and expectation on the other that the boundary of the state would be revised by the Boundary Commission, perhaps by transferring a district or even a whole county. It was important, therefore, that district majorities be maintained in order to hold on to the territory. The nationalists' greatest grievance was the very arithmetic of the situation in which they were involved. They were asked to behave as democrats, to accept majority decisions where, in their view, both local and regional boundaries had been rigged to ensure that they would be permanently outnumbered. They had not been consulted about any of this, and they had acquiesced only on the understanding that it would not be for ever.

At the same time, nationalists viewed the new northern administration with scepticism if not actual truculence and hostility, and chose to regard it as temporary and transient. Some councils continued to send their returns to Dublin (as did Downpatrick Rural) and found themselves disbanded and commissioners sent in. When they were reinstated, they found that boundaries had been changed, and that the voting system, and majorities, had been determined for generations ahead.

G.B. Newe, the only Catholic to serve as a member of a Stormont cabinet, once told me a story of being, as a youth in the Glens of Antrim, present at a meeting in Cushendall when some of the older men of the parish asked the then Bishop McRory what their attitude should be to the new government. He told them to ignore it because it would collapse in a year or two. Even in the fifties, I heard a veteran nationalist county councillor inducting a newly elected member who was innocent in these affairs: 'Every time a unionist makes a proposal which involves spending money, get up and second it quickly. For the more they spend, the quicker they'll be broke. And when they're bankrupt we'll get our way.'

Few of these great issues arose in Downpatrick, where there had been a tradition of sticking fairly rigidly to matters that were within the competence of the council, of avoiding contentious political debate, where possible, and minimising the symbolic gestures and posturing that tended to give offence. For some years the council had avoided an election by agreeing a panel of candidates to fill all twelve places, seven nationalists and five unionists, or to put it more crudely, but more accurately, seven Catholics and five Protestants. There being no independents and no other parties, all twelve were returned without an election. Casual vacancies were filled by co-option in a way that preserved the balance. The chairman and vice-chairman were invariably Catholic and there were no committees that did not include the whole council.

There was a similar arrangement in nearby Newcastle, where no elections were held for years until in the late 1950s a controversy arose about a proposal to widen the main street, which transcended sectarian interests. Suddenly the status quo was challenged, an election was fought between the pro-street-wideners and the anti-street-wideners, which the progressives won. It is symbolic in many ways of the dynamic of local government that no action had been taken by the time the council was disbanded and today, forty years later, the main street remains unwidened (and unspoilt).

In the first election after the Second World War in Downpatrick, a Labour vote had emerged and two Labour candidates (who happened also to be Catholics) were elected. That changed the balance of power, with nationalists and unionists having five seats each. Labour voted with the unionists to elect a unionist chairman and so broke the nationalist hold on the office. At the next election, in order not to be outvoted, and to ensure the return of at least seven members, the nationalists put up nine candidates and worked for their election. In the event, all nine were elected. Catholic voters also voted for Catholic Labour candidates and unionist representation was reduced to one. At the next election it was eliminated entirely.

Incidentally, one of these elections was the only occasion in my life when I heard an overtly political sermon from the pulpit at election time. Of course, then and subsequently, one heard sermons about the control of schools or moral issues such as divorce, contraception and abortion, but not often, and these were political in a general sense. There was too the almost ritualistic recital on the Sunday before an election, of the Christian duty to vote, but no direction was given, though some may have made the silent assumption that the audience would know what to do with their vote without it having to be spelt out for them. But on this particular occasion, a rather excitable and eccentric curate preached a 'red menace' sermon against the puny, emerging local Labour Party, and launched a disgracefully vituperative attack on the leader, a devout church-going man who sat through it all: treachery, thirty pieces of silver, and the final shameful peroration that Judas had the decency to go and hang himself. In the event, Labour topped the poll.

The council was therefore Catholic rather than Nationalist, even the Labour members. The only difference was that the Labour members were less likely to look over their shoulders at the parish priest, who was a particularly dominating figure in the community. The nationalism of both groups was only faintly tinged with green, and not all the time. Councillors were not given to excessive involvement in political display or rhetoric. One effect of not having an ideological opposition was that they tended to disagree among themselves, and personalities tended to be stronger than party whips. In fact the only time they were completely united tended to be when there was a threat to remove British servicemen either from Ballykinlar camp or from the Bishopscourt air force base. Both these

27

encampments were important sources of employment for local people, and the servicemen and their families mixed freely in the town and were good customers of the local shops, pubs and dance halls; and many servicemen married local women and returned to settle in the town when their term of service had expired. There was no sense that the troops were an army of occupation, and a nationalist councillor saw no contradiction at protesting at the rundown of the bases. The soldiers were not, of course, involved in local security or in the enforcement of law and order: that was the province of the police or, to the extent that facilities were being guarded or road-blocks mounted, of the B Specials. Full-time servicemen were seen to be a cut above this.

B Specials were generally despised if not derided. They were unpopular with the regular police, who felt that they let the side down, and were unpopular with Catholics, oddly enough, as shirkers who had sought a safe haven in case of conscription which would have involved them in real fighting. I remember one articulate coun-cillor excoriating the local commandant for having 'warmed his arse at the brazier in a B Special hut in Crossgar for the duration of the war' instead of having served in France or the Western Desert.

The aerodrome had been built during the war, when it provided employment for hundreds of men during construction, and fortunes were made by subcontractors and suppliers of sand and gravel. Despite a large investment of public money it never seemed to be operational in any regular sense. Subsequently runways were exten-ded to accommodate larger planes which never came, and the airfield remained as a white elephant of mammoth proportions. At the same time a radar tracking station was developed nearby and the two func-tions combined in a civil and military air traffic control station which played an important part in controlling air traffic across the North Atlantic. The drome was watched jealously from Downpatrick for any change in function, any diminution in status, against the dream that the length of the runways and the fog-free weather would lead to its development as the main civil airport for Belfast and Northern Ireland.

One result of the absence of Protestants from the council was the absence of that voice from the chamber. True, discussions were rarely partisan, and very rarely indeed of an overtly political nature. The councillors believed in getting on with the job, and most of the work was done in public. They were, however, close to their electors who had invariably voted for a religious label, or a personality, and the concerns of their constituents tended to press closely upon them: jobs and housing. They were not in my experience bigoted or partisan or unfair men. They tried to do their best, but they were more aware of the needs and worries of their own constituents than of any other group. In this they were not markedly different from other councillors in Northern Ireland. They did not see themselves as being active in politics in any real way: the divisions at regional level were cast in stone and they simply accepted them, national politics were inaccessible and unattainable given the dominance of the local Westminster seat by the unionists over the years. The absence of non-nationalists on the council was regretted as a by-product of the electoral system (which nobody was rushing to change). There was no wish to discriminate, and a real wish to be responsive to the expressed needs, particularly, of the Protestant churches. It became one of the roles of the officials to ensure that the concerns of unrepresented sections of the community were aired before decisions were taken; the town clerk became a channel of communication, particularly with the churches.

One such occasion arose in 1964 when the Archbishop of Canterbury, Dr Michael Ramsey, visited Down Cathedral for the St Patrick's Day pilgrimage. I thought it would be disgraceful if such a distinguished man could not be received by the council and the efforts of the cathedral clergy to celebrate the Patrician connection with the town could not be publicly endorsed. One evening, after a council meeting, I told the members privately that I understood that the cathedral authorities would welcome some sort of civic reception for the Archbishop of Canterbury, but were afraid to suggest it in case the council was unwilling to respond. The councillors very quickly, and unanimously, expressed a desire to do the decent thing, and left it to me to convey their views to the church. Next morning, in the paper shop, I bumped into the senior churchwarden and told him that the council was very anxious to recognise Dr Ramsey's visit in some way, but were reluctant to make any public move that might embarrass the church or cause controversy. An hour later I had a phone call from the bishop and arrangements were in train. The council met the archbishop in the porch of the cathedral before the evening service. In one sense it was a blow for ecumenism and decency, in another a concession to narrowmindedness. In those pre-conciliar days, Catholics did not participate in Protestant services, and so the councillors, decent men all, withdrew, public duty done, and left the Protestants to their prayers.

I am glad to say that the council representation at the cathedral became an annual, and indeed a normal, event, with full participation in the services as the benign effects of Pope John XXIII's papacy were felt.

One outcome of the visit of Dr Ramsey was that John Doris, the chairman of the council, and I were invited to take afternoon tea with the archbishop at a Church of Ireland study centre in Murlough House, outside Dundrum. He was an immensely interesting and impressive man. On the way in, across the narrow causeway, in the dusk of a March evening, we suddenly found ourselves surrounded by police, which was unusual for the time. In the shadows I heard a voice saying that we were all right, we were from Downpatrick. I asked one of the policemen who I should not have been. He replied, 'Oh, sir, there's a man called Paisley.'

On the way out I made my first contact with biblical fundamentalism. A little old lady who could have been anybody's maiden aunt, with a fur collar, steel glasses and a tight hat, was picketing the entrance with a huge placard which declared, 'THE WHORE OF THE VATICAN FORNICATES WITH THE RAM'.

An interesting feature of relationships with the churches was the lack of any civic culture in the Catholic ecclesiastic tradition. Catholic clergy were so accustomed to ignoring the civic authorities, or inured to being snubbed by them, that even in a town with a substantial Catholic majority and with an all-Catholic council they found it hard, with honourable exceptions, to develop the sort of constructive relationship with the council and its officials that seemed to come as second nature to the Protestant churches. It was noteworthy that on civic occasions representatives of the Protestant churches would attend and participate; Catholic priests tended not to come, to participate with ill grace, and to have little interest in the development of any sense of community or civic spirit that was not based on the Catholic parish.

The monthly council meetings in Downpatrick had developed a rhythm of their own which in retrospect can be seen to verify Parkinson's Law that work expands to fill the time available. Downpatrick was one of those towns where the pubs closed at nine o'clock. Council meetings started at 7.30. By some strange alchemy, council discussions tended to finish at about 8.50, so that members who wished to do so could retire to their favourite pub before the official closing time. A change in the licensing laws in the early sixties which delayed closing time until 10 p.m. had the apparently unconnected effect of prolonging council meetings by another hour.

Council meetings were public in the sense that they were open to the press. Theoretically the public could attend also, but the fact that the room was barely able to accommodate twelve councillors round the table plus a small number of staff and a couple of reporters meant that there was no space left for a public gallery and no members of the public were admitted – save very exceptionally as a delegation or a deputation on some issue.

In these circumstances the role of the local papers was important. They did report very fully the discussions at meetings, and there was a real sense of decisions being taken under public scrutiny and subject to a degree of accountability. This was, I have often reflected, one of the main differences between working as a senior officer in a local authority and as a senior civil servant. In local government, advice was given at meetings in the presence of the press. The whole town knew who had advised the council on some particular course of action or dissuaded them from some other. Human nature being what it is, and the public taste for scandal and recrimination, the bad advice was more often remembered than the good, the disaster more often than the unspectacular gain. But there was a sense of taking responsibility for what you had to say, no hiding behind an unpublished and unseen minute in a ministerial brief or the opaque protection of the doctrine of ministerial responsibility.

When I started, I discovered that there was an arrangement whereby newspaper reports were cleared at proof stage by the town clerk. This, I am satisfied, was an effort by the newspapers to ensure accuracy or to avoid the possibility of libel and not an attempt by the council to impose censorship. In either event, the dangers of the practice were obvious and I stopped it. I was content that the

31

journalists should be able to check their notes against the draft minutes before publication, but otherwise I thought it important that they should be responsible for presenting their own view of the proceedings.

Local councils were accountable in other ways too, in being close to the people and in the impact of the rates. Costs were contained because the impact was immediate and apparent. The office was modest – the citizens would not have stood for grandeur, and the staff was small – a typist was the equivalent of a sixpenny rate. Striking the rate was a serious business for the councillors, who agonised over a halfpenny increase, knowing that they would be accosted in the street by irate ratepayers on the first sound of the increase. In a way they were too cost-conscious. Downpatrick had boasted of being the lowest-rated town for some years. There had occurred, some years before, the unusual spectacle of the townspeople (or at least the business people) giving a dinner to the councillors for their success in keeping the rate low. Of course, if there is no expenditure, even on essential works, the rates will not rise. But what faced the council in the fifties was a backlog of work on water and sewerage schemes, on housing and redevelopment, much of which might have been done earlier, and which had now to be tackled. Recreational provision was nonexistent, and little attention was paid to the environment.

I remember once, as a teenager, helping my father in his office one day and remarking how lucky he was not to have a boss. He pointed to a woman walking down the other side of the street. She was poorly dressed, slatternly and down-at-heel, and she was rather looked down on in the town because of her lifestyle. 'Do you see that lady?' he said. 'She is a ratepayer. She is my boss, and there are a thousand others.' I never forgot that lesson in accountability.

3

'GODS MAKE THEIR OWN IMPORTANCE'

D OWNPATRICK AT THE TIME WAS JUST beginning to pull out of
its century or more of decline. It had begun to find itself
again as the war revived agriculture, and the construction
of aerodromes and army camps provided employment. The building
of schools and health service developments after 1948 provided
a new role for the town, a new sense of purpose, and an increasing
number of steady, well-paid jobs. The town's population, which had
peaked in the 1820s and declined steadily for over a century, was
rising again, though it would not reach the 1826 level again until
the 1960s.

The 1947 Education Act was a stimulus to growth. The town
became an important centre for education for the surrounding area,
new schools were built, there were jobs for teachers and ancillary
staff, who needed houses, there was a small influx of graduates, and
more money in the local economy.

The welfare state was good for Downpatrick. In addition to the
schools, the extension of the local hospitals was to provide a pool of
secure and well-paid jobs which provided a degree of economic
stability. Both the first and second industrial revolutions had passed
the town by, but it still had a lot going for it. A particular advantage,
which was to stand the test of the troubled times ahead, was a decent
and tolerant people, a tradition of good-neighbourliness, and an
absence of rancour and overt conflict. The confluence of the traditions that had formed the personality of the area were symbolised in

the meeting at the town hall corner of English Street, Irish Street and Scotch Street.

The 1950s saw the start of a consistent programme of public works. The main social problem was bad housing, and the council tackled this as a first priority. Downpatrick had been one of the first councils to adopt a points scheme for the allocation of houses. Like all such schemes, it was fair, provided you agreed with the criteria on which it was based. In Downpatrick the main problem was overcrowding and it is not surprising that the scheme favoured those with large families. There was also a bias in favour of local residents, again not surprisingly as councillors were reluctant to face the opprobrium of housing 'blow-ins' while their own long-suffering neighbours and constituents were unhoused. Although objectively based and intended to be so, the scheme had the effect of favouring local residents with large families – who tended to be Catholic. Partly for this reason, and partly for the less worthy one of lack of councillor control over the outcome, the scheme was dropped in the middle of the 1950s. It had exemplified the difficulty in framing any scheme for the distribution of scarce public goods that does not become impossibly rigid and that does not produce undesirable counter-effects which had not been anticipated or intended. Not to have a scheme at all proved to be equally undesirable. Allocation meetings became interminable wrangles and anomalies that could not be explained or justified by any reasonable standard were an embarrassment. Nor did it make life any easier for councillors. People who had been allocated houses regarded that as no more than their entitlement, and were rarely thankful, while the much greater number who had not been successful excoriated the council for not having housed them.

All this created trouble for officials too. Councillors, like most Irish public representatives, had a habit of not putting people off with a bad answer. It was easy to promise support individually to all comers. Unsuccessful applicants were mystified when, having canvassed the support of all councillors and being promised a vote by each, they were not ultimately successful. Neither were the councillors, human nature being what it is, too anxious to explain the reasons for their defection, or for the applicant's failure. 'Well, I voted for you anyway' was easy to say. One result of this was the harassment of officials who could be cornered in the council office, with no chance to escape up the nearest alleyway. In the end, without breaking confidences, we were reduced to explaining the arithmetic of the allocation system: 'If seven councillors vote for you, you get a house, if only five, you don't.'

As a result of all this, there was strong official pressure on the council to adopt again a points allocation scheme. Councillors too saw the mess they were in and the difficulty in justifying the way in which decisions were made and some of the outcomes. In the end, they introduced a modified form of the original scheme, intended to be more flexible, to cater for families of different sizes and in different circumstances, and to give more weight to health problems and disability and slightly less credit for length of residence in the town. It was not perfect, but it was a great improvement on arbitrary choice or political muscle, and it was at least defensible as an attempt at objectivity.

Not that it always worked in that way. Brian Faulkner was MP for the area and he received many representations from applicants to support their case for housing. He dealt very fairly with these, sending the letter on to the council and asking what the prospects were of the person being rehoused. It was a great convenience to be able simply to compute the applicant's points, and to say how many were currently required for success in that particular category. Faulkner would transmit this information to his correspondent as a fair statement of the position. Nevertheless, if that person got a house in the normal operation of the scheme, such is the Irish belief in the power of 'influence', of the 'focal sa chúirt', of the obsequious knock on the back door of the Big House, that this outcome would be attributed not to the fairness and objectivity of the system, but directly to the intervention of the MP.

The council was still almost alone in Northern Ireland in operating a points system, and it was increasingly a comfort as house allocation became a bone of political contention, as councils across Northern Ireland were accused of discrimination and as the civil rights movement of the late sixties articulated an increasing demand for the fair allocation of public housing.

The Housing Trust, set up by the Stormont government after the war to build public housing across Northern Ireland, did not build any houses in Downpatrick urban district, mainly for want of space, and because the council itself was so actively engaged in public housing. It did, however, build extensively in the rural district just outside the urban boundary. The Housing Trust operated a more flexible letting policy, catering for incoming workers and for smaller families. The result was that the trust estates tended to be predominantly Protestant and the council estates predominantly Catholic – the beginnings of separation in a town that had not been marked by division of this sort. In addition, the trust operated a housing management policy in which suitability as a tenant and compatibility with neighbours were more important criteria than housing need, and this introduced a class difference in the estates also. This was both a strength and a weakness of the Housing Trust. It could point to spotlessly clean estates where there was little trouble between neighbours and contrast this with some of the council estates. What they did not notice was that they had removed from the council estates the standard-setting tenants, the Joneses with whom other people might have tried to keep up. These factors were not as marked in Downpatrick as elsewhere, but they illustrate some of the factors that have led in many Ulster towns to the segregation on which sectarianism breeds.

Another factor that tends to encourage segregated housing is the separate school system. Mothers want to be able to leave their children to school and to have them within easy walking distance. If there are separate denominational schools, inevitably the Catholic families will cluster round the Catholic school and church and the Protestants round the state school. In order to prevent Downpatrick segregating in this way, we hit on the idea of encouraging all the schools to locate on or about the same central campus. The Catholic church authorities would have accepted this in principle, but the county education committee people would have none of it (for no very serious reason other than that they always preferred to do their own thing) and so the schools were located at opposite ends of the town.

I remember the town clerk of Lurgan telling me with some satisfaction how the council there had met the wishes of the parish priest by building houses near the Catholic church and schools and allocating them to Catholics. As a result, Lurgan became a segregated and deeply divided town with the fault lines running down the middle of the main street, a recipe for the trouble which was to erupt a few years later.

One feature that has struck me increasingly over the years is that Ulster Protestants do not seem to be happy living in an area where Catholics are in the majority. Middle-class Catholics are content to live in middle-class Protestant areas; perhaps to do so is a confirmation of upward social mobility. Middle-class and professional Protestants, on the other hand, tend to move out and re-establish themselves among their own – from Malone Road in Belfast to Cultra, from the Cityside in Derry to the Waterside. This rather dents the theory that sectarianism in Northern Ireland is a working-class phenomenon.

One example of the classic tension between positive discrimination intended to benefit a disadvantaged group and fairness to the individual adversely affected by it arose in the treatment of casual housing vacancies in Downpatrick. Generally, when a tenant died the house would be allocated to a surviving family member living in the house. This was a means of preserving community links and encouraging stability. Often, however, there were no surviving relatives. In these cases, or when the previous tenant had simply moved away, the house was available for letting. The councillors were aware that if these vacant houses were allocated on a points system they would almost certainly go to someone with a large family and more than likely a Catholic. They were anxious not to appear to be discriminating against Protestants, and they were anxious to maintain at least the existing number of Protestant tenants and a mixed community in council estates. They therefore adopted a policy that in casual vacancies, a Protestant tenant should be replaced by another Protestant. There was an 'A' list and a 'B' list, and allocations were made, on some judgement of need, from within each list. This was ostensibly fair, although not publicly discussed. It soon produced the ridiculous situation where a house on the 'B' list was allocated to a single person with no dependants, because there was no other eligible applicant, while a large family living with in-laws in overcrowded conditions could not be accommodated. Much against their will, since they feared being accused of discrimination against Protestants, the councillors were persuaded to drop the policy and to allocate all houses on the points system.

There was a similar difficulty in relation to transfers. Tenants often wished to transfer to another house – perhaps for an extra room, or for a smaller house, or to be near parents, or work or school. This resulted in a drift of Protestants to one end of the town, and the council, anxious to avoid a divided, segregated town, tried to resist the movement by refusing transfers that would tend to increase segregation. Unfortunately, at the time the policy could not be openly stated, it was difficult to defend in individual cases, and it had to be dropped. It does show the difficulty of trying to interfere with the free choice of people, and of trying to change attitudes by social engineering.

Although the council was a multipurpose authority, housing took up about half of its officers' time. Housing, too, was by far the most satisfying activity to be engaged in. There was a sense of completeness in conceiving the scheme, buying the land, briefing the architect, letting the contract, watching the houses grow, taking possession, allocating tenancies and seeing the thing through to completion over a period of two or three years. There was also the satisfaction in seeing the improvement in social conditions and the way a family was able to flower and prosper when taken out of overcrowded, insanitary conditions and given a new house. This was often seen in a sense of well-being, a greater take-up of educational opportunities and a general rise in the standard of living. I became firmly convinced that the recipe for social stability was for people to have jobs, a good house, and a stake in the community. Although I personally approved of the state providing houses, I soon reached the conclusion that it would be better in the long term to give them away to tenants – both in ensuring continuity of occupation and stability in estates, and in giving people a sense of property and belonging. It would also avoid the costs of maintenance and repair which were bound to escalate over the years. These were not popular ideas.

I thought too that in any case, there should be a balance between local authority housing, owner-occupied housing, and houses built privately for letting. In an ideal world there might be equal proportions of each. In the event, private houses for letting had been virtually extinguished in Northern Ireland by successive Rent Restriction Acts (another example of a high-minded policy having a perverse outcome) which over-protected tenants and made letting an unprofitable exercise. Downpatrick at the time was not prosperous enough to provide many owner-occupiers, and in any case the boundary was so tightly drawn that the better sites were in the rural district. This meant that by the late sixties over 60 per cent of the dwellings in the town were council-owned.

This trend had been exacerbated by redevelopment. As a declining town, Downpatrick had large areas of substandard but overcrowded housing. These were small houses in narrow streets of great character with local names like the Gullion, the Shambles, Back Lane, Mary's Lane, Gaol Wall, Pound Lane, Saltbox Row, Fountain Street. Downpatrick was early in the field after the passing of the 1956 Act that facilitated large-scale redevelopment and slum clearance. Unfortunately this was the period in which complete clearance was in fashion. Admittedly it would have been difficult to rehouse people at the densities of the old small holdings, but nobody tried very hard to do so. Housing standards and the space required about houses were laid down by regulation and it was hard to challenge them. It was only later, when the Northern Ireland Housing Executive assembled its own expertise, that these regulations were challenged and house types were varied. Councils generally worked with private architects who had limited experience and relatively small offices, who wanted the fees to be based on repetitive house types, and who were content to go by the design manual. Councils too did not have somebody like Charles Brett, a forceful and gifted man with a great feel for architecture and design, who later, as chairman of the Housing Executive, took public housing by the scruff of the neck and imposed standards of design and layout that were vernacular and sympathetic to existing townscapes. In Downpatrick we were lucky enough, in redevelopment, to avoid the worst excesses of high-rise building, but we did – and I much regret it – clear whole streets of character which had made the town what it was. No attempt was made at rehabilitation. I don't think it crossed anybody's mind to think of it, and in any case the subsidy structure favoured new-build, and the people wanted new houses and not old ones tarted up. The majority of houses were admittedly beyond recall: too small, of poor construction and badly sited. But some few could have been saved and the street patterns could have been respected and traditional views and townscapes preserved and maintained.

We did try to keep communities together and we were mainly successful in this, and in maintaining as far as possible the links between elderly people and their extended families. People did get better housing, conditions were improved and health and well-being were encouraged. Given the hindsight of years of experience, however, it could all have been done more sympathetically.

The relationship between chairman and town clerk is a key one in any local authority. While the officials are there to serve all the members and no single party, the chairman is the key figure, both in procedures and in ensuring the efficient disposal of the public part of the business. His personality too will have a great bearing on the way in which members behave – amicably or with animosity, and since his is often the public face of the council, it helps if it is a restrained and dignified one. I was fortunate to work with four exceptionally good chairmen, all of whom, in their different ways, put their stamp on the office and on the town.

My first chairman was E.K. McGrady, who had held office with only a couple of breaks for the best part of two decades. He was also a member of the county council and many committees and boards, and had run unsuccessfully as an Anti-Partition candidate against Brian Faulkner when he was first elected in 1949. He was very experienced in local government, a man of stature and of grave courtesy. He took his duties very seriously, and spent every Thursday afternoon (his half-day from his grocer's shop) reviewing the business of the council and the agenda for the next meeting.

His method of presiding at meetings was masterly, aided by a slight deafness, which I thought was tactically intensified from time to time. He had an innate sense of when it was appropriate to put the question and when to rein in a member who was going too far. During an irrelevant or rambling discussion in which he was not interested, he would sit back at the top of the table discussing the previous Sunday's football match with me, and then, at precisely the right moment, he would intervene to say that the subject had been sufficiently discussed. He was a wise and decent man and I owe him a lot. I learned much from him about handling meetings and committees and the interaction of agencies and bodies.

We lost E.K. McGrady's valuable experience as chairman as a direct result of our first redevelopment scheme. McGrady owned a public house right in the middle of the redevelopment area. When plans were first mooted, the redevelopment acts provided protection for the holders of liquor licences, with a guarantee of a new licence without the necessity to prove need. Subsequently, and before the Downpatrick scheme was finalised, a more restrictive regime was introduced: publicans affected by redevelopment no longer had an absolute right of renewal, they could bid for one of a restricted number of new licences in the area, but with no guarantee of success. And they had no right to a new licence elsewhere. The gossip in the trade (both licensed and local government) was that the change had been effected following pressure from the Licensed Vintners' Association, which was dominated by Catholic pub owners in the upper Falls, who did not wish to see their smaller inner-city rivals following their displaced customers to Ballymurphy and Andersonstown. They were reputed to have made a sizeable contribution to Unionist Party funds. In any case it meant the end of the chairman's pub and the chairman, who, having very honourably presided while the council carried through the preparations for vesting, resigned from the council in order to oppose the proposals at the public inquiry. In fairness, his concern was not about money, but about the great symbolic value of the licence, and about the little pub he ran in the evenings as a club for his friends and neighbours.

E.K. was succeeded by John Doris, a chemist and a nationalist, who died suddenly in office. A former athlete of note, he was a man of great compassion and decency with a wonderful sense of humour and a loud ringing laugh. He was a man of inventive mind and a very keen photographer. Many of our discussions on policy took place in his darkroom as he developed films. He was a justice of the peace too, and, being the JP living nearest to the police station, was often called upon for special courts or to remand people. I remember once accompanying him when a soldier was being charged with rape. He spoke to the victim, trying to make it as easy as possible for her, and to ensure that she understood what was going on.

'Just tell me, daughter, in your own words, what happened.'

The victim, a country girl, replied with Chaucerian brevity and bluntness: 'A sojer rid me!'

Eddie McGrady, later the MP, was by far the youngest chairman. He had, in fact, been a pupil of mine. He was, I think, the best chairman I ever sat with for getting through an agenda in an orderly and methodical way, and in briefing himself for the business. When he withdrew as part of the civil rights protest following internment, he was succeeded by Jim Clements, who had been chairman for a spell as a unionist in the late 1940s and had since been re-elected as an independent. All of them were first-class chairmen, honourable and able and a pleasure to work with. All made a point of discouraging party political attitudes and ideology in the discussion of urban affairs, and the council was remarkably free from acrimony.

Whilst the council was virtually all nationalist in the 1950s, the 1960s saw the emergence of a number of independent councillors, some of whom, paradoxically enough, formed a group. In the first instance, two popular GPs sought election and topped the poll, one a Catholic, one a Protestant. It became more fashionable to stand for the council, and at the next election five independents (three Protestants and two Catholics) were returned along with a liberal and a unionist, the remainder of those elected being nationalists. This formed possibly the best council I worked with, one that operated harmoniously and with much mutual respect, and which raised the tone of public debate about issues and improved the image of the council as a body dedicated to the welfare of the town and likely to get things done.

When I joined the council, and for most of my time there, it had a very small staff: the town clerk and an assistant who doubled as a secretary/bookkeeper and a part-time surveyor, an abattoir manager, a part-time rate collector and a part-time rent collector who was paid on commission. Over the years we added a typist (and the assistant became finance officer), a housing manager and a couple of rent collectors.

There was one office, which was open to the public. This had drawbacks in the way that business was conducted, and in a lack of privacy, even when this was necessary and desirable. The bonus was in the first-hand contact with the consumer, an immediate contact with the needs and desires of the customers that obviated the need for opinion polls. We didn't need them, we heard it all too often from the horses' mouths.

Administration had not advanced much beyond the steel pen. The legal basis for the work was laid down in the Towns' Improvement Acts and the Commissioners' Clauses Act of the 1840s and in the 1878 Public Health Act. Forms and procedures were prescribed by the Public Bodies Order of 1904. I remember being struck on my first day with the convention of ending letters to the Ministry of Development with the obsequious *envoi*: 'I have the honour to remain your obedient servant'. I did not see why I should profess to be anybody's servant, much less an obedient one, and I simply substituted 'Dear Sir . . . Yours faithfully'. The roof did not fall in, affairs continued to be administered, and gradually the other side responded in like terms and we progressed to 'Dear Mr . . . Yours sincerely'. Hardly earth-shattering, but little straws in the wind of change. One convention I could never warm to was the use of surnames in address. I never wanted to be 'Dear Hayes' and to be addressed by my surname in conversation always irritated me, as indicating that the speaker was patronising me or speaking down to a social inferior. This I know is oversensitive, but as my grandmother used to say, 'You can't wipe out centuries of serfdom in a single generation.'

Whilst the shortage of money and the small staff meant that the council operated as economically as possible, there was very little concept of managerial efficiency. Audits were held to ensure financial probity and that councils operated strictly within legal limits. The doctrine of *vires* was supreme. Anything not placed specifically on councils as a duty by statute was *ultra vires*, and councillors and officials indulging in such activity, however laudable, sensible or beneficial, laid themselves open to surcharge or worse. No council could incur expenditure in excess of £100 without the prior written approval of the Ministry of Development. All of this was a curb on activity and the imagination and discouraged councils from taking a lead in the development of their areas.

The stress on the legality of actions meant that the audit was conducted as a legalistic scrutiny of correctness rather than as a review of efficiency or effectiveness. Auditors tended to have a legal rather than accountancy qualification. This was lucky for me in that my first local government auditor was a civilised man called Maurice Collis, one of the distinguished Dublin medical family, a distant descendant of the eponym of the Colles fracture, and a cousin of the travel writer of the same name. He was much more interested in books than in bookkeeping and this suited me since I knew a good deal more about literature than public finance. He had served in the First World War and a very touching ritual took place each year at the close of the audit when two local ex-servicemen who had been in his unit in France turned up to see 'Captain Collis, sir'. Having signed the books, the auditor would take off with them for a drink. I might still see his car parked outside the office at nine o'clock that evening.

The audit was conducted in the public office, along with the other business. Once when I offered the auditor the comfort of a private room in the council chamber, he declined saying, 'But I meet the most interesting people in your office.'

My work was enjoyable and very satisfying – more, I think, than any other job I did. But as I grew into it and learned the ropes, it ceased to engage me fully. I would have gone to seed if it had not been for some outside interests. Some of these were associated with work or were an extension of it, others were quite different, spare-time or hobby pursuits, but none the less rewarding for that.

Part of the problem was the inability to progress. Unionist councils did not employ Catholic town clerks. It was as simple as that. In any job, one should have the prospect of advancement, the proverbial field marshal's baton in every soldier's knapsack. In local government, this meant moving from a small town to a larger one, and so on to the higher reaches of the profession. But religion was a block. Nor was it any better in Catholic-controlled councils: these tended to be in small towns anyhow, but they also had a strong tendency to appoint only locals.

At one stage, I thought of moving to one of the new town commissions, which seemed to herald a new era of physical planning and development, a manifestation of the new vision of Terence O'Neill, and a departure from the old habits. I applied for a post with the Craigavon new town and did not get an interview. In conversation later with the chief planning officer of the Ministry of Development, an engaging and witty Scot called James Aiken, he let me know that he knew about my candidacy, but he opined that while I knew a lot about local government and planning I was not strong enough on Bible studies. *Plus ça change!* I did get an interview for Ballymena/Antrim, but no appointment. For a senior post in Down County Council, among people who knew me and were accustomed to ask my advice at member and officer level on local government law and procedures, for the most senior job they had advertised in years, I had a perfunctory interview which lasted less than ten minutes, and no appointment. County councils were almost the last strongholds of privilege in Western Europe. People were 'got into' the Courthouse, which was the equivalent of Myles na gCopaleen's 'Guinness clerkship of the third class', a soft sitting-down for life. Boys and girls who had failed exams in the county school were spirited into jobs without advertisement or competition, and people who had failed in business or other walks of life, or who had retired from other pensionable occupations, found rest and recreation there and gainful employment – so long as they were the right sort.

I remember one conversation in a men's toilet after a conference dinner. A well-known and colourful chairman of Antrim County Council, Millar Cameron, a buccaneering character, a supporter of O'Neill and one of the early adherents to Alliance, whom I had got to know well through my work on committees, told me in what I suppose was meant as a compliment, and kindly meant, but I thought it patronising, about an appointment to a senior post with his council: 'I told them there was an honest pape in Downpatrick they should look at.' Slightly bitterly I asked him which of those categories the Antrim County Council had found the more off-putting – honesty or papacy. Shortly afterwards I applied for an assistant town clerk job in Belfast without, I think, getting an acknowledgement. The successful applicant, a good friend, Bill Johnston, who subsequently became town clerk of Belfast, said to me one night, 'I hear you were looking for my job in Antrim.'

'No, Billy,' I said. 'I was looking for your job in Belfast.' He simply roared with laughter that anybody could be so naïve.

Put down like this it all seems like bottled-up bitterness. It is not, or was not like that. I record it simply to exemplify the rigidity of the system, and as a bench mark against which may be measured subsequent changes in attitudes and opportunity. At the time I was, I think, phlegmatic – not sure that I wanted to leave Downpatrick, where I was happy and satisfied (and single, without family responsibilities) but anxious to test the system for change from time to time, pushing out the walls of the room, like a beaver waiting for the dam to burst, a salmon waiting for the spate to bring him upstream. But at least I had a job. This gives an idea of the frustration that was experienced by those who had neither jobs nor prospects, and which was to build

45

up into the head of steam that propelled the civil rights movement on to the public stage and blew down the whole house of cards.

My reaction, not a conscious one, I think, but a form of compensation, was to develop other interests both inside and outside the job. Work with the council tended to be cyclical around the monthly meeting, or yearly about the time for estimates and striking the rate, and there were other times, once a reasonable system had been established, when things tended to tick over. This allowed for a good deal of flexibility in the way the job was tackled, and a town clerk who had good relations with his council, who kept things going, and dealt with any unforeseen difficulties as they arose, could manage the business more or less in his own way.

Outside work, one of my main interests had been Gaelic games – football and hurling – both as a player and as an administrator. I was deeply involved in the organisation of leagues and championships and in developing teams shortly before I became town clerk. I had also become secretary of the Down County Board of the Gaelic Athletic Association, the GAA, an entirely honorary post, which took up most of my spare time.

The chairman of the council was a very keen follower of Gaelic games, and would sometimes conduct a whispered discussion about a game in the middle of a boring meeting. A lady who got hopelessly into debt with rent arrears was helped by being given a contract to wash the county team jerseys at a rate that was calculated to pay her rent. As the Down team prospered and more games were played, her mountain of debt was reduced and finally eliminated. Sometimes, however, the GAA intersected with council work in a ludicrous way. Another non-rent-payer, a staunch unionist, held the view that pursuing him for rent arrears was a form of religious and political discrimination. When threatened verbally with court action, he welcomed that prospect on the grounds that the county court judge, George Hanna, a former Minister of Home Affairs who had protected the right of Orangemen to parade over the Longstone Road in County Down, would see him right. In the event, the case came to court at Newtownards a few days before the 1960 All-Ireland Football Final. Our solicitor, Michael Johnston, was one of the oldest solicitors in practice in Ireland. He had, he said, given George Hanna's father his first brief, and he was a very keen bridge player.

George Hanna was an international bridge player. Before the case was called, there was a brief by-play in open court about the forthcoming Portrush Bridge Conference. At the end he wished me well in Dublin on Sunday. In between he had given the tenant a roasting for not paying his rent, and had given judgment for the council. As we left the court, my assistant, who had borne the brunt of many verbal attacks over the years, could not resist saying to the tenant: 'Well, the judge did not do much for you.' Which brought the snarling reply: 'How could you expect justice there? A judge who plays cards all week with one of them and football on Sundays with the other!'

4

WIDENING THE FOCUS

IT IS NOT POSSIBLE TO BEGIN TO comprehend Irish life, especially Irish rural life, without some attempt to understand the role and function of Gaelic games and the salience of the Gaelic Athletic Association (GAA) as an organisation. Founded in 1884 partly to ensure the survival of traditional games such as hurling and Gaelic football at a time when other games including soccer and rugby were beginning to organise themselves, partly as an expression of nationalist separatism, and partly as a front for the dormant Fenians, it has for over a century now teetered on the margins of nationalist political movements, whilst it has become the dominant sporting body in rural Ireland.

Sport does represent perhaps the most evident manifestation of popular culture – as persistent as religion in some areas, perhaps even a substitute community opiate as religion declines, and certainly attracting more coverage from the popular press and the broadcasting media. Soccer has by and large tended to be the game of the urban working class and rugby that of the aspiring urban middle class (only in Limerick does one find a popular adherence to rugby which makes it a game of the people, the expression of the combined will of a community to be recognised, as in the Welsh valleys). However much the skill and sheer attractiveness, and the added dimension of glamour of international competition in these two games, there is a quality of excitement in Croke Park on All-Ireland Final days which is not to be experienced elsewhere. Indeed, I would say that someone who has not experienced a Munster hurling final at Thurles or a *fleadh cheoil* in Listowel or Ennis or wherever has missed a vital part of contemporary Irish culture and knows less about the plain people of Ireland than he might otherwise do.

The GAA has its uncritical supporters and its blind opponents and a broad spectrum of adherents in between. It makes great claims for itself as a saviour of the games and of the soul of the nation, and in pursuing the second goal is sometimes in danger of forgetting about the first or, at best, ending with such habiliments of pomposity as to make communication with the young people it is intending to attract to the games more difficult.

Those concerned in any sport break down into three broad groups: those who play, those who follow and those who administer. These last tend, more often than not, to be the voice of the sporting establishment, to be more concerned with organisational and procedural matters, to regard themselves as the guardians of the purity of the tradition, to take themselves unduly seriously, to be generally conservative, older than the players, more committed than the followers. In the GAA this is a very dominant group, which shapes the widespread public perception of the organisation as conservative, backward-looking and ultra-nationalistic. The real spirit of the organisation is otherwise: most players and followers are attracted to the games, they get on with what they enjoy, and are prepared to put up with the rhetoric as the price one pays for enjoyment. All games tend to produce a cadre of administrators, some professional, others virtually so, whose main objective is the preservation of their own positions. These people stay on for years: most of them were not top-class performers, many decided early on to climb the less physically demanding but more byzantine ladder of administration, and those who did have grown further and further away from the new generations of players. Athletics seems to be rife with this. So too are rugby and soccer. Gaelic games are no exception.

The captain of the Northern Ireland soccer team Danny Blanchflower had a wonderful story of a team whose eleven international players were accompanied by forty officials. I have an early personal memory of playing on a Down hurling team in an Ulster final when there were so many officials on the bus the players had to stand. Another feature of the GAA is that, unlike rugby, there seems

49

to be no continuing place for old players, however eminent their contribution; they tend to move away when their playing days are over, leaving the committees to be run by small men, national school teachers and country curates. I remember seeing the serried ranks of the GAA's Central Council on television on the occasion of the organisation's centenary, and reflecting that they looked like the reviewing party on Lenin's tomb during the Moscow May Day parade. I further reflected that the GAA and the USSR's Komsomol must be the only youth organisations in the world to be run by a gerontocracy.

Having said all that, the GAA has made an enormous contribution to Irish life over the last hundred years, in providing healthy games for generations of young men and boys, in providing a network of grounds and facilities at virtually no cost to the public purse, in acting as a stimulus to community development and growth in areas of depopulation, in providing a focus for local loyalty both at parish and county level, and in providing a link with Irish exiles. It has secured the survival of hurling as a game of incomparable skill and grace, and the development of Gaelic football as a major game in Ireland; it has nurtured handball as a minority sport, and it has encouraged the emergence of camogie as a game for girls. Where it has been weak is in being inward- and backward-looking, trying to drive into the future with eyes firmly fixed on the rear-view mirror, in having diffi-culty in coping with urbanisation, and when it attempts to go beyond the organisation of games and act as a general cultural policeman and gauleiter.

I have progressed through all three phases of attachment. Having been a player and administrator, I am now the sort of supporter I used to sneer at who comes out only on fine days, to support a winning team in the last stages of its progress towards the cup, or when stand tickets are supplied or the occasion is great enough.

The relevance of all this is the extent to which involvement in the GAA enabled me to use up my surplus energy and to develop, both personally and as an administrator and manager. At the same time as being town clerk at Downpatrick, I was secretary of the Down County Board and a member of the Central and Ulster councils. This exposed me to a wide range of personalities and gave me a great grounding in the procedures of meetings and in dealing with people in all sorts of situations and moods. Years later, when a colleague remarked at my nonchalance at a very difficult meeting of the Public Accounts Committee at Westminster, I explained to him that if you had had to stand as an amateur official at a GAA county convention and explain to a mountainy delegate why his club team had been suspended, you could face any challenge with equanimity. At least the members of parliament, however hostile their questioning, were likely to stop short of physical attack.

The GAA activity, too, brought me into every part of Ireland, and provided a network of contacts and friendships which endured over many years. Meetings generally took place at night, Central Council on Friday evenings and Ulster Council on Saturdays. With games on Sundays, the GAA not only absorbed a good deal of time, but it fitted in very well with my official work schedule. Ulster council meetings were carried out entirely in Irish, and in them I was able to deploy the Irish I had picked up on holidays in Waterford over the years. The insistence on the use of Irish meant that the other members of the council tended to be teachers or priests, as the only people likely to have fluency or practice, and it also tended to lessen further the likelihood of former prominent players being involved. As in so many of these cases, however, discussion about important issues such as money tended to bring a reversion to English. My experience on these councils made me warm to Gerry Fitt when at one stage in the development of the SDLP he complained of being 'up to my arse in country schoolteachers'.

The great man of the GAA at that time was Pádraig Ó Caoimh, known more commonly as Paddy O'Keeffe, the general secretary, a man for whom I had inordinate respect and affection, and who has been for me a role model in much that I have attempted then and since. He was a man of great breadth and vision who had almost singlehandedly taken a small organisation by the scruff of the neck and steered it through a period of growth and development, meeting and coping with new challenges, and helping an extraordinarily conservative organisation, run by amateurs and worse than amateurs, to adapt to changes in society and to professionalise both its operation and its presentation. Those who do not recognise the GAA of today in this description should try to envisage what it would have been like without his contribution. Paddy O was the continuing rock of consistency and continuity in an organisation whose president, nominally

51

its head, was elected for three years and then generally left office. Paddy O was thus better known as a figure in society than the president, and some presidents resented this. He had over the years built up the prestige of his office and had acquired both status and sapiental authority. At the same time, perhaps oddly in the circumstances, he was closer to the players than the presidents and most of the other senior people, and this kept him young in mind and spirit. He had a strong sense of what he wanted to achieve and the organisational skill to bring it about. He was courteous and diplomatic and had a great capacity to defuse conflict or disarm opposition with a quip or a joke. He had time for those whom others ignored – the old, the poor, the very young, the disadvantaged, the infirm – he liked a story and he always had time to listen. He gave leadership to a disparate group who, at Central Council level, were often in forty minds, he coaxed coherence and decisions out of them, and he got things done with a very small staff, in spartan offices, and with a minimum of fuss. His handling of difficult committees was superb, and his relationship with successive presidents was, I often thought afterwards, like that between a permanent secretary and a minister: deference without servility, advice, support and encouragement, joy in helping the high-flier to achieve his aims, patience with the plodder who with help might get there in the end, persistence in keeping the show on the road nevertheless, and the ability, without appearing to do so, to prevent the vainglorious or the ill-equipped from making bigger fools of themselves than they might otherwise have done. He had many of the qualities of a senior civil servant, and most of those of a civilised, decent man.

The GAA in Down itself was in a poor shape after the Second World War, although there were some very good players, some good teams and some very good games in both football and hurling. But there was no consistency or continuity, the county was divided between east and south, discipline at games often broke down, and county teams had not won an important competition for years, indeed had hardly won a match of any consequence. In the order of merit of counties, Down languished deep in the lowest quintile, and on the roll of honour it was not mentioned except for a Junior All-Ireland football title in 1946, the potential of which had been dissipated.

I joined the county board, having been secretary of the East Down League, just after I started teaching. I was by far the youngest member, but gradually we started getting other young members who had been at secondary schools in Downpatrick or Newry, who were still active players, who had been to university or training college, and who were not content to preside over failure and lack of effort. The main concerns of committees were legalistic rather than athletic: petty arguments about who had started what row at which match, or what team had not used Irish watermarked paper for its lists, or what team had fielded an ineligible player, or why the league was un-finished or hopelessly out of date, or why somebody's nephew should or should not have a place on the county team; there was collective relief when the county team was beaten in the first round of the championship so that we could all get back to watching the rest of the All-Ireland as spectators.

Amongst all this, gradually, through the input of newer, younger and less easily satisfied members, the debate moved to the higher ground of what was wrong with the games in Down and what could be done. We started an All-County league to raise standards, and gave teams for the first time ever a published fixture list at the start of the year, which was adhered to. We arranged for a supply of capable referees who turned up and submitted reports, and raised standards of performance and discipline. We started a Barony League to break down club rivalries and to give good players an opportunity to play with their peers. We encouraged the development of the games in the emerging intermediate schools and at underage and local level. Meanwhile, one effect of the 1947 Education Act was to increase the numbers of boys attending the local grammar schools, where, par-ticularly in Newry, football was well coached and of a high standard. Eventually there was a pool of good players and time to turn attention to county teams.

In the mid-1950s, a small group within the Down County Board, fed up with being beaten year after year, disgusted by the defeatism of the majority, and determined to put Down's name on the map of Gaelic football, conceived the idea of trying to produce a team that would win an All-Ireland. We decided that it could be done, with careful planning and preparation, about five years hence, and we set about this, surreptitiously at first. A panel of twenty-five players was assembled who were willing to face the drudgery of two nights' training a week for most of the winter, training facilities were provided, a series of challenge games was arranged with teams outside Ulster, and hope and confidence were engendered. There was soon a compact between the players and the managers that if the players honoured their commitments, the selectors would stick by them, and that as a group we had our own programme which would involve periodic defeats, setbacks, disappointments, but which in the end would bring success. This venture was regarded as so fanciful, so foolish, so fraught with disaster by the Cassandras of the county board that we were allowed to get on with it without the trouble of having to repel those who would usually try to interfere.

In the event we did bring it off. Down won the All-Ireland championship in 1960, four years into the programme, and again the following year. In the process we produced one of the most exciting teams ever to play Gaelic football, we attracted the largest crowd ever to a match in Ireland, we developed a new style of play and many innovations in training methods and preparation, we lifted the spirit of the whole community for a brief period, and we were an inspiration to young people, and brought life and colour to many.

It was only many years later, when I began to read the books by the gurus, that I discovered that we had, all unwittingly, been operating a system of management by objectives. However we stumbled on it, apart from the application of common sense, which I regard as the essence of management, I think I learned more about managing people from that group than from anything else I did: how to set objectives beyond the normal expectations of people, but achievable with effort and determination, how to motivate people, how to mobilise resources of training and support, how to sustain people in disappointment and defeat, how to put the activity in the context of a wider and more serious world, how to deal with interference, tensions and defeat within the group, how to cater for the special individual needs of a wide variety of people, how to dull the edge of disappointment without blunting the thrust of ambition, how to bond people into a group with a single purpose, with a set of standards, and with self-discipline, and how to remotivate them to do it all again.

It has often struck me since that if you want to learn about the practicalities of man management, there is no better place to do it than with an amateur team, where the pool of players cannot be expanded by purchase or poaching, where the core activity is a pastime, where people have their lives to lead, livelihoods to earn, an education to complete, family and other responsibilities, where the reward systems are limited and nonmonetary, and where training and preparation involve tedious and difficult travelling arrangements and have to be undertaken after a long day's work or study. I think I learned more from this group than from any other. As publicity about the team grew, there was also the burgeoning interest of the media, especially the emergence of television, which provided me with experience in dealing with journalists, in handling debate and in the public presentation of issues.

People generally are anxious to associate with a winning side and the success of the team attracted support from many quarters, often in a surprising way. I remember once, after Down had won the National Football League for the first time by beating Cavan in the final, the captain took the cup home and placed it on the family sideboard. There it was seen by the local postman, an Orangeman and a B Special, whose local pride and pleasure at a neighbour's achievement were reflected in the congratulatory message 'Jesus, we took it off the friggers!'

Seriously, though, the success of the Down team did attract support right across the board. The GAA was perhaps the only organisation that provided a focus for loyalty to the county as a unit, and most people who were interested in sport of any kind supported the team, and interest went very much wider. For our part, we tried to make the team accessible to all. There was no great tradition of rhetoric in the GAA in Down, and the team and those most closely associated with it were more interested in football than in flag-waving. They were proud to represent the hopes and aspirations of all the people in the county, and to receive the support of all, irrespective of politics or religion. In a way it was an early venture in ecumenism, in cross-community relations. We tried to ensure, for example, that all councils in the county could get tickets for the finals, and not just the Catholic- or nationalist-controlled ones, and we tried to ensure that nothing was said or done that would damage or rebuff the good will that was so evident. One long-time supporter, a father of two players, complained to me that he was embarrassed, on behalf of his Protestant friends who had gone with him to support the team, by the singing of a Catholic hymn, 'Faith of Our Fathers', before the games at Croke Park. Given the raucous expectations of the average football fan, keyed up with expectancy for the game and impatient for the start, this was as inappropriate as the playing of 'Nearer My God to Thee' before Wembley finals, which was also the practice of the time. However, there was a particular sectarian point in the context of Northern Ireland, and we took action accordingly to encourage the GAA to end the practice, which it did. Ironically, it required a chauvinistic interpretation to clinch the argument: it was pointed out that the author, Father Faber, was English, and that the fathers 'chained in prison dark but yet in heart and conscience free' were English too, and not, as the singing crowds had been led to believe, Irish all along.

Although I gained a great deal from my GAA experience, in the end, I got tired of trying to change a very conservative body at national level; meanwhile the zest of the action in Down had been dulled by the fact that many of those who had derided our early efforts had now climbed on to the bandwagon of success and wanted to take control. What had previously been possible was now questioned by nit-pickers, decision making became cumbersome as committees muscled in, and it felt as if we were having to push the stone the whole way up the slope again. It is also one of my weaknesses to lose interest in a subject when I know how to do it, or have acquired a certain competency. This could be described more positively as seeking new pastures, or fresh challenges or renewal, but in either case it produced a succession of five- or seven-year itches when what had been tolerable, or even enjoyable, became progressively more boring, routine became drudgery, and bores became impossible to bear any longer. In other ways the glitter had gone off too.

The GAA had for most of the previous seventy years maintained a ban on participation in, or even attendance at, cricket, soccer, rugby and hockey matches, which were characterised in the cant of the time as 'foreign games'. Down had been trying to change this rule for a decade and a half without success, although the tide was turning and the rule was to go within the next ten years. I found it less attractive to remain deeply involved in an organisation that required its members to be shackled by regulations characterised by meanness of spirit and lack of vision. My friend and mentor Paddy O'Keeffe had died. I applied for his post as GAA general secretary, not in any hope of success but only so that I could say to myself that I had made my effort to change things. In the event, in a welter of canvassing in which I did not indulge, I received a derisory single vote (and that not from the Down delegate). I take a perverse pride in having been so rejected, and of having secured the vote of one of the few distinguished players in the room. In the end, my problem was solved for me by the Down Convention which, in an orgy of vote-rigging, having first replaced me as Central Council delegate, relegated me from secretary to assistant secretary. At this point I got the message – that they wanted to drop the pilot – and I withdrew from active participation: without recrimination, but not without some hurt and disappointment at a certain lack of grace in the transition. In the event, the ban was removed within ten years and I have continued to draw much pleasure from Gaelic games as a spectator and much satisfaction from the many friends I made through them.

Closer to the work front there was enrichment and expansion. The tradition among Downpatrick councillors had been to keep to themselves as a council, not to bother too much with the world outside, and not to get involved in regional organisations that sucked you into the establishment and were dominated by unionist councils and councillors. Downpatrick councillors were generally nationalistic, but they did not fit comfortably into the harness of a party, even if the tack of the Nationalist Party had been any more than a loose rein at times of parliamentary elections and a saddle for the candidate.

The Downpatrick councillors were really independents, but they still were suspicious and found it difficult to relate to what appeared to be the better-organised, more self-assured unionist councillors who exuded the confidence that comes with power (however circumscribed) and continuity in office (however modest). The local Westminster MP hardly existed in the council's mind. This was because the council's dealings were with Stormont; Westminster was not in the least interested in what went on in Northern Ireland, and the debates in Westminster seemed far removed from, and irrelevant to, the work of the council. It was also because the Westminster members, although grandly described as Imperial Members of Parliament, were entirely undistinguished men, party hacks in safe seats who did not need to make the effort to placate the voters so long as they satisfied the selection committee every four years or so. Captain Orr, the MP for South Down, was a nonentity, and deservedly so. George Currie, the MP for North Down, had a house in Downpatrick, but he would never have been recognised on the street. Willie Orr never appeared except at election times and on Orange platforms. It is ironic that having been unrepresented by Willie Orr for so long, the decent people of South Down were then misrepresented by Enoch Powell as he paddled his own eccentric and manic canoe.

The local Stormont MP was a different matter – and yet much the same. He was a unionist. In his rising years, Brian Faulkner was a fairly strident exponent of hardline unionism, an enthusiastic Orangeman, a supporter of the right to march regardless of local feelings, and one who took a tough line on law and order. The councillors viewed him with some suspicion, and the chairman, E.K. McGrady, who had stood against him in a tough Stormont election, found it hard to approach him as a petitioner in relation to council business. This reflected the idea at the time, held on all sides, that members owed a prior duty to those who elected them, the notion of a tribune of all the people being not very well developed. It was seen to be the policy of unionist governments and unionist ministers to encourage and facilitate development and economic growth in unionist areas and not elsewhere, and it was not thought to be worth the effort to approach them only to be rebuffed, or sidelined, or strung along.

As it happened, Brian Faulkner was an assiduous constituency MP. Perhaps the most bizarre manifestation of this occurred after many of the hurley sticks in Downpatrick had been broken in an attack on his overexuberant supporters who wished to march through parts of the town where they were not welcome; the local stockist sought Faulkner's support in an application for an import licence for replacements, and got it. Faulkner's representations on behalf of constituents brought a constant stream of letters at official level to the council office. I soon found that he was a man of considerable integrity who would accept a straight answer when the facts were put to him. I also found him ready to make representations to other government departments on our behalf. This began a working relationship, and a friendship which lasted until his death.

My instinct in relation to bodies like the Association of Local Authorities was to join everything, to participate, to make people aware of the existence of Downpatrick as a place that mattered, and to influence developments and policies in a way that would benefit the town and its people. The local authority associations provided another outlet and another set of personal, professional and political contacts. There were three associations. The county councils considered themselves a cut above the rest, and rarely fraternised. The rural districts had their own set of interests, which were usually in rivalry with the towns. And the Association of Local Authorities comprised the medium-sized and small towns, including those that had puffed themselves up as boroughs so that the mayor could wear a chain and the councillors robes, plus or minus Belfast and Londonderry. Belfast wished to swim in the larger sea: to associate with boroughs in England and to float in and out on a current of self-interest. Londonderry had aspirations in the same direction. They tended to take a reactionary line on most things, and to become increasingly embarrassing bedfellows as the protests of their own citizens became more vocal and more specific.

Local government abounded in strong characters. Some were chairmen who had been in office for years, and protected their turf like robber barons. Some were men of great ability and force of character who could provide local leadership and take on government ministers and departments at a political level. The results of their efforts could often be seen in the relative prosperity of their areas, the quality of the infrastructure and of public buildings. They were, it is true, generally representative of the areas with a good record of employment and relative prosperity. It is an interesting question whether they were the products of their environment or the creators of it. There is little doubt in my mind that it is easier to develop a civic culture on a sound economic base than in the midst of a depression but that, once going, economic development and civic leadership can interact to develop and sustain a sense of well-being and of pride in community. Whether these men were creators or catalysts, it is hard to say, but they did leave a mark on their towns. They were generally people who had done well in business, they had no great vision for the future except that of the small shopkeeper – the vision that the town should be run like their business – they were not very democratic, they were in safe seats, and would not have fought for office, and some, in the county councils, were actually co-opted.

There were some very able local government officers too. They were tough, self-confident men who had tended to stay with the same council, who had been in office for years, longer than any of the councillors, who were generally authoritarian and paternalistic in a sphere where there was no tradition of challenge from either the councillors or the consumers. They could get things done – or stop them. Where they were interested in housing, for example, houses got built. Allocation was another thing.

I had begun to develop an interest in the study of local government systems which led to lecturing on Further Education courses, and more widely. It also brought me more on to committees and working parties as councils in the sixties geared themselves for changes which were seen to be inevitable, but which were to be resisted nevertheless.

The sixties was a period of tension between Stormont which was centralising, and to an extent modernising, and which saw the local councils as an obstacle to progress, and the desire of local government to remain local. One of the difficulties, of course, was that some councillors desired to remain local in order to resist the moves towards a more equal society.

I was involved in several delegations from the Association of Local Authorities to Stormont in relation to proposals and counter-proposals for local government reorganisation, which was a constant theme in this period. On one occasion when the urban authorities were invited to meet Bill Craig, then Minister of Development, I suggested that they might prepare a position paper. They reacted strongly, these staunch unionist warhorses. Craig, they said, was a dictator who would come and lay down the law. Whatever he said, they were not going to accept it, and would tell him so in no uncertain terms.

The minister, on the contrary, was all sweetness and light. 'My mind is open, gentlemen,' he said. 'Tell me what your ideas are.'

This was too much for them, and they did not know how to respond. Instead of a dialogue, we were reduced to individual contributions as the minister went round the room trying to elicit some sliver of common ground. We had been invited for lunch, and it proved very difficult to fill the time available; having heard about the defective sewers in Newtownabbey and the state of the pier in Bangor, we limped off to pre-lunch drinks at the earliest decent moment.

Such delegations brought me into contact with senior people in the civil service, especially those in the Ministry of Development. Chief amongst these was John Oliver, one of the outstanding civil servants of his period, who dominated thinking about planning and urban development and the structure and form of local administration. I was to work more closely with him in the future and I developed a great affection for him and great respect for his intellectual range and grasp. In the early days the department was called the Ministry of Health and Local Government and the permanent secretary was Ronald Green, a civilised man of enormous quality and great intellectual distinction. I always thought it a reflection on the system that he did not become Head of the Northern Ireland Civil Service when lesser, greyer men were preferred. He had the glamour of being a polymath member of the Northern Ireland team on 'Round Britain Quiz', along with James Boyce. Years later, when I was permanent secretary of the Department of Health and Social Services (DHSS), I represented Ireland on the same radio programme; it added to my pleasure to be in a sort of apostolic succession to Ronnie Green.

I was very anxious at this time to involve the council in new developments and in pilot schemes, especially if extra funding was being provided. My view was that if somebody in authority wanted to spend money, even foolishly, they might as well do it in Downpatrick as anywhere else. On one occasion the Ministry of Development was anxious to prove a theory that the life of an Arcon prefab house (such houses had been built in hundreds after the Second World War with a life expectancy of ten years) could be extended by putting it in a brick envelope and roofing it. We offered one of our prefabs and, with the help of a local builder, proved that the job could be done for £500. This produced a stream of visitors, from the architects up to William Morgan, the Minister of Development. One day it was announced that the permanent secretary would come in state to see for himself. I had never met a permanent secretary and did not know what to expect. It was a wet day, Ronnie Green made a perfunctory inspection, and then retired to the hotel for tea and a drink. We had a long chat about Yeats and Joyce which was much more enjoyable than the nuts and bolts of building construction. In the course of conversation, we agreed that a knowledge of literature and a feeling for poetry were not the worst means by which to try to understand the problems of societies.

5
BEFORE THE DELUGE

ONE OF MY LIFESAVERS IN THE SIXTIES, after I had left the GAA and was looking for something to expend my energy on, was the Ulster Countryside Committee. This was a statutory body set up to advise government and the planning authorities on the designation of national parks and areas of outstanding natural beauty. The group met once a month for the six years that I was a member and was a club of interesting and convivial people, and a very powerful learning experience. The chairman was Professor Muskett, a plant pathologist from Queen's University, who had made his name in a radio gardening programme, on which he signed off with 'Good night! Good luck! And good gardening!', and as chairman of a Best Kept Small Towns Competition. He had an evangelical manner and a burning mission to protect and improve the environment. He had a tendency to pose questions with an ontological scope. 'What are we here for?' he would ask in the middle of a meeting. If you replied that the meeting was considering the designation of the Lagan valley as an area of outstanding natural beauty, he would interject testily: 'No! No! I mean on this terrestrial globe. Why are we here?' He was a little man of great courage who would face down a crowd of irate farmers or developers as he held on to his brief to prevent sporadic building in the countryside.

Among the others were two geographers, Ronnie Buchanan from Queen's and Des McCourt, a former Irish rugby international, from the New University of Ulster. Des had been prominent in the protest about the siting of the new university. He had strongly supported Londonderry as the location, and was violently anti-O'Neill because of what he saw as his pusillanimity on this issue. McCourt once caused outrage in the dining room at Stormont, where we had been for one of our meetings, by ordering, in a loud voice, 'An O'Neill steak, cut off the rump and well roasted.' He was, however, a sensitive and gifted geographer who had made a special study of rural traditional house types.

Then there was Wilfred Capper, a green before it was popular or profitable to be so. Wilfred left his own mark afterwards through the Ulster Way, which he charted, walked, negotiated and signposted. At this time he was the voice of outrage at every intrusion in the countryside, at every right of way obstructed, at every tree felled. His mildest reaction to any threatening proposal was 'Monstrous, chairman, monstrous!' He spent most of his working life in an endless guerrilla warfare and in unflagging denunciation of the Ministry of Agriculture, which was his employer. There was George Cathcart, from Fermanagh, who represented the Farmers' Union. He was a wonderful raconteur who knew his way through the undergrowth and the backwoods of the Unionist Party. Ken Parkin, the chief forestry officer, was an enlightened man who turned many of the state forests into recreational areas and opened them up to a wider public. And there was Paddy Falloon, a hotelier who, having re-created the Crawfordsburn Inn, was now developing a first-class hotel in an old beetling mill at Dunadry. Paddy was a man of passion and great feeling, with a love for the arts and a gift for language. But perhaps the most interesting member, and the one most surprising to me, because strangely enough we developed a great affection for each other, was Lady Brookeborough, the wife of the former prime minister. I found her to be an intelligent, open and courageous person. Over time we were able to discuss the most contentious subjects without rancour, including the policies of successive unionist governments and of her husband. She defended his notorious speech about employing Catholics – 'I wouldn't have one of them about the place' – by putting it in a context where her babies were under threat, her husband and herself felt under siege, the big houses were under attack, and politicians were particular targets.

We developed an interesting barter trade based on Basil's partiality for Ardglass herrings. I would bring herrings and prawns to meetings to be exchanged for artichokes from Colebrooke and yellow tomatoes. I asked her once why her son John was so antagonistic to Terence O'Neill. 'Well, John is a backbencher, a member of the party, a supporter of the government. He meets the PM in the corridor at Stormont, who walks past him without speaking. Then he comes home and turns on the television and there is the prime minister announcing some other great initiative which his backbenchers haven't heard of.' This story illustrates many of Terence's shortcomings as a party leader: his lack of personal warmth, his difficulty with personal relationships, his inability to communicate, even with his friends, his defensiveness in the face of criticism and his inability to mend fences within the party.

Lord Brookeborough was a director of the tobacco company Carreras, which periodically sponsored the Downpatrick Races. On one occasion when she and Basil were attending the races, Lady Brookeborough invited me to take her on a tour of the interesting buildings in Downpatrick instead. As we approached the Southwell School, a gossipy bystander called me over to tell me of a sensation at the racecourse – Basil Brooke had dropped dead. And there I was with the widow. I told her that he had been taken seriously ill (which turned out to be true) and brought her to the Downe Hospital where the expert care of Johnny Boyd pulled him through. He spent some time in the hospital and developed a great rapport with all the staff. Despite his notoriety, he had a common touch which enabled him to speak to people in a largely Catholic area in a way that made them feel that he was interested in them. This was precisely the talent that Terence lacked. I often wondered why Terence could not have come to an arrangement with Brian Faulkner by promising him the succession after a few years' working together. They would have been a formidable combination. Years later I mentioned this to Jim Malley, who had been O'Neill's private secretary at the time. 'But he did,' he said. If he did, Brian must not have been listening, and I don't think many other people heard it either.

One by-product of my years on the Countryside Committee was that I acquired a thorough knowledge of the region, gained as we visited beauty spot after beauty spot in order to survey and designate areas of outstanding natural beauty, and tramped fields and lanes along with a remarkable planner called Cecil Newman in order to assess the impact of power transmission lines or other intrusions into the landscape. There were meetings, too, with conservation groups and farmers, persuading them of the value of nature conservation and protection of the landscape. In this we were vigorously opposed by the Department of Agriculture – a great surprise to me who had innocently expected government policies to be a seamless garment. After one meeting at which Professor Muskett had been mobbed by angry farmers in Fermanagh, we discovered that they had been summoned and stirred up by a circular letter sent out in franked envelopes from the local Agriculture office in Enniskillen. On another occasion, on a deputation to the Ministry of Agriculture to try to persuade them to withdraw their objection to the designation of the area between Clough, Castlewellan and Newcastle as an essential foreground to the panorama of the Mournes, I heard the permanent secretary lay bare the essential policy of the ministry. They were on the side of the farmers. If bungalows were a better cash crop than grass or turnips, then that is what they would support.

Another by-product was my nomination to the Salzburg Seminar for American Studies in Austria, one of the seminal and stimulating events of my life. This seminar comprised two people from each European country and an American faculty, which spent four weeks in residence considering a topic of relevance to the problems of the day. Our session concerned urban and regional planning. I was reluctant to go at first, but Ronnie Buchanan pushed me, and John Oliver made the way easy too, by encouraging Downpatrick Council to grant me leave and to pay the course fee. At first I was overwhelmed by the sheer scale of the discussions: the Americans were talking about the problems of a continuous builtup area stretching from Cape Cod to Norfolk, Virginia, about 120 million people, while my concern was with the urban district of Downpatrick. The group soon melded, however. We were in Schloss Leopoldskron, which had been used as a set for the film version of *The Sound of Music*, the town was nearby, a Mozart mass could be heard in the cathedral, there was skiing, the Salzkammergut, and the opportunity to take the train at weekends to Munich, Venice or Vienna. I made many enduring friendships with some of the interesting Americans on the faculty, especially Paul Ylvisaker, then head of the Urban Affairs Program of the Ford Foundation, who remained a close friend until his death in 1992.

I remember one discussion about the optimum size of a city. An eccentric urban geographer from Durham was advancing the thesis (with which I quite agreed) that economic poles of growth should be cultural growth points as well. He went further, however, in arguing that since only one in five million people was an Einstein, and one in a million a Shakespeare, and one in 100,000 a Dickens, then a city of five million people would give you the possibility of an Einstein, five Shakespeares and fifty novelists. I intervened to tell him about Listowel, a small town in the south-west of Ireland which had four Abbey playwrights, four novelists, battalions of poets, and regiments of short-story writers.

Shortly after I returned, I met the legendary Dublin character Pope O'Mahony. He called me across the street: 'You'll never have any trouble getting into America. The Americans will conclude that you have been sufficiently brainwashed.'

Another diversion in the mid-1960s were civic weeks. The trades council in Downpatrick, in an effort to raise public consciousness about unemployment and to halt economic decline, promoted the idea of a civic week. At a public meeting which I attended to hold a watching brief for the urban district council, I found myself elected chairman of a committee to organise the civic week. The committee was composed of people who were new to public activity, and they brought a freshness and enthusiasm to the exercise, while the fact that I had the resources of the council staff to call on lent organisation and stability. The week was a great success. I still remember the last evening, with ballad groups singing at braziers strategically placed around the town to encourage street entertainment; there was music in pubs too, and John D. Stewart, then a local television personality and columnist, said it was like Spain, and at the final midnight folk concert in the cinema the groups were judged by a young traditional singer called David Hammond and Cecil Newman, who had been my old sparring partner in Salzburg.

Politically more interesting was the invitation to Terence O'Neill to open the civic week, and his acceptance. At the opening on the Courthouse steps, O'Neill was flanked by Brian Faulkner and Bill Craig. It was his first official visit to a nationalist town, and he was well received. Indeed he was so attracted to the idea of civic weeks that he began to promote them elsewhere, and in that way debased the currency. The head of the Government Information Service at the time was an incurably romantic optimist called Eric Montgomery who persuaded O'Neill of the desirability of creating an innocuous middle-ground culture which all could share, which married Scottish dancing with Irish, which invented its own tartan, which stressed Ulster links with American presidents. The apotheosis of this culture became the Ulster American Folk Park. At this time, however, the idea was in its infancy and O'Neill made some mileage out of it.

The second civic week saw an invitation to the Governor of Northern Ireland, Lord Erskine. This was a slightly more risky political undertaking because of the trappings of royalty and of protocol, but it too went off well. We always tried to avoid situations to which one group or another might take offence, and to play down symbols and totems. This was particularly the case with flags, emblems and toasts. In order to prevent a rash of union flags breaking out on public buildings and government offices, which might provoke either counterdisplays or actual removal, we invested in a supply of the flag of Saint Patrick, a red cross on a white background. We then gave one to the occupant of each building which had a flagpole and explained that we were trying to promote Saint Patrick as a tourist attraction and as an internationally recognised symbol for the town that bore his name. Would they mind flying his flag for the duration of civic week? All agreed, and what might have been a divisive incident was avoided.

So good did we get at dealing with these incidents that when in the late 1960s the Twelfth of July demonstration was held in Downpatrick at a field on the new Belfast Road, we were able to agree with the organisers and the police a route that ensured little disruption of traffic and no irritation of the bulk of the townsfolk, and absolutely no trouble. Indeed, uniquely, the council was thanked from the Orange platform for its efforts to facilitate the demonstration and to make the day a success.

As a result of the Salzburg experience, and as a developing interest, I became more involved in the regional planning debate, in working parties on local government reorganisation, and more generally as a lecturer on these topics for the Workers' Educational Association (WEA) and adult education courses.

One important milestone was a series of winter lectures on public administration in Northern Ireland organised by Ted Rhodes at Magee College in Derry. I gave a long lecture, spread over two evenings, on local government. This whetted my appetite for this sort of thing; it forced me to organise my thoughts and my reading, and it resulted in my first publication in any sort of academic guise. The booklet of lectures appeared about the same time as the first White Paper on the reorganisation of local government which, Harry Calvert said in a review in the *Northern Ireland Legal Quarterly*, was made to look like comic cuts by comparison. I don't think John Oliver ever quite forgave him, or me.

I remember giving a lecture at Castlereagh College one evening and finding, to my surprise, that the treasurer of Belfast Corporation was in the audience. Afterwards he enunciated a theory of local government by which the strategic approach of the Belfast Corporation suddenly made sense. Cities, he argued, were not for people. People were expensive, you had to provide them with expensive services. What the city needed was shops and offices and industry which would produce high valuations and rate revenues. People should be pushed outside the boundaries into the county areas which would have to provide the expensive schools and clinics and housing. There you have the explanation for the imbalance of development in Belfast and the anomalous appendages of Castlereagh and Newtownabbey, plus the lack of any strategic vision for the organic growth of the city as a whole.

At a later conference at Magee College I met for the first time Councillor T. Dan Smith, then mayor of Newcastle upon Tyne and a commanding figure in local government in Britain. He was the driving force behind the regeneration of the North-east, and a strong advocate of regional planning and decentralisation. He seemed very much a man of the future. Sadly, a few years later his involvement in the Poulson affair brought him a jail sentence and disgrace. But in Derry, in the mid-sixties, he was a colossus such as we had never met, asking the questions none of us had hitherto heard voiced on a public platform from an establishment source in the presence of the mayor: about the failure of the corporation to build houses for its own people, about discrimination, about the unionists' throttling of growth in the city rather than lose political control. Smith had groups of people burrowing away all day, devilling and ferreting out statistics for his address, and this seemed to me a new, constructive and potentially effective way to bring about changes and to end abuse.

In the summer of 1968, I attended an international conference on housing and planning in Dublin. It was a glittering affair, but I found it disturbing in many ways. There was an evening programme for foreign delegates to 'meet the Irish', for which the small Northern Ireland delegation (Cecil Newman, Ronnie Buchanan and myself) posed a problem. We did, through some personal acquaintance, get invited to a party in a private house in Dublin 4. It was at the high tide of TACA, a fundraising support group for Fianna Fáil, which seemed to have an inordinately large membership of property developers, builders, architects and others who had made money out of the property boom and the astute manipulation of the planning process. There was an oversupply at the party of mohair suits and conspicuous consumption. I found it all very vulgar, and after a while we left and went to a convenient pub to meet our own Irish. The final night of the conference included a reception in the state apartments of Dublin Castle, hosted by the then Minister of Local Government, Kevin Boland. While we were there, the castle gates were besieged by protestors from the Dublin Housing Action group, a front for the then Marxist rump of the IRA. Hearing them outside chanting:

> What will we do with Mr Boland,
> What will we do with Mr Boland?
> Hang him up and burn the bastard...

in the splendour of the state apartments it was as if one were listening to the Paris mob howling outside the Tuileries in the weeks before the French Revolution. In the end we were smuggled out through a back gate, leaving the field to the protestors. All of which led me later to give some credence to the theory that the emergence of the Provos in the North had been encouraged by some Dublin ministers in order to divert the energies of the IRA from agitation on social issues in the South.

On one occasion in April 1969, a fraternal delegation of English town clerks was being hosted by their Northern Ireland counterparts over a weekend, and I had arranged for them a tour of the County

Down coast on a Sunday afternoon, ending with a picnic beside the Silent Valley reservoir. At about eight o'clock in the morning, I was phoned by Norman Agnew, secretary to the Water Commissioners, calling off the trip because of the explosion of 'IRA bombs' at the reservoir. I remember wondering, a couple of days later, when the precise location of the bombs had been described, how the IRA had been able to acquire sophisticated and detailed knowledge of a plant that employed virtually no Catholics, so as to be able to place the bombs in the most internally sensitive part. I was not surprised to hear later that the bombs had been placed by loyalists in an attempt to bring down O'Neill.

I remember John Oliver telling me in Strangford one night that the gossip in Whitehall was that Harold Wilson wanted to intervene in Northern Ireland, but was being held back by the coat tails by Roy Jenkins, the Home Secretary and biographer of Asquith, saying, 'Prime Minister, Prime Minister! Ireland! A graveyard for political reputations!'

In the spring of 1968, I was asked along, with Fred Boal of the Geography Department at Queen's, to conduct a course on planning over a few weekends for the National Democratic Party, the NDP. This party included people who had been in the New Ireland Movement at Queen's (one of whom, Conor Bradley, was a former pupil of mine), young professionals, mainly Catholic, and people from the Irish National Teachers' Organisation like Gerry Quigley and Joe MacMullan, and Eddie McGrady, who had become council chairman in Downpatrick. Many of them moved later into the SDLP and some to Alliance. The lectures arose to some extent out of a series of induction talks I had given to new councillors in Downpatrick, which had proved to be so popular that the older councillors asked for them too. These told them what their powers were, analysed the social and economic needs of the area, outlined what had already been done, and indicated the possible priorities for developments and the constraints on action. I did not regard it as political involvement to provide the same course for the NDP. I saw myself as providing a professional input, and this was strengthened by the participation of Fred Boal. I would have done the same for other parties if they had asked me.

The NDP was the first stirring of political awareness on the part of the young emerging Catholic professionals, who were disgusted by the lethargy and nihilism of the old Nationalist Party, unwilling to accept the status quo which condemned them to perpetual inferiority, and anxious to do something constructive. They had just made a disastrous pact with the Nationalists which left them free to contest only those seats that they had no hope of winning.

At a coffee break in one of the course sessions at the Wellington Park Hotel, Austin Currie, then a young Nationalist Party MP, described his plans. He was going to wait for a particularly blatant case of discrimination in the letting of a local-authority house, and then he would seize possession before the tenant moved in and squat for as long as possible until ejected by the police. The resultant publicity, he believed, would focus attention on malpractice and force some change in the law and practice relating to house allocation. I did not think then that I was hearing the blueprint for the first civil rights activity. A few months later, in June, the newspapers were full of events at Caledon, where Currie had squatted in a council house allocated to an unmarried Protestant woman.

When the troubles started in Belfast in the summer of 1969 there was an immediate influx of refugees to Downpatrick. Having anticipated that this would happen, we made preparations. I was extremely anxious that the good relationships that had built up in Downpatrick would not be shattered as a result. It was particularly important that people should not bring their sectarian squabbles with them from Belfast. In order to prevent this, I wanted to encourage a cross-community approach to the problem, so that Catholics would not be looked after only by the Catholic Church, and Protestants by the Protestant churches. In the event, nearly all those who came were Catholics. We agreed that all the churches would combine, with a reception centre in the Church of Ireland parish hall, and dispersal centres in the Presbyterian hall and the Catholic scout hall. Feeding was arranged by women volunteers in the school meals kitchen, which the supervisor opened up after we had threatened to break in anyhow. In fairness, the position was speedily regularised by the chairman of the County Education Committee as soon as he could be got in touch with. Incidentally, the officer whose responsibility this might be thought to have been could not be located until his office opened on the Monday, which might be thought to be as good a way of dealing with a crisis as any other.

The main influx of refugees came on a Friday and Saturday; on the Sunday a notice was read out in all the churches asking people with a spare room to offer to take in a family for a few days. The response was overwhelming, and was genuinely cross-community, and we were able to accommodate all who came.

One day in the office I was phoned by the Rector of Ardoyne Monastery saying that there was a shortage of food. He asked me to try and get some in Downpatrick and to bring it up. Sticking to our cross-community approach, I phoned the Agnes Street Methodist church on the Shankill Road and spoke to a young minister called Harold Good. I explained the position and said that I was willing, if the need existed, to share what we had with the Shankill as well. He thanked me, and said there was no immediate need. I then approached a couple of businessmen and raised £100 with which I bought food. I borrowed a lorry from a local builder, Hugh O'Boyle, who also supplied a driver. I did not want him to risk making the journey on his own, because the reports coming in from Belfast, and particularly the Crumlin Road, were frightening. Neither did I wish to put pressure on any of the council workmen to go, so I went myself. I left after work on a Friday and got to Ardoyne about 7.30.

The Crumlin Road was indeed frightening, with burnt-out buildings on either side, flames smouldering and flickering along both frontages, barricades across Disraeli Street and Butler Street, a smell of cordite in the air, and smoke and dirt and dereliction. We turned into Butler Street through a gap made in a makeshift barricade, and were directed to Holy Cross School. The driver, Paddy Fitzsimons, a former county footballer, was known to many of the locals who worked in the docks or in builders' suppliers where he was accustomed to pick up materials. Many of them would have known me through football too, so we were recognised and welcomed and given a safe passage without much difficulty.

One man said to me: 'Where are the guns?'

I said, 'We have no guns. We brought butter.'

I got the chilling reply, 'What the fuck use is butter to us?'

We unloaded nevertheless and got offside as quickly as we could. A couple of days later the troops were deployed in Ardoyne, much to the relief of the locals, and in response to requests made by the rector, the bishop, and almost anybody who could raise a shout in the place.

At the end of July there had been trouble on the streets in Downpatrick, for the first time since 1949. This had arisen mainly from rather stupid policing after a civil rights march, and a build-up of aggro between local youths and the B Specials. What you had really was two groups of louts, defined by religion, one lot of whom had uniforms and guns and the power to stop and harass the others on their way home from dances late at night. There was also a copycat element, of people wanting to act as they saw others doing on television, and behind all a real concern that great things were happening of which they wished to be a part. There was an element of agitation too. The myth was being created before our eyes, reinforced by the television news, of gallant Catholic youths under constant attack by police in Derry. This created a demand among the armchair strategists for action in other towns in order to draw the police off from the Bogside and to attenuate their strength.

When trouble appeared about to erupt in Downpatrick, a group of councillors, led by Eddie McGrady, along with the local clergy, made a concerted effort to get people moving off the streets. One local hero, a drunk and a noted womaniser, who had not darkened the church door for years, told one of the curates to fuck off when the curate tried to persuade him to go home. When asked by the priest why he was there he replied, 'I'm a Catholic, amn't I?'

Later in the evening, the action moved to the police barracks. The police had rather stupidly arrested a drunk who had shouted abuse at them, visibly roughing him up in the process. Eddie McGrady and I went to the barracks to negotiate his release, and found ourselves inside the Alamo. The place was full of B Specials with presumably loaded rifles in an acute state of funk. What they would have been like if released on the public, I did not care to imagine. There was quite clearly ill-feeling between the B men and the regular RUC, who wished to distance themselves from the whole affair. We persuaded them to release the man into his mother's custody and persuaded the crowd to go home on the assurance that the police would take no punitive action. They had just about got home, as had I, when an erroneous statement on the radio news carried an announcement of the earlier trouble and a promise that further arrests were expected. This brought the lads out again.

I took some wry satisfaction from the fact that the senior police officer who was depending on us for help to prevent his barracks from being attacked was one who many years before had persisted in following me around in the belief that my GAA activities were a cloak for more subversive activities.

At some time during the evening, I sensed that the people in Bridge Street, a small Protestant enclave, were extremely afraid. I also discovered that night that I was a coward. I had a deep fear of physical confrontation and a deep distaste for violent action, especially if it was directed towards me. I found myself, to my shame, drawn to the back of the crowd instead of to the thick of the struggle. Since then I have always had to steel myself to face up to these situations. On that occasion I think I rationalised my fear into a solicitude for the Bridge Street people who were conveniently far from the action. However imagined my emotions, their fears were real enough. They were terrified, huddled into a few houses, fearful of reprisals and of being burned out or attacked. I got three clergy from the various denominations and went round from house to house reassuring families, visiting old people, and drinking tea.

One house had been liberally decorated outside in red, white and blue, every coign and keystone covered; the painting round the doors and windows and on all the adjacent kerbstones represented hours and days of devoted labour. The lady of the house was embarrassed at the presence of a priest to whom she was dispensing liberal cups of tea. Her natural courtesy required her to make some gesture. 'I don't know how it got that way, sir, I was down the street for an hour and the young fellows must have got hold of paint somewhere and done it.'

I said I would spend the night at my mother's house at the end of the street, which I did, a night punctuated by the reports of a scarecrow gun in the fields near the town, which was even more frightening than the reality. For a few nights after that, we arranged for mixed parties of Catholic and Protestant men to call round the area at intervals to reassure the people. There was no more trouble in Downpatrick but elsewhere in Northern Ireland things were very unsettled.

6

MIX AND MATCH:
COMMUNITY RELATIONS

I WAS WALKING ALONG THE Circular Road in Downpatrick one
Saturday morning in the autumn of 1969 when I bumped into
Brian Faulkner, then Minister of Development, who was doing
his shopping. We chatted for a few minutes about the deteriorating
political situation. As we were parting he said, 'I've put your name
down for something. I can't tell you at the moment what it is, but
I hope you'll accept. There's not much in it, but it might be quite
useful and interesting, and it might lead on to other things.'

A couple of weeks later I had a phone call from the office of the
newly established Ministry for Community Relations asking if the
minister could come to see me in private. Since there was little real
privacy in the council offices, I arranged to see him in the hotel across
the road. The Minister for Community Relations was Robert
Simpson, a general practitioner from near Ballymena who had just
been appointed. It was rather a contradiction in terms, given their
exclusivity over the previous fifty years, for a unionist government to
contemplate a Ministry of Community Relations. Apart from that,
there were very few senior or experienced politicians who could be
considered for the minister's post. Most had put themselves out of
court by their speeches on election platforms and in various Orange
halls and fields up and down the country. The order over the years
had been noted neither for the mellowness of its views on Catholics
nor for the moderation with which these were expressed.

Dr Simpson had emerged as minister in part because he had not compromised himself by partisan rhetoric. His first act was to resign his membership of the Orange Order as being incompatible with his role in drawing the communities together. I suspect that his heart had never been much in it and that he had joined in the first place to secure his political position rather than from conviction. In any case he came across as a sincere and concerned man with the sort of compassion one finds in a good country doctor. I grew to like and respect him during his relatively short period as minister. He was interested in books, and dabbled in travel writing and in writing in a popular way about medical matters and minor ailments. He was not a very imaginative man, and had no great vision of the possibilities of his role, which he had not conceptualised beyond a general sense of decency and the belief that if people got to know one another as individual Ulstermen and Ulsterwomen, group prejudice would lessen and tolerance would flower. He was nevertheless a courageous man to take a post which was not at all popular in unionist circles and which his hardline friends and neighbours, whose fear of sell-out was endemic, would regard as appeasement.

Not all, indeed not much, of this emerged at our first meeting. The minister, along with his permanent secretary, Bill Slinger, explained that in addition to the ministry a Community Relations Commission was being set up. This I knew from the communiqué issued following the Callaghan visit at the end of August promising a Community Relations Board, and from the general gossip of the marketplace. Simpson explained that the membership would be fifty–fifty Catholics and Protestants, that it would be independent of government, with its own budget and staff. He told me of the people who were being invited, or who had agreed to serve, and he finished by asking me to chair the new body. This he justified on the basis of my career in local government, my knowledge of local administration, and my contacts with local officials and councillors. These, in the received analysis of the time, were seen as the most recalcitrant, the most likely to oppose the policies of toleration and fair employment, and the ones most in need of persuasion. Simpson also referred to the normally good community relations in Downpatrick, to the successful civic weeks of the sixties, to the way in which refugees from Belfast had been accommodated earlier that summer, to my contact with departmental officials, and to my interest in and former connections with the organisation of Gaelic games. He told me that the prime minister and cabinet were anxious that I should do the job, and that the chairman of Downpatrick council, Eddie McGrady, had been consulted, had welcomed the appointment, and had agreed to ask the council to release me for a day and a half a week to take up the post.

Following the hint from Brian Faulkner, I was not entirely surprised to be asked to join the commission. I was very surprised to be asked to chair it. Years later I found out, as happens in these cases, that I was not the first choice for the job. That had been Ian Higgins, a Catholic QC who had been involved in the Scarman Tribunal, one of the inquiries that were rampant at the time. He had turned it down. In any case he later became a judge.

To the extent that I had thought about it at all, I had some doubts about the utility of the approach and some scepticism about being able to do anything useful. However, the whole society was in turmoil and seemed to be about to slide into sectarian conflict, if not civil war. There still seemed to be time to haul it back from the brink before the shooting started. And then there was Edmund Burke's observation, recalled from a collection of essays read in school, that all that was required for the triumph of evil was for good men to do nothing.

For years too, the Catholic community had been complaining about exclusion from public office, and here was, perhaps, a first attempt to redress the balance. Apart from which, I was bored. The job in Downpatrick was proving progressively less stimulating and challenging, local government was in a state of flux, perhaps even in terminal decline, I was increasingly interested in political developments and in the wider scene, and I relished a challenge. Whilst I was not sure that I could do any good at all, and whilst I could not be sure that the commission was not being proposed as a sop to public opinion in Britain, and as a palliative rather than as a cure for severe systemic dysfunction, or as a prop and a cloak for an administration that was doubtfully reformable and had better be left to fall through its own ineptitude, I did not think I could refuse. If there was even a 10 per cent chance of doing good, and the same odds that the institution was genuine and the minister honest, given the sad state of the country and the suffering of people already affected by rioting and strife and the prospect of worse to come, I thought I must take it. In the event of failure, or of my having been misled, or having duped myself, the main casualty would be my own reputation, for what that was worth.

Having heard that I would consider the proposition favourably and was likely to accept, the Minister for Community Relations surprised me by asking, 'You are a good Catholic, aren't you?' Even if the tide was turning and what had been a handicap was now a bonus, and used to the oblique subtlety with which religion and origin were cued or identified in Northern Ireland, I was a little shocked by the bluntness of this approach. While I was not surprised that religion had been an issue, given the promise to balance membership of the commission, I had thought this was a statistical matter rather than a test of the quality of belief. I fenced.

I said that I thought there were only three or four good Catholics in the world and I did not know any of them. I was about to proceed to a disquisition on comparative sanctity when he applied the public and, for a Ballymena man, the clinching test. 'But you go to church, don't you? And pay your dues?' Having assured himself on these fundamental proofs of faith and morals, he left satisfied. Next day I asked Bill Slinger what had been bothering his minister. He told me that he had a horror of the headlines in the *Irish News* if he had appointed a lapsed Catholic, or an agnostic or a communist.

I remember on the evening the appointment was announced, being asked by a rather patronising television interviewer, 'Does this mean that Catholics are now taking these jobs?' I told him that I could only speak for myself and not for the generality of Catholics, that this was the first time I had been offered a job and I had accepted it. I was sure that there were others who, if asked, would respond, and that no society could afford to cut itself off from the contribution of skill, experience, intelligence and potential of one third of the population.

An interesting bench mark of the move of public opinion is the reaction to my appointment. I had many letters of support. In particular, I received a letter from every GAA club in County Down, and many outside it, congratulating me on taking up the post and wishing me well.

I don't think that would happen today. Perhaps people have become more cynical, perhaps just weary, perhaps we have all been round the track too often.

★   ★   ★

We started the Community Relations Commission on 3 December 1969 in an empty room on the fourth floor of Bedford House. There was no furniture. The secretary, Dill Henderson, had been seconded from the civil service, a serious-minded principal officer called Paddy Farrelly having consulted me and minuted solemnly that the chairman had 'no objection to a woman, as such'. We made up the script as we went along, and gathered staff, initially from the civil service.

The commissioners were just the sort of people a government department selects, although even more so then than now, from among those it knows, or from among safe people in constituencies it is trying to draw on. The make-up of the committee, I suppose, reflected the way in which the idea of a commission had emerged, or had been thrust upon the administration. It reflected too a view of community relations that owed much to early experience in US cities where there were civil rights problems. There, the response was the conference, called together by the mayor, of what seemed to be the stable elements in the community: the banks, the churches, the solid citizens and the representatives of the moderate blacks. The failure of this model on its original testbed did not prevent it being imported by the Home Office as a response to emerging problems with race in Britain, or its application without further modification or testing to the much more complex conflict in Northern Ireland.

Almost by definition, therefore, the membership of the commission excluded activists. None of the people who had been active in promoting civil rights were there: none of the people who had marched, or had been on the streets, or who had spoken up prominently in the cause. There were no active politicians, because the commission had to be seen not to be political, and no churchmen, to emphasise its neutrality, I suppose, from what was seen to be the divisive religious labels that had characterised the conflict in the north of Ireland for generations, if not centuries. There were no young people on the commission. I, the chairman, was the youngest, and I was forty-two.

There were two retired politicians, both women who had lost their seats in the Stormont parliament through the removal of the university seats in 1967. Sheelagh Murnaghan had been a Liberal and Bessie Maconachie a moderate Unionist. Despite, or perhaps indeed because of, their political backgrounds, they were among the best members.

Sheelagh Murnaghan had been a lone voice crying for reform in the Stormont parliament for a number of years. She had been a long-serving Irish hockey international and still retained some of the aggressiveness of her no-nonsense style of play. She dressed in rather butch tweeds and smoked mannikin cigars and was not afraid to tackle anybody in debate. My memories of her had been of a lonely figure on opposition benches denuded by abstention on the nationalist side, facing government benches thinned by unionist apathy and indifference, if not actual antipathy to the policies she was advocating: fair employment, fair representation, distributive justice, fairness to minorities, especially travellers (or itinerants as they were called then), and an end to discrimination. Had she been heeded to at any time in the sixties, most of the demands of the civil rights movement would have been anticipated and dealt with, and much conflict, destruction and death might have been avoided.

Sadly, when her political base was removed with the loss of the university franchise, in what was generally intended as a liberalising move, she sank without trace politically and ceased to be a force in public life; thus was silenced one of the few truly liberal voices around. I suppose that her appointment to the commission, and that of Bessie Maconachie, was not only a matter of maintaining a gender balance on the commission, but an attempt by a minister to compensate former political colleagues for whom there was genuine respect on all sides.

Sheelagh Murnaghan had a tremendous heart, full of compassion, and she had a strong sense of justice. Unfortunately she had not the capacity to exploit all the situations to which her instinct led her. She was a woolly thinker, an appallingly convoluted and imprecise speaker, who confused activity with action. One day she told me how she had travelled to Newry with a traveller and spent ten hours securing a reduction of £10 in the price of a van. When I pointed out that in much less time in the Bar Library she could have earned £20, paid the traveller his £10 and saved herself a lot of time and trouble, she seemed to think I had missed the point. Maybe I had.

On the first Christmas after the inception of the commission, Sheelagh proposed, and the rest of us weakly agreed, that we should show ourselves to the Belfast citizenry by a tour of pubs along the so-called peaceline, at that time a straggling temporary fence of corrugated iron sheeting erected at the main flashpoints to separate Catholic and Protestant areas. This we did, Sheelagh leading the way, respectable middle-aged men in business suits, and Bessie Maconachie, into pub after crowded pub shamefacedly introducing ourselves to the drinking public who, momentarily released from the stress of conflict in seasonal revelry, could not care less who we were, while we wondered whether we should order drinks for the house on the public purse, and whether the system of accounting for public finance would allow us to do so, and visiting a house where a woman (very shrewdly, I thought) asked us if we had brought her giro from 'the Supplementary Benefit', and switched off quickly again when she heard that we brought only good will and a message of peace. I had never felt such a fool and we quickly withdrew. Sheelagh thought it had been an excellent effort.

The commission membership included a former president of the Law Society, a recently retired director of the Northern Ireland Tourist Board, two businessmen, one Protestant and the other (by far the more conservative) a Catholic educated at Downside, the Roman Catholic public school in England. There were, I think, four members of the Queen's University Senate, representatives of a group I grew to typify as Queen's liberals, who saw themselves as being above the struggle that was going on in Belfast but who, as senators, had presided over a university which, as it transpired, had a quite shameful record of unfair employment practices against Catholics over the years.

The commission's membership was completed by the inclusion of the two ombudsmen *ex officio*. Sir Edmund Compton, the Parliamentary Commissioner for Administration at both Stormont and Westminster, was a mandarins' mandarin. He rather dulled the cutting edge of his own office by opining in his first report that the Northern Ireland administration was 'meticulous to a fault'. It did not help to engender confidence among those needing his protection when the appointed watchdog rolled over on his back and purred like a cat. He was later to produce a shameful and infamous report on the abuse of detainees under interrogation, in which he made an entirely specious distinction between ill-treatment and torture on the grounds of the intention or not of the perpetrators to inflict pain. He came to commission meetings very infrequently and made no significant contribution. Years later, not long before Compton's death, I was in the same room as him at a gathering in London to celebrate the coming of age of the Ombudsman's office. I found that I could not bring myself to speak to him.

John Benn, on the other hand, the Northern Ireland Commissioner for Complaints, made an enormous contribution. He attended every meeting and event involving the Community Relations Commission, and he was more radical than most of the other members and more ready to face up to government departments and outside agencies. A former permanent secretary of the Department of Education, a native of Bolton who had been in Northern Ireland since joining the schools inspectorate in the thirties, John played a major role in developing the policies underlying the 1947 Education Act (the Northern Ireland version of Butler's 1944 Act). This, in extending the scope of free secondary and university education, and in producing a generation of young Catholics who were educated beyond the willingness of the society or the capacity of the economy to employ them, had created probably the most potent ingredient of the civil rights movement and a motor for political change. Later, as permanent secretary, he had negotiated and carried through the settlement with the Catholic Church that had increased the rate of capital grant for Catholic schools from 65 per cent to 85 per cent. He once told me that it was a great source of pride to him that the Catholic bishops, suspicious of unionist politicians and distrustful of local education authorities, at least had confidence in the Department of Education. He was shocked when I remarked that there were many people, including many Catholics, who trusted neither the hierarchy nor the ministry when it came to the control of education, and that he had retarded the process of opening up the schools system by consolidating power in clerical and denominational rather than in lay and secular hands.

John told me a story of how, as an inspector of schools, he had been instructed by one of his former ministers, Dame Dehra Parker, a formidable old unionist battleaxe and James Chichester-Clark's aunt, to commission an impartial history of Northern Ireland, 'written from the unionist viewpoint of course'.

So much for the membership of the commission, but what about policy? It was clear that the ministry had no real idea what community relations was about. Indeed, it is probably not unfair to say that the government did not see community relations as having much to do with civil and human rights; rather, it was all to do with socialising and getting to know you. Any idea that the government itself, or the system, was in any way responsible for the conflict was far from government ministers' minds. In a classic case of overkill, not having given a thought to community relations for the previous fifty years, they had plunged in with both feet, or were run in by Whitehall and set up both a ministry and a commission of community relations. And since neither had a precise remit, or any clear direction, it was not surprising that they often bumped into each other in the dark.

Neither at ministerial nor official level was there any real attempt to conceptualise what they were about, there was no attempt to analyse the problems, or to develop a strategy to deal with them. The minister, Dr Simpson, was qualified on grounds of decency: he acted thereafter as if community relations was an activity that was somehow outside politics – when it was in fact highly charged. Bill Slinger had been an assistant secretary in the Industrial Relations wing of the DHSS (and formerly the Ministry of Labour) for some years before becoming the commission's secretary, with a good track record on negotiations and good relations with trade unions and employers. He was essentially a decent man, but not the person to provide the rigour of analysis that the new department needed. I often reflected on what might have been if his colleague assistant secretary, George Quigley, had been deputed to steer the new ship.

The ministry, being not particularly interested in or capable of policy formulation, did as all governmental species do when in doubt: they concentrated on action, or at least on activity. But that was supposed to be the commission's task. The commission, for its part, finding that no other body was developing policy, tried to provide a theoretical and analytical framework for what it was doing. And this brought it into conflict with the ministry, which did not like being out-run, or out-jumped, or out-thought.

On beginning my new job, I went round everybody whom I thought might have a constructive view on the nature of the problems in the community or on how we might tackle them. This included community workers (thin on the ground at the time), those who had been active in the civil rights movement, policemen, teachers,

84

clergy, businessmen and academics. My most surprising encounter, perhaps, occurred when I went to the Social Studies Department at Queen's University in search of ideas and guidance, unpublished matter, theses, student essays even, anything that might throw light on the dynamics of the conflict, only to be told that there was a rule in the department that precluded discussion of these issues as being too divisive. Well, there are ivory towers, and towers of fake ivory.

At an early stage in the work of the Community Relations Commission, I was approached by a deputation from Dungannon complaining about discrimination in housing by the local urban district council. The group was led by Dr Conn McCluskey and his wife Patricia, who had been the real pioneers of civil rights in Northern Ireland. They had started the Campaign for Social Justice in the early sixties to document discrimination and to lobby Westminster MPs. They were decent, earnest people who sought no preferment or office for themselves, and who laboured tirelessly and unselfishly for justice. They left the civil rights movement in disgust when it was taken over by a combination of reactionary right-wing republicans and trendy left-wing agitators.

In response to their complaints, I spoke to Brian Faulkner, then Minister of Development, who called in to see me in my Downpatrick office on his way to Belfast one morning. He said he had been considering taking housing powers off the Dungannon council and giving them to the Housing Trust, but for political purposes he would prefer to persuade the chairman of the council to request him to do so rather than to be seen to exercise punitive powers, which he was not very sure that he had anyhow. A few days later, he phoned me to say that the Dungannon council would shortly be requesting the Housing Trust to take over the management of its housing stock, and the trust was willing to do so. I had arranged to see the Dungannon deputation that afternoon. When I told them the outcome, the McCluskeys were delighted that fair administration had been achieved. Others of their group rounded on me for protecting the council from the showdown and public castigation it so richly deserved. This was a lesson that people are often happier with their grievances than with their relief, and that winners in Northern Ireland achieve satisfaction mainly from dancing on the graves of their vanquished opponents.

Another part of my task was to establish the credibility of the commission with various constituencies. One early meeting involved an encounter with the Central Citizens' Defence Committee, the CCDC, which had emerged behind the barricades in Catholic areas. The meeting was held in a former de la Salle monastery in the middle of the Falls Road area, a house I had often visited during my teaching career with the de la Salle Brothers. It was a winter's night, dark and cold with no streetlights. The roads were littered with debris, burnt-out cars and pieces of aborted or incipient barricades. The entrance to the house was, I think, sandbagged, the windows were heavily shuttered, the front door lined with metal. Having been scrutinised through a wooden flap, I was admitted to a crowded, smoke-filled room, with a narrow space against one wall and the rest of the room packed with men on chairs and others standing at the back and round the walls. I don't remember any women, though there may have been some. They were an interesting and varied crowd, ranging from manual workers to unemployed men to teachers and clergymen. There were several people whom I recognised as having been reputedly prominent in the IRA in the forties and fifties, and some who were clearly the local hard men of the moment.

The atmosphere was one of fear and concern rather than menace. These were men who had seen their community under attack from Protestant mobs and from the police and B Specials. They felt violated and exposed. They had responded to threat by throwing up barricades made from buses, burnt-out cars, kerbstones, building materials and anything else that came to hand. They did not trust the police, detested the Bs and felt that the hand of the government was against them in all things. The arrival of the British Army in mid-August had provided a period of respite. There was a wary but highly suspicious relationship. Some of the citizen defenders were prepared to envisage a new beginning, others were highly distrustful of all authority, some, echoing Bernadette Devlin, were waiting for the inevitable clash between army and community, and some shadowy figures in the background, not many, had guns and were ready to use them. Politically they ran the gamut from traditional nationalist to republican labour, to Northern Ireland Labour to Sinn Féin in one or other of its feeble manifestations.

I sensed very little political ferment, not much vision, the aggression that comes from fear, a sense of being cornered, a sense of having survived one onslaught too many and a determination not to allow another, a feeling that on top of unemployment, bad housing and discrimination, sectarian attacks and oppressive policy were the last straw. Yet, surprisingly perhaps, the general will was to look forward, and whilst the sceptics had their say, and some others might have silently reserved their positions, there were those who wished to look forward, to give peace a chance and to take developments at face value.

The meeting was chaired by Tom Conaty, a prominent Catholic businessman, a fruit importer who had emerged with great credibility during the previous couple of years. A man of considerable courage and integrity, he was a straight talker who let you know very quickly what was on his mind. He was, I supposed, at one level a representative of the Catholic Church. Although there were local priests in the room, he was thought to be closer to the bishop than they. He worked in double harness with Canon Padraig Murphy, who had been a curate in Downpatrick in the fifties. Murphy was a big man, physically, with a large head and white hair, who had become known on television as a spokesman. He had a strong physical presence, and he was perhaps the most authoritative voice on the social, economic and security concerns of his community. Tom Conaty based his negotiating style on his dealings with orange merchants in Smyrna and Cyprus. He always believed that the other side had more to give, and would do so if pushed hard enough. Stirring stuff when he told it, but not very conducive to compromise.

At this stage, control of the CCDC was being wrested from the hands of the original street committee men. The Catholic Church was fighting to take control from the few IRA men who had emerged as citizen defenders. Jim Sullivan, who had been chairman, and his fellow founders were ruthlessly squeezed out of office as the CCDC grew into an umbrella organisation covering other parts of Catholic Belfast, where organisations were centred on the Catholic parish rather than on the street, which were much less republican and much less politically aware than the lower and middle Falls. At the same time there was division in IRA ranks as the more political incumbents were being challenged by more militant recruits. This was the beginning of the split that was to lead to the emergence of the Provisionals.

I have often thought that the Catholic Church, in their fear of red communism, let the Provo cat out of the bag. They were more comfortable with the good, clean, honest-to-goodness Catholic Irish boys in the Provisionals, even if they did carry the odd gun, than they were with the closet Marxists of the 'official' IRA. Whether wittingly or not, the cat soon became a tiger which was incapable of being caged, controlled or ridden by anyone.

I knew many of those in the room through Gaelic football, and this gave me a tiny foothold. Many of them had played for or been associated with Antrim clubs, and were natural leaders of their communities. It was a tough meeting. Those present gave me a fair hearing, but a fairly tough grilling afterwards. I explained that even at this early stage, the approach of the commission went far beyond tea and cakes, that we were concerned to encourage the removal of barriers of misunderstanding between the communities (which was of less interest to them) but also to ventilate issues of economic and social deprivation, fair employment and human rights (all of which engaged them rather more). In the end, they rather grudgingly gave me the benefit of the doubt; they agreed to co-operate with the work of the commission, or at least not to impede it, and to suspend judgement until we had had time to prove ourselves, or until time showed that the whole process was another piece of cynical manipulation by the Stormont government of which I was, if not a willing tool, at least a credulous dupe.

There were many meetings of a similar type over the next couple of years. I remember going to a meeting of the east Belfast presbytery where, after I had spent some time explaining how independent we were of government, an old retired minister stumbled to his feet and complained about the Macrory Committee which had been set up to review the structure and powers of local government. 'When you go back to the prime minister,' he said, 'tell him that they have got to be stopped.' It appeared that he was reflecting the views of one councillor in County Antrim, 'a loyal man, who had wrought hard for the party in the Bannside all his days', who had been interrogated about his council's record on discrimination in housing.

'They were arrogant men,' he said of the committee members, 'arrogant men. The way they spoke to him, he might just as well have been John Hume.'

One occasion when I tried to introduce a facilitator exemplifies the difficulties that arise in this sort of work through stereotyping and false impressions. On the first occasion that the army came into conflict with loyalists on the Shankill Road, there were some hard feelings, some broken heads, and much recrimination. The protests of pastors on the Shankill brought an echo of sympathy from the people of the Falls, who thought they knew a bit about this sort of treatment, and it began to look like a moment when people might be brought together. I spoke to Canon Murphy and to the Reverend Donald Gillies, who seemed to be on the point of meeting, and suggested that it might be helpful to have a facilitator from outside who would structure the conversations and prevent a collapse into recrimination. I undertook to provide help if they were of a mind to talk, and to remain silent if they were not.

Both sides were willing to talk. Both agreed to field a team. But in the end, the Shankill people withdrew. This arose, I believe, because of their stereotype of the Catholic as a mendacious fellow who was handy with words and would talk you down in any argument. Therefore, since it was a zero-sum game, and they did not want to return home the losers, it was better not to enter into discussions at all.

In this seminal stage, we were very much guided by Estyn Evans, the father figure of social geography and regional planning, who had written sensitively and perceptively about identity, tradition and folk culture. He rather shocked me by prescribing the use of bulldozers which would start at Castle Junction and flatten the segment of Belfast including the Shankill and Falls Roads; the area would subsequently be planted as an urban forest park which would effectively separate the warring factions. We never got far enough into the discussion to find out what was to be done with the people so displaced. Estyn enunciated a theory when we were driving one day through drumlin country in north Armagh about the effect of landscape and geomorphology on character and attitudes. The great plains, he argued, lent themselves to long perspectives, to great vistas which induced breadth of vision and nobility of spirit. People, when they could see them, raised their eyes and their minds to the contemplation of the far-off hills and mountain peaks. But the small hills of Armagh and Tyrone, and the dreary steeples of Fermanagh cut off the views of the mountaintops, narrowed the vision, and produced a race of narrowminded, introspective bigots who could not, or would not, look round the next corner. It was an attractive theory, which promised to explain a lot, except for the fact that the people of the American Midwest, which was broad enough and flat enough for anything, did not immediately come to mind as examples of liberality or of the free imagination. Perhaps he was echoing Thoreau's dictum that there are none happy in the world but beings who enjoy freely a vast horizon.

One of our first initiatives was to offer house room and support to John Malone, who had been detached from his headmaster post to develop community relations programmes for schools, under the guise of a moral education curriculum, or maybe it was the other way round. I persuaded him to act as the commission's adviser on education and as a general counsellor.

John Malone was one of the really great educators. A member of an old Downpatrick family, he had become headmaster of Orangefield, a new intermediate school catering for the east of the city. John set about transforming this into a comprehensive school in all but name. In doing so he set new standards for secondary schools in Belfast, and more widely. He employed interesting people as teachers, and gave them their head, he was accessible to pupils and engaged their interest. He was the headmaster who persuaded the future Beirut hostage Brian Keenan to return to school after he had left to begin an apprenticeship as a heating engineer, and he was widely revered by teachers, especially those who were less than fully happy with the complacency of the system. John worked for a couple of years developing and piloting a curriculum which anticipated by almost twenty years the later developments in Education for Mutual Understanding. He raised hackles in the educational establishment, however, by his insistence that community relations work had to go far beyond the curriculum, and had to involve school structures and government and the manner in which the school engaged with the individual pupil. He expounded unfashionable ideas about the dignity and worth of pupils who had been labelled as second-class by the selective system, and his pioneering work was disgracefully ignored by the sceptical and non-practising pundits in the Ministry of Education.

John was, from an early stage, an extra and willing pair of hands. I remember him, one Monday morning, telling me a story that illustrated the doubtful value of the simplistic mix-and-match approach to community relations. The Rotary Club, or some such group, had arranged a community relations concert in the Grosvenor Hall to which old people were to be bussed from various parts of the city. John, acting as a conductor on one of the buses, was helping an old lady aboard in Dee Street when she asked suspiciously, 'Will there be any of the other sort there?' When John explained in his patient and charming way that the general idea of the concert was to meet people of 'the other sort' she went along willingly enough. The concert was a huge success and was acclaimed by the organisers as a great contribution to community relations. Still, as the tired old lady was being escorted to her door in Dee Street, she turned to John and whispered, 'All the same, don't you think they might have had their own night?'

Adventures like the Grosvenor Hall concert impelled the commission to adopt a strategy of community development. I had been impressed by the work of the rural development group Muintir na Tíre in the South, based though it was largely on the Catholic parish. There had also been an address by Dr Hendriks of the Netherlands at a conference in Magee College organised by Ted Rhodes in the late sixties which described Dutch attempts to build communities in the newly reclaimed polderlands, and articles written by G.B. Newe. Paul Ylvisaker, whom I had met at Salzburg in 1965 and who was now with the Ford Foundation, was another formative influence, and I had read about the experiments in co-operativism in Antigonish in Nova Scotia and in Mondragon in the Basque country. It seemed sensible to us to respond to the felt needs of communities, to help them to organise themselves and to relate in a constructive way to government agencies. One metaphor I used at the time was that it should not be necessary to burn down the City Hall to get a lock fixed on your back door. In the end, it was easier to convince the communities of the truth of that proposition than the Belfast Corporation. We also hoped that as they learned to deal with functional issues like housing, urban transport, economic development and employment, communities would see that these issues transcended sectarian divisions: there were poor Catholics and poor Protestants, old age, poverty and unemployment were not unique to one community, and there was a benefit in coming together to deal with common problems. In this way we hoped that the great constitutional and ideological issues that divided people could be put on hold while communities got on with the ordinary business of living. In this way too, trust, a delicate plant, might begin to take root and flower, providing a basis for exchanges on more fundamental matters in the future.

Another aspect of our diagnosis was that there was a lack of leadership at local level, and a lack of community self-confidence, which conditioned people to react defensively to any perceived threat and to almost any approach from the outside. We believed that any worthwhile programme of community development would address the problem of local leadership, and in developing indigenous leaders who could articulate the hopes and fears of the community, and help them to move towards a more constructive relationship with government agencies and with modern society, we would be laying the basis for a new approach to politics and community organisation, and a civic culture of co-operation rather than conflict.

This, quite clearly, and somewhat to the dismay of the ministry, shifted the priority slightly for some of our activities, from cross-community work where Catholics could be paired with Protestants, where bums could be placed on seats and counted, towards work which, initially at least, might involve only one community. But it seemed to us more sensible to help people to determine their own priorities, to help them to come to terms with the problems they found, to help them to find themselves and gain confidence, and to give them the tools and the training before sending them off to encounter others in the hope of reaching a wider understanding.

Having decided on policy, we set about recruiting staff. Early in 1970 we appointed as director of the commission an engaging Welshman called Hywel Griffiths, whom I had spotted a few years earlier at the Magee conference, and a team of field officers. These were interesting and energetic people from a wide range of backgrounds – from a Hoover salesman to a Presbyterian clergyman, and included teachers, academics and community workers. They were selected because they were different, because each in his or her own way had reacted to the situation in Northern Ireland and had tried to do something about it, because of the links they had developed with the communities, because of their ability to talk to ordinary people, because they were not frightened of authority, and because they had the ability to take responsibility in a nonhierarchical organisation. They came from different political backgrounds, which we did not inquire into. Most, I suspect, had a radical edge, all were committed to the nonviolent resolution of conflict, and all had a very highly developed sense of social justice. They were very special people whom Hywel quickly trained and welded into a team. All of them worked very hard, and most went on to do other interesting things when the commission was finally wound up. John Darby, a history teacher, was recruited as a research and publications officer and so began an illustrious career in the study of conflict.

The field workers had an important secondary role, to act as the antennae of the commission, to pick up the signals in the community, and to give early warning of the movement of public opinion on a micro scale. This they did very well. They quickly became trusted by the communities, and were able to operate in even the most dangerous areas on both sides of the so-called peaceline, irrespective of religion. That also provided me with up-to-date information on the state of play in most parts of Belfast and elsewhere in Northern Ireland.

From the beginning, community work was easier in Catholic areas. I suppose there were some Protestants who saw the whole community relations exercise as a sop thrown to Catholics to quieten the civil rights movement. Others saw community relations as some sort of admission of guilt, others as an affirmation that relations had not been good and that it was necessary to do something about that. One heard, invariably from councils that had not employed a Catholic for generations, the bland assertion, 'Of course, community relations have always been good around here.' It reminded me of a picture associated with the collapse of a system-built tower block of flats at Ronan Point in the East End of London a few years before. The building had succumbed to a minor gas explosion and had collapsed like a house of cards. The borough surveyor was interviewed on television, against the backdrop of the collapsed building, declaring, 'The building complied with the building bye-laws.'

There was a sense too in which people in Catholic areas saw that there was something in community relations work for them. For the first time in some cases, somebody in authority was prepared to talk directly to them and to listen to their needs. A great deal of energy had been released in these communities by the civil rights movement, which had politicised them, and by the felt need for defence and mutual support that had grown up behind the barricades. They were, in a sense, looking for direction, for structures, for a means of channelling all this energy. Community development provided a means, and the field officers were there as facilitators. In the beginning there was some tension between them and the Catholic Church, which tended to claim the right to organise people on the basis of the Catholic parish, and which resented interference that might dilute the strength of that bond. Whilst we respected the strength and importance of that linkage, the organisation of social, educational and other services, including the voluntary sector, on denominational lines had seemed to be part of the historic problem, encouraging people to look inward for support to their own group, discouraging dissent or any breaking of ranks, and inhibiting contact across sectarian barriers. This of course is one of the classic dilemmas of community development in a divided society: to balance the desire for self-sufficiency, self-confidence and a secure identity with the need to relate in the wider society to other communities holding utterly different sets of values.

At an early stage, the contest for leadership in the community became three-sided with the Provisional IRA competing with the Church for the hearts and minds of the people, seducing the young with the glamour of action and involvement in a struggle that the folk memory, partisan history and the bar-room ballad had invested with an aura of romance and gallantry. At the same time, the silent acquiescence of their elders was secured by intimidation, by peer pressure, by a deep-seated aversion to informing and by the fear of external attack, in which case any and all defenders would be needed. Or, more crudely, to paraphrase an American maxim associated with the Vietnam War, 'Get them in the kneecaps, and hearts and minds will follow.'

There were, I think, deeper reasons for the failure of community development as a strategy to attract Protestant support. In part this may have happened because politics had atrophied in Protestant areas through a belief (mistaken, as it appeared) that the Unionist Party in power would look after its own. It may indeed have done so, but not visibly those at the bottom of the ladder, and not to the extent of eliminating poverty in Protestant areas, or of providing decent housing on the Shankill or in Sandy Row or the lower Newtownards Road. There was a feeling that it was impolitic to rock the boat in case the constitutional position was called into question. There was less desire than in the Catholic areas to challenge authority, and no tradition of having done so. Unemployment rates too were higher in Catholic areas, which provided a pool of intelligent, underused people who were waiting for an opportunity to do something constructive. In Protestant areas their counterparts were more likely to be in jobs where they could exercise their leadership potential as shop stewards, and their political activism through the trade union movement.

There was also a religious, perhaps a theological, factor. Protestantism, as a system of belief, puts much more emphasis on individual responsibility, Catholicism puts a higher value on community. This, I think, made it a more typical response for Protestants to seek relief through individual efforts (and to be perhaps less tolerant of those who were seen not to be exerting themselves) and for Catholics to seek the comfort and the diffusion of duty that comes with community. A generalisation, perhaps, but, for whatever reason, the development of community structures in Protestant areas has consistently moved more slowly than in comparable Catholic areas.

There may have been something in the make-up of the Community Relations Commission too. At that time the Catholic community (certainly in Belfast, and most of our concern was with Belfast) was more closely knit in class terms than the Protestant community. The members of the small Catholic middle class, mostly doctors, lawyers, teachers, priests, publicans, were more closely integrated into their own community than were their Protestant counterparts, were closer to their community's fears and aspirations, and could articulate these for them and speak to them with some hope of being heard. This, of course, has changed. One of the great shifts of the past quarter of a century has been the emergence of a Catholic middle and professional class that has done quite nicely out of all the changes, that has moved both geographically and spiritually away from its roots. It has begun to lose contact with the working class, and that has created divisions of class and wealth in a community that was once more coherent.

Such divisions already existed in the Protestant community of the late 1960s. I remember being appalled at the audience reaction in a meeting in suburban east Belfast, organised by Alliance, or its forerunner the New Ulster Movement, or Protestant and Catholic Encounter, PACE – who all tended to have a common membership. I spoke, along with Austin Currie and Brian McRoberts, who was then aspiring to be MP for West Belfast. The audience reflected the temper of the time in that this middle-class, 'liberal', mostly Protestant audience spent most of the time baiting McRoberts as a reactionary unionist. I was content to sit on the sidelines for most of this, but what did concern me was the mockery and scorn that greeted his attempts to depict the problems of people on the Shankill, the poor housing, the low standard of health, the almost total lack of educational opportunity.

It may be, therefore, that the Catholic members of the commission were better able to reflect the concerns of Catholics in areas of conflict, and to communicate to them the general aims of the commission, than were their Protestant colleagues on their side.

I tried to repair the omission by suggesting to the Minister for Community Relations the appointment of a prominent soccer player, a folk hero who could speak to Protestant youths in east Belfast, where tartan gangs were beginning to emerge, and at a time when the aggressive behaviour of young football fans was a constant source of anxiety, and a potential flash point every time Linfield played a team with a substantial Catholic following, or at a ground which caused their followers to traverse Catholic streets on the way to or from the match. To my disappointment, the minister appointed Mike Gibson, an Irish rugby international, a great man in his own sphere, but little good for my purposes. What was more important, his name meant very little to the youths we were trying to influence.

At one time, incidentally, I thought that George Best, then at the height of his wondrous powers as a footballer with Manchester United, who had grown up in east Belfast, would be a useful and charismatic figure to involve in some way. By devious means, including the Anglican Dean of Manchester who was vice-chairman of the English Community Relations Commission, and through contacts in English Catholic organisations, I spoke to Manchester United's manager Matt Busby and told him of my plan. He said it wasn't a very good idea and not to bother my head.

Another interesting character who appeared at this time was John Burton of the Institute for the Study of Conflict in London. His presence had arisen from an initiative early in 1969 when Michael Hurley, an engaging Jesuit who had founded the Irish School of Ecumenics in Dublin, asked me to find a mixed group of trade unionists to take part in a workshop. This I did with the help of Billy Blease, secretary of the Northern Ireland Committee of the Irish Congress of Trade Unions. Burton had been head of the Australian Department of Foreign Affairs at a very young age, and had represented Australia at the founding meeting of the United Nations in San Francisco in 1945. Having become very close to Dr Evatt, leader of the Australian Labour Party, a Foreign Minister and subsequently prime minister of Australia, Burton had retired from the civil service to enter politics, and had become an academic researching conflict in various parts of the world. He had developed a model of conflict resolution that encouraged people to work together on functional matters in which they had a common interest, until they built up enough trust to deal with the more divisive issues. I had read one of his books and invited him in to work with groups in Belfast. He brought two assistants, John Bayley and Ron Wiener, who each went native in quite different directions. Ron produced a classic study of urban redevelopment in *The Rape and Plunder of the Shankill*. John identified more and more closely with republican groups until, along with some colleagues in social research, he was eventually accused (wrongly, I think) in a headline article in the *Andersonstown News* of being a British spy and forced to flee to the less threatening climes of English Maoism.

At this time, too, I met Ian Paisley for the first time. I had been doing quite a few television interviews and radio spots, and getting a considerable amount of press coverage for community relations work. This produced a lampooning attack, complete with a cartoon, in the *Protestant Telegraph*. Under the heading 'This man is dangerous' I was described as a monster who had crawled out of some County Down necropolis, who glared mirthlessly at people from the television screen, and who was more dangerous than the IRA to the interests of Protestant Ulster. I was advised to sue, but I couldn't see much point. At least it was publicity, and a bit of a laugh, although I thought it odd to be called humourless by a puritan paper. The worrying part was the possibility of incitement to violence. With sectarian killers on the loose, I preferred not to be labelled an 'enemy of the loyalist people', the term 'pan-nationalist' not having then been invented, or as some sort of fellow traveller with the IRA.

Whether any representations were made to the newspaper, I do not know, or whether the police took any action on incitement (which I doubt), there was a phone call from Dr Paisley asking if he could come to see me. He explained that while he nominally controlled the *Protestant Telegraph* he did not exercise day-to-day management. He had been unaware of the attack on me and of its particularly virulent nature until, he said, 'Eileen saw some reference to it in the *Irish News*.' I found this description of the breakfast-time reading of the Paisley family both interesting and amusing. He went on to apologise most handsomely for what had been said, and I accepted the apology and that was the end of that.

This was the beginning of a long, if not close, relationship with Ian Paisley. He is a complex personality. I have often thought there are about six Paisleys. Two of them are very nice people, two quite awful, and the other two could go either way. What I have to report is that he never told me a lie, never breached a confidence, and that as a constituency MP he worked unceasingly for all his constituents irrespective of religion. True, he could be, and was, a rabblerouser. He very often filled the atmosphere with an inflammable vapour that other people could and did ignite, but then Ulster has always had, always seemed to need, a roaring parson, like Cooke, or Roaring Hanna or A. Wylie Blue. In public he often appeared a driven man. In private he could be affable and very amusing. He did not, I think, use his church as a platform or constituency from which to gain political power. Rather, he entered politics to secure the fundamental religious values to which he is attached.

7

'MUCH HATRED, LITTLE ROOM'

THE YEARS 1969 TO 1972 WERE AN exciting time in Northern
Ireland politics. One advantage of being chairman of the
Community Relations Commission was that one met most of
the interesting people who came to Belfast: politicians, journalists,
academics and churchmen. Most of them were looking wildly around
for some expression of moderate or neutral opinion, for some shred
of hope, some sliver of good news they could bring away with them.
Academics and journalists were the best because they could be
persuaded to return for a recap at the end of their tour, and would
often convey the gist of what had been said to them by people who
would not talk to the commission or to official representatives.

At this time too, Lord Grey, the Governor of Northern Ireland,
was a good friend. He had come to Northern Ireland in 1968, a
former colonial civil servant whose instinct was to run things, who
knew the nature of official briefing and who wanted to receive views
from a more independent source. He was anxious to diversify his
dinner table, and since most senior politicians who visited were entertained by him, this gave me an opportunity to meet senior British
politicians, ministers and former prime ministers and chancellors and
to have a channel that bypassed Northern Ireland government departments. I often travelled to Hillsborough in the evenings with a friend
and neighbour, Sir John Anderson, a retired general, a former Chief
of the Defence College, and first Colonel-in-Chief of the Ulster
Defence Regiment, the UDR. He was a very decent, straight man

with a great sense of fairness. He was also a good source of army gossip. He shocked me one night by explaining that the army was encouraging the IRA to grow so that it could become big enough to take on and defeat (in a pitched battle, I suppose). If this reflects the level of strategic thinking about counter-insurgency, it is no wonder the struggle has lasted so long.

Lord Grey phoned me one day soon after my appointment, to ask whether he could visit an area on the Donegall Road that had been badly affected by flash flooding. I had not appreciated until then that even on a small matter like this, he could only act on the advice of Northern Ireland ministers. Apparently the Ministry of Home Affairs was not anxious that he should visit, and it soon became clear to me that he was angling for an invitation that he could not politely refuse. This I rapidly issued and he arrived in his be-flagged limousine fifteen minutes later. The only condition I made was that we should travel in my wife Joan's battered Triumph Herald rather than in the state coach. It is perhaps hard to credit, given how rapidly things deteriorated subsequently, that in late 1970 the governor was able to walk about with a minimum of fuss and without the area having been invested by the security forces.

The sense of togetherness engendered in combating the common threat of the floods momentarily united Catholic and Protestant. It also convinced me of the importance of a superordinate goal in conflict resolution. If the Cave Hill were falling down on Belfast, Catholics and Protestants would combine to keep it up, and would not have time for lesser squabbles. The problem was to convince them that metaphorically at least the sky was falling on Belfast as a result of the increasing and continuing violence.

Lord Grey once told me that the first prudential act of a newly appointed colonial governor was to check that the nearest port had a pier capable of accommodating the frigate that would come to remove him, and that the route from Government House to the quayside could be secured to allow for early and rapid evacuation should it become necessary to bring down the flag. He did not actually say that he was applying this advice to his own position in Northern Ireland, but it certainly suggested an awareness that things could worsen, and that doomsday could not be ruled out.

An early visitor, in June 1970, was Reginald Maudling, who

appeared to be overwhelmed by a situation that defied rationality and logic. 'Tell me,' he asked, 'what makes the IRA tick?' This was the time when he uttered his memorable farewell to Ulster on staggering back to his plane: 'What a bloody country! Give me a double whisky.' What you got from Maudling was the impression of a massive intelligence, only partly in gear, which moved sideways towards the problem, like a crab, and then scuttled back into its hole without actually coming to grips with it.

I thought it a pity that he was so pilloried for his remark about seeking 'an acceptable level of violence'. It may not have been the most sensitive expression, but it was the comment not of a careless cynic but of a totally rational man. It is not possible to remove violence completely from human society. To have reduced the conflict substantially would have been a great achievement. In any case, there is in every society a tolerable level of violence – otherwise we would not put up with the number of deaths that occur in traffic accidents, or the amount of domestic violence that goes virtually unnoticed.

Another visitor was the Labour Party leader Harold Wilson, not long after his defeat in the 1970 general election. A small man, vain about his memory for people and places, he boasted that he had been offered a job as an economist in the Northern Ireland Civil Service just before the Second World War, by the then head, Sir Wilfrid Spender, and he glowered from behind a cloud of pipe smoke, nodding his head with pleasure as people recognised Spender's name and confirmed the possibility of such an offer having been made, and congratulated him on the wisdom of refusing it, despite the clear loss to Northern Ireland, and on having preserved himself for an unimpeded progress to the dizzy heights he now occupied, or had recently, and soon would again.

After dinner he had the engaging practice of speaking separately and privately to the other guests, quizzing them on the state of affairs locally and briefing himself on a wide variety of fronts. He had a great capacity to listen, which he did courteously, and to absorb information. He showed a willingness to be informed, and he did not disclose his own views, except in the form of hypothesis or as a flown kite.

During his visit, I made bold to ask him what it was like to be out of office. He snarled: 'It's political masturbation.' This prompted me to remark that now he knew what it was like to be in opposition in Northern Ireland. Worse still, the longer you were at it, the more likely you were to become blind and impotent.

Another visitor in the spring of 1971 was James Callaghan. I met him at dinner one night in the house of Mon O'Driscoll at Carnalea. O'Driscoll, a stockbroker and chairman of the Allied Irish Bank (AIB) in Northern Ireland, had been a member of the Macrory Committee and was financial adviser to Bishop Philbin of Down and Connor. For dinner he had assembled a varied group of churchmen, which included not only the bishop but also Monsignor Mullally, who was much more aggressive, the Reverend Eric Gallagher and Canon Eric Elliott, Jamie Flanagan, then a senior policeman, Harry Tuzo, head of the British Army in Northern Ireland, and some businessmen – no politicians. Callaghan got down to business quickly after the meal had ended. He produced what looked like a school exercise book and interrogated each person round the table in turn, taking notes all the time. After the discussion broke up he continued talking separately to people, sucking them dry of information. Callaghan had become rehabilitated in 1969 through his intervention in Northern Ireland: he had appeared as a statesmanlike figure, a whale among minnows when he bestrode the scene, a fair and rational man who could speak to a crowd from an upstairs window in the Bogside and calm the multitude. After a while, the shine wore off the image, as the problem was seen to be much more complex and difficult than he had at first surmised and as atavistic feelings and pent-up emotions were triggered and released which defied logic and the application of rationalist liberal arguments. At this stage, however, the aura was still intact and he did come across as a big man who was still interested in the progress of the reforms he had seen as his creation, and who was anxious to see things through, on a bipartisan basis, to a fair conclusion.

He came to see me the next day in the commission office. He told me he had been struck by the fact that of the dozen or so people round the table the previous evening, only Jamie Flanagan and myself had expressed a pessimistic view of the likely course of events. He then, to my surprise (he was accompanied by Ron Edwards the national organiser of the British Labour Party) spoke extremely disparagingly of the officers of the Northern Ireland Labour Party, the NILP, then entering a period of terminal decline. He was very critical

of David Bleakley's decision to accept office in Faulkner's government, and he finished by offering me the leadership of the party.
Whether that was actually in his gift was another matter. I was not
in the least interested. I told him that I regarded my present role as
an interlude before returning full-time to administration, that I
preferred to influence events as an official rather than as a politician,
that there seemed to be enough people competing to lead political
parties and few enough in a position to effect change at the administrative level, that I was not attracted by ideologically based politics,
and that if I were looking for a political vehicle, I would probably
prefer something more roadworthy than the NILP which had split
itself on the silly issue of opening the swings in children's playgrounds
in Belfast on Sundays. I gathered that Callaghan's politics were more
pragmatic than ideologically based, but when I asked him what I
would live on while the political base was being prepared, the conversation flagged. I suppose he wrote me off as a spineless civil servant
who was afraid to take the leap out into the real world of politics.

About this time too I had dinner in London with Professor David
Donnison, then director of the Centre for Environmental Studies.
The other guests were Shirley Williams and her husband Bernard. I
found them both very attractive people. She went on a bit about how
Faulkner and the Unionists, every time they came over to London,
thought that the Home Office had thought only about Northern
Ireland in the meantime, while really they had many other problems.
I suggested that if the Home Office had thought about Northern
Ireland a bit more than the efforts, half a day a week, of half a principal, who also had to look after the Channel Islands, the crisis might
not have come as such a surprise. She suggested that a whole series
of further reform packages would have followed the Callaghan
package had Labour won the 1970 general election, but she did not
go into detail.

Quite the most impressive visitor at this time was Edward Heath.
True, he was prime minister when he visited, but he came across as
an honest, concerned man who really wanted to do something about
the situation. His style was to move from table to table, eating a
course at each, in order to hear as many people as possible. Basically
a shy man, he was better one to one, and came across as brusque
and humourless in company. He did speak directly. At one table of

businessmen and lawyers who were all protesting their innate liberalism, he responded to one man who asserted, 'Of course, we're all liberals here' with the crushing retort, 'There are ten thousand workers in Harland and Wolff and only three hundred Catholics. I don't see anything very liberal about that.'

One of the problems of the 1970 change of government at Westminster was that nationalist representatives, who felt that they had been on an inside track following Callaghan's visits, suddenly found themselves out in the cold. People who had had ministers' ex-directory telephone numbers suddenly found themselves out of contact. They had expected to like, and be liked by, Labour ministers. They expected the reverse of the Tories, who they thought would cleave to their former partners in the Unionist Party, who would be toffy and unapproachable, and probably not worth the effort anyhow. This cooled the atmosphere for a time, and the situation was worsened when, a couple of days after Maudling's visit at the end of June 1970 the army mounted an extremely stupid siege and curfew in the lower Falls in a search for guns in Balkan Street.

There are a small number of turning points which, if avoided, might have prevented the whole thing sliding downhill. This was one of them. This was the single episode that ended the Catholic honeymoon with the British army in west Belfast, which tipped the community towards reactive violence, and which opened the way for the emergence of the Provos. If there ever was a case of sowing dragon's teeth, this was it. People were imprisoned in their houses for three days, and saw their homes broken up in a search which produced a handful of small arms, and which mobilised women from the upper Falls to march through the military lines to bring bread and milk to their beleaguered sisters. It is hard to remember any other incident that so clearly began the politicisation and alienation of a whole community.

The GOC at that time was General Sir Ian Freeland, a little martinet much given to lecturing the public. He did not help the general acceptability of the army when he allowed two particularly stupid unionist ministers, Captain William Long and Captain John Brooke, to be photographed inspecting the war zone in an armoured car. Long was an absolute ass, an Englishman who had come to Northern Ireland after the Second World War and worked his way up through the Unionist Party machine. He was at this time Minister of Home Affairs (Bill Craig having been sacked) and had previously been Minister of Education. Paddy Shea, who had been his permanent secretary at Education, told me a hilarious story about coming into the Private Office one day to find the minister on the hearth rug practising firing from the prone position. Ministers had just then been supplied with personal firearms. John Brooke was not any brighter. The son of the former prime minister of Northern Ireland, he had eventually arrived at a parliamentary secretaryship which gave him responsibility for government information, for the dissemination of good news, and for quelling rumour, which was rife. One of his bright ideas was that the Government Information Office should use the commission's telephone number as a cover in its dealings with the public. When he phoned to discuss this, I had to disabuse him fairly strongly, while inquiring about his mother's welfare.

The army had arrived to hold the ring while the politicians sorted things out. None of them, I think, thought of it as a long haul. Having come to protect the Catholics from attack by loyalists, plus or minus the B Specials, they were generally more sympathetic to the Catholics at this stage. They were all of them genuinely appalled by what they saw on the ground: poor housing, overcrowding, chronic unemployment, lack of open space, shortage of amenities, poor services and general social malaise. They were convinced that if social conditions and unemployment could be dealt with, peace would follow quickly. In the manner of military men, it was a short leap from analysis to the identification of an objective, from the selection of a strategy to the deployment of resources and achievement. They had little understanding of, and less patience with, the operation of a civil bureaucracy in what was, despite all appearances, peacetime.

Having said that, they were at least on the ground, in contact with and listening to local people. In a very short time they had marshalled the facts and conducted the surveys that gave them a better picture of life in the poorer areas of Belfast than most of the civil and public servants who were supposed to be dealing with them. There was in Stormont what I came to call the Massey Avenue syndrome: most of the people responsible for the development of social and other policies lived within shouting distance of the Stormont Estate, rarely strayed north of the estate, and were highly unlikely to have set foot in those parts of the inner city or the peripheral housing estates where their policies had the most impact – or lack of impact.

One illustration of this was the introduction of the telephone hotline as a response to rumour and intimidation. I called the official concerned one day and asked him how it worked. He said it was very simple: you just picked up the phone and dialled a particular number. I said that he did not understand – I was in Bombay Street, the nearest phone box on the Springfield Road was vandalised, as was the next one outside the Royal Victoria Hospital, and the one after that. Meantime there was a hostile mob between me and the end of the street. What was I to do? He simply could not conceive of a situation where every house did not have a telephone.

There were some highly intelligent soldiers whom it was interesting to meet. Anthony Farrar-Hockley, the commander of land forces, had been captured in Korea and subjected to torture by the Chinese. He had a vigorous, inquiring mind. I met him first at a supper in Palace Barracks along with Mike Grey, a colonel in the Parachute Regiment, and got into a long discussion about the provenance of the republican tradition after 1798. We had only got halfway there at midnight and I left it at that, only to be phoned next day with an invitation to continue the discussion over dinner a couple of days later. Farrar-Hockley was strongly in favour of the emergence of Sinn Féin, led as it was by Tomás Mac Giolla (or as he called him, Tommy Gill), as a political party, and he believed that if the few hard men in Belfast could be encouraged to go political they would make more progress. What he did not realise was that the unionists were generally less threatened by violence that could be contained, in traditional fashion, by a few more companies of B Specials, or internment, or a few more strands of barbed wire, than by political activity, and while the objection officially was to the pursuit of republican ends by violent means, the elimination of violence would rapidly show (as had happened with the civil rights movement) that it was the political end which was itself objectionable.

Farrar-Hockley also underestimated (or lacked intelligence about) what was happening within the republican movement. The IRA had, in fact, largely gone political under Cathal Goulding and Roy Johnston, and had been seen to be powerless in 1969 when Belfast communities under attack from loyalists needed defending. After the burning of Bombay Street, the taunting graffiti had declared, 'IRA = I Ran Away'. Subsequently there had been festering resentment in Belfast communities at what they saw as the unrealistic ideological posturing of a politicised leadership in Dublin while the real need in Belfast was for defence and for a reversion to the good old republican principle of the gun.

Belfast's black humour was never very far beneath the surface, and quickly emerged in the nomenclature of the various groups and splinters. The militant republicans, having discovered the inefficacy of Chairman Mao's *Little Red Book* in the face of a charging loyalist mob, and having detached themselves from the political ideologues, split and formed a 'Provisional Army Council'. In itself this was a deliberate echo of the Provisional Government of the Irish Republic proclaimed in Dublin in 1916. This soon became shortened to 'Provo', then familiarly 'Provie', then, finally simply 'the 'RA'. The rump remaining, who became known as the 'Official' IRA, became known as 'the Stickies' because of their use of self-adhesive lapel badges for their Easter lily emblems. This was soon shortened to 'the Sticks'. Both were paramilitary organisations with their parallel, collateral or simultaneous frontagers, masquerading as political parties, Provisional Sinn Féin (soon to drop the adjective) and Official Sinn Féin, which was to evolve through the Workers' Party to Democratic Left.

There were conflicting messages coming from the streets, and the field workers were constantly being tested out by hard men, emerging hard men and local heroes. Generally the Officials were trying to keep young people off the streets, and the Provos were trying to egg them on, both to politicise them, and to draw the soldiers into conflict with the community and to prove a need for defenders.

Gerry Fitt told me an amusing story one night to illustrate how you could tell a Stickie group from a Provo one. The Officials generally called their branches, or *cumainn*, after Liam Mellows or James Connolly, while the Provos called theirs after Cathal Brugha or Patrick Pearse. One night, after a riot in the New Lodge, in which the Catholics were the aggressors, a colonel called to see Gerry to complain. 'Mr Fitt,' he said, 'I regret to say that I attribute almost the total blame for this disgraceful episode to the Patrick Pearse chaps. Now, Mr Pearse, I am sure, is quite a reasonable man, and if you would introduce me to him . . .'

'Imagine that, Maurice, right there where you're sitting, listening to that sort of shit, on the sofa in my own bloody kitchen!'

One bizarre watering hole at this time, and a main point of contact with Westminster outflanking the Northern Ireland system, was the office of the UK Government Representative. Originally this office had been set up by Callaghan, who left Oliver Wright behind him as a progress chaser. Wright had been ambassador to Denmark, and in fact, while it lasted, the UK Rep post was consistently filled by a senior Foreign Office person. Wright described the relationships in very patronising terms on being asked, in an interview before his departure, whether his role had not been that of 'Big Brother' to the Stormont administration. 'Good gracious, no,' he replied. 'Nothing like that. Big Brother's little brother, perhaps.' The office was maintained for a couple of years at the Conway Hotel, which became a stopping-off point for Catholics and liberals and others who had had little communication with the Stormont regime and who saw such visits as a means of influencing the system. It was also a means whereby the British government collected its own information on the situation. Here too, there was an anxiety to involve the commission as the professional guide to the middle ground and for the value of the contacts the field officers had with the local communities in working-class areas.

Wright was succeeded by Ronnie Burroughs, and then by Howard Smith, who had been ambassador in Prague and was later our man in Moscow and head of MI6. The office moved to a more permanent location in a house at Craigavad called Laneside.

As a cabinet minister, our first Minister of Community Relations, Robert Simpson, was barely ranked; like his successors, he could do little more than plead with his colleagues that they should do the decent thing. On one occasion, in 1971, when the commission had been pressing for some time for the introduction of legislation to outlaw incitement to hatred and violence, the minister confirmed that he was making no progress and suggested that I should speak directly to the Attorney-General, at that time Basil Kelly QC, later a distinguished judge and Lord Justice in the Northern Ireland Court of Appeal. Kelly took me to lunch in the old Grand Central Hotel, and there, under a massive Humbert Craig landscape that looked like a British Rail travel poster, over Dover sole and Chablis, he explained to me in great detail that he could not recommend the introduction of such a piece of legislation because of the difficulty of proving intent. When pushed, he reflected that it might be that the act might only be capable of being used against Protestants because they were the people who were offending in this way at the time. I told him it was a little like refusing to legislate against housebreaking because only burglars would be caught. In the end, an act was passed through Stormont, and it did prove ineffectual, probably for the respectable legal reason he had adduced. In fact only one prosecution was ever taken under it, against leading Belfast loyalist John McKeague and two others for publishing a loyalist songbook that included such sentiments as 'the only good Taig has a bullet in the back', or words to that effect. He was acquitted, and after that the prosecuting authorities lost whatever minimal enthusiasm they had for the measure.

In an attempt to influence policies at official level, I instituted a periodical meeting with senior civil servants in the social policy departments. Over dinner, they gave me the opportunity to explain the developing strategy of the commission to an influential group, and to meet people like Ken Bloomfield, John Oliver, George Quigley, and Paddy Shea, who was a particular favourite of mine. Shea was a remarkable man, the son of an RIC head constable, a Kerry man, who had retired at the disbandment of that force and settled in Newry. Paddy had been educated there by the Christian Brothers and, unusually for that school and that time, had gone straight from school into the Northern Ireland Civil Service. His promotion had been blocked for years by his religion, but he found a congenial job running the works service, and being responsible for public buildings. Here his friends were architects and artists; he was himself a man of taste and culture, an attractive writer and a dramatist. Almost too late for him, the liberal hour arrived, the logjam broke; under O'Neill there was a search, perhaps a need, for a Catholic permanent secretary. Paddy's time had come, and with it a well-deserved and very long overdue promotion to permanent secretary at Education in succession to John Benn. Paddy Shea wrote a beautiful book, *Voices and the Sound of Drums*, about his childhood and his early days in the civil service, which is a minor classic. John Oliver wrote a book about his career called *Working at Stormont*, and Ken Bloomfield contributed *Stormont in Crisis*.

I was surprised to hear at these gatherings that there was no formal means for co-ordinating policy at permanent secretary level in the Northern Ireland administration. Ministers were jealous of their powers and were not anxious, and neither were successive prime ministers, to allow policy to be formulated by anybody but themselves. This probably enhanced the role of the head of the Department of Finance, and the Cabinet secretariat, but it also allowed the development of departments as separate fiefdoms, each doing things its own way and with little regard for the overall impact of policies.

One very odd experience occurred when the commission decided to do some work with the media. We were concerned not with controlling the news but with its balance and presentation (perhaps a euphemism for news management). We were anxious to encourage journalists and writers to reflect on the problems of reporting in and to a divided society, and on the new challenges that were being thrown up by the salience of the image over the word in the visual media. There were those who blamed all our problems on the media – who believed that what had been kept in the dark for decades could continue to be suppressed, and that conflict would then subside. There were those who saw publicity as the oxygen that sustained the terrorist, and believed that if it could only be turned off, so too would he. There were bitter arguments about censorship, and about failure to support the established order in crisis. We did not want to get into any of this. But we were concerned that the very words and images used in reporting an incident could themselves be inflammatory and provoke retaliation; rumour and speculation could be allowed to fester, and ideological positions could be parroted without challenge.

For these reasons, we proposed a one-day seminar on reporting in a divided society, to which only journalists were invited. The seminar was chaired by Alastair Burnet, then presenter of Independent Television News, ITN, whose editorship of the *Daily Express* was yet to come, and along with it the knighthood and the pejorative label Sir Cringe. We also had Professor Jim Halloran who was just then beginning his media monitoring and research work at Leicester. We were surprised when some people from the local newspapers who had initially expressed interest and support withdrew without explanation. On investigation, it turned out that they had been lobbied by the Government Information Service at Stormont and advised not to have anything to do with us. Since these people had come to exist rather supinely on the uncritical rehashing of GIS handouts and selective leaks and nods and winks, the fear of non-cooperation or cold-shouldering, if not blacklisting, was enough to keep them on side. In the event, there was a good turnout of the better and more independent journalists from the London and Dublin broadsheets. Unfortunately, these were the very people who were prepared to think deeply about the professional and ethical problems of their craft, and who needed the seminar less than the friends of the GIS who stayed away.

At one stage, in order to secure the representation of Ulster Television, UTV, at the seminar, I took Brum Henderson out to dinner. An interesting and convivial man who had built UTV up as an independent voice which gave space for both communities, he mellowed during the evening and enunciated what has become another of the private bench marks against which I measure movement in community relations in Northern Ireland. He had been arguing that things had been improving steadily, if not spectacularly, until the civil rights movement came along and upset everybody. Why, even the *Irish News* had been beginning to notice Protestant weddings, and the *News Letter* to report Roman Catholic funerals!

Robert Simpson was anxious to encourage artists to embrace the theme of community relations. He set up a sort of rolling dinner party to discuss how a programme could be formulated, which included such people as the young Seamus Heaney, Rowel Friers, Estyn Evans, David Hammond, George Thompson, Sean O'Boyle, Paddy Falloon and others. The crack was so good, and Paddy Falloon's hospitality at Dunadry so lavish, that the group never got down from the philosophical plane to actual business. After the third dinner, the minister resigned and the idea lapsed.

On one of these occasions, I remember Sean O'Boyle, a great man of learning and the saviour of much of Irish traditional music, whispering to me after he had made an intervention, 'That was all right, wasn't it? I didn't let us down?' Which pointed up the sad lack of self-confidence to which the system had reduced even the best Catholics.

Robert Simpson's successor was a different sort of person: David Bleakley, a small man with a gift for the commonplace and the trite, and a command of the instant cliché. 'What I say is, if you don't stand for something you fall for everything.' Everything was apocalyptic: on the edge of the cliff, at the crossroads, the last chance. Bleakley was appointed, early in 1971, under a provision that allowed a person who was not an elected member of parliament or a senator to hold office as a minister for a maximum period of six months. David soldiered on for six months, and then resigned a few days before his time was up, in protest, he said, against internment, which had been reintroduced seven weeks earlier, and about which he had remained silent. He was followed as minister by Basil McIvor, a courageous man who had won in a mixed constituency on the O'Neill ticket.

Before Bleakley's appointment, I had gone to see Brian Faulkner, by then prime minister, to argue against the need for a ministry at all. I argued that the present ministry was too peripheral to have any effect, that finding a way for people to live together in peace and harmony was the central problem for government in Northern Ireland and should be shouldered by the prime minister. I urged him to disband the ministry and to set up a unit in his own office headed by some effective person like George Quigley or Ken Bloomfield or Robert Ramsey, which would interrogate all departments on the community relations aspects of their activities, and become whistle-blowers and progress-chasers. He agreed with my analysis, but said he could not afford, politically, to make the change. The ministry had been set up as one of the Callaghan packages of reforms and it would seem as if he, Faulkner, the arch-reactionary, was trying to turn back the clock.

One issue relating to the arts at around this time concerned a young painter called Brian Vallely. His father had been one of my boyhood heroes as a fullback for Armagh and Ulster, and he was himself at this time a young painter of great promise and I had bought one or two of his paintings. He had recently become very involved in the civil rights agitation through the group People's Democracy, PD, and had taken part in demonstrations that had ended in scuffles with the police. He had an unfortunate habit of allowing the pole of whatever banner he was carrying to fall on the heads of unsuspecting police-men. The result was a series of court appearances at which he was bound over, requiring the posting of bail bonds. He became a frequent visitor to my office and several of the pictures I own, and which have given me much pleasure over the years, were first traded in order to raise the bond. The patience of the judicial system ran out at last and he was given six months in jail when a suspended sentence was activated by a further brush with the police.

I was approached by the Kerry writer Bryan MacMahon, an old friend, who told me that PEN International had been asked to intervene to defend a persecuted artist. I told him that Brian was not exactly a prisoner of conscience but that I was already working on his request, which was to be allowed to continue to paint while he was in prison. I spoke to Robert Simpson and reminded him of Yeats's *The King's Threshold* and of what happens to rulers who fall foul of artists. The result was that I went to see the governor of Crumlin Road jail, a very concerned and humane man called Major Mullan. The only time I had been in the jail before that was when the chaplain asked the 1960 Down team to bring up the Sam Maguire Cup to display at the Christmas concert for the prisoners. Even as a guest, I had felt trapped and claustrophobic when the lock slammed home behind me for the twentieth time. There were still a few IRA men in jail then, at the tail end of the 1956 campaign, although they were released not long after that.

On this occasion, even being in the governor's office was enough to give me claustrophobia, but I kept at it anyhow. He was quite prepared to allow my friend to paint, but said that the prison was overcrowded and he did not have any room to use as a studio. Unfortunately, at this time, Brian was painting huge canvases about five foot square.

In the end we arrived at a wonderful civil-service-type compromise. Brian was engaged to paint frescoes in the prison dining hall from 10 o'clock to 4 each day at a rate of 2s. 4d. per hour, with paint and brushes supplied by the authorities. From 4 o'clock until dark he could paint in his cell, but could not use the prison's materials to do so.

Things went on quietly for a time, then another problem arose. Brian had spent the previous year on an Arts Council bursary which required him to put on an exhibition in its gallery within six months of the year's end. Unfortunately he had been finding alternative forms

113

of expression in political protest and did not have enough pictures to mount a show. Apart from which, he was in jail.

Brian's wife, a most resourceful person, went round to people like me who had bought his pictures in the past, and borrowed back enough of the better ones to form an exhibition. Then Major Mullan turned up trumps. He discovered a clause somewhere in the small print that enabled him to give a prisoner near the end of a sentence twenty-four hours' leave to prepare his affairs for release (a rule normally applied to people coming to the end of a long sentence). So Brian was let out for the exhibition.

At the last minute, the governor got cold feet. The drawings Brian had done in prison were, not surprisingly, dark and gloomy – all steel stairs and bars and close confinement. The major got worried in case he was allowing plans of his jail to be smuggled out in the guise of artist's sketches. A phone call reassured him, however, and the exhibition went ahead, with the drawings included. The evening was a lively one, marked by traditional music and much political crack, but it was also marked by the absence of the Belfast arts establishment, with a few honourable exceptions. One of those who did stand by honourably at this time was Tom Caldwell, a moderate unionist MP who had come into politics to support O'Neill. Tom was a major in the UDR, and spoke with a slightly plummy accent, but was good-hearted. Once, when he was writing a letter to the court in support of Brian Vallely, he asked me whether I thought he should go in person to speak for him. I said it might help with the court, but it would destroy Vallely for ever with the PD.

Meanwhile, work at the commission brought much interest and many contacts. One protean figure was John McQuade, a unionist alderman and MP, who was cruelly lampooned in the *Honest Ulsterman* which published each month a blank page with one or two expletives on it, under the running title 'The collected speeches of Johnny McQuade'. He was the member for Woodvale, who represented the Shankill Road, and he came into my office with a neatly rolled umbrella saying, 'I know what you are, but it does not make any difference to me.' He had been a Chindit in the Burma campaign, and favoured a very tough security policy. At his mildest, he reminisced about his war service in India, and about winning the boxing championship of the Indian campaign, beating a Catholic soldier from the Donegall Road with whom he had struck up a close comradeship. 'I never talked to him after. I seen him once in Shaftesbury Square, but of course we never spoke.' It was a story that encapsulated the tragedy of Belfast apartheid, when people who had fought together with mutual respect against a greater tyranny could not find the means to make simple human contact at home. I had great respect for John's integrity on another issue. When in 1971 some unionist politicians decided to boycott Stormont briefly as a protest against Faulkner, John McQuade, who could probably least afford to do so, was the only one not to draw his salary.

Another visitor was Maurice Foley, a backbench Labour MP who had been a junior minister at Defence in the last Wilson government. He arrived at the door of my house in Strangford one Sunday evening, having been recommended to me by one of my cousins, Murt Kelly, who had captained a Kerry All-Ireland team. Foley was one of the midwives of the Social Democratic and Labour Party (SDLP) and did a lot to help the party to coalesce (or at least to emerge). His period at the Ministry of Defence had given him some understanding of the army and some contacts, and he told me once that the army had calculated that they could accept the deaths of 300 army personnel in Northern Ireland – after that they would pull out if peace had not been established.

Foley had been prominent in Catholic youth organisations in England, the Jocists, and was ardently pro-European. One day in 1971 I drove him over to Armagh to see Cardinal Conway, who asked me to join them for tea. The cardinal was complaining about the networks by which Northern Ireland was governed, and from which Catholics were excluded. 'Did you know,' he asked, 'that Faulkner's wife, the governor's wife and the GOC's wife meet for tea every Monday?' The implication was, how in the face of such a distaff army could Catholics hope for anything?

Maurice was bland. 'Isn't it an interesting thought, your eminence, that if the Vatican Council had come a generation earlier, the cardinal's wife might have been among them?'

Perhaps this is a good place for some reflections on the attitudes of the churches to our work. In public they were generally supportive and, at the top, prepared to talk and to be helpful. The head of the Catholic Church in Ireland at the time was William Conway, a fine man who had two relevant blind spots. One was that he was a canon lawyer who would not tell you the time of the day in public in case it committed him to something, though in private he was very warm, humorous and friendly. His other blind spot was his closeness to the community in the Falls Road, where he had grown up in very difficult times in the late twenties and early thirties, a community that felt itself constantly under attack, and which was consequently defensive, suspicious and introverted. He was nevertheless a man of stature. He was particularly supportive to me on my appointment, advising me to do my best but not to hope for miracles (an odd formulation, I thought, for a Christian churchman), and he was extremely interested in social and economic issues and very ready to discuss them. We had a sort of bond in both having been students of a bizarre and eccentric professor of English Literature called Baxter, and in both being honours graduates in English from Queen's. You felt that as a Belfast Catholic, concerned with survival and with making a living in a unionist-dominated society, he was not entirely comfortable with the more simplistic and greener nationalism of the Armagh clergy, who were accustomed to regard a cardinal as something of a blow-in.

The bishop of Down and Connor, at the time, William Philbin, was a saintly man and a scholar who was totally miscast in the role. He had come with high hopes to Belfast with a track record of social concern and what seemed to be a new realism that 'the true patriotism is expressed in a favourable balance of payments'. He was snubbed by the lord mayor when he wished to pay a courtesy call on the City Hall, he was attacked when he drew attention to the imbalance in employment in Harland and Wolff, and he failed to penetrate the isolationism of the Down and Connor clergy. As a result, he retreated into his shell, to his study and his Greek eclogues, and emerged in public statements as a slightly prissy man, or in petulant responses to individuals when his admonitions were disregarded.

The role of the clergy in Down and Connor was an interesting one. Down and Connor, unlike most other Irish dioceses, did not send its clerical students to Maynooth until they had graduated at Queen's. Indeed in the early seventies, Philbin was so concerned by what he saw as the radicalism of Maynooth that he did not want to send students there at all. What could have been a source of strength by having the clerical students at Queen's meet and mix with people of different religions, and backgrounds, was negated by housing them conventually in St Malachy's College and discouraging participation in university affairs, apart from lectures. The Down and Connor priests tended not to serve abroad. They were drawn from closed communities, educated within them in a segregated system, propagated in a sort of enclosed clerical hothouse, and returned straight to the community again in a position of status and leadership, where their views were not questioned or challenged. This was a recipe for the continuous reinforcement of values – the bad as well as the good. In a good sense, it meant that the clergy might be closer to the people, but the system also induced a lack of vision, an unwillingness to take risks, and an inordinate dwelling on old sores. It also seemed to be very difficult for the Catholic clergy to get involved in civic affairs.

In the Catholic Church, there seemed to be a great gulf between the colonels and the sergeant-majors at parochial level. Of all the churches I found them the most difficult to get involved in community relations work. Community development they could see the point of – indeed welcomed, so long as the focus was the parish and the parish priest or his curate was the linchpin. They were not particularly interested in developing strong local lay or alternative leadership. And they had virtually no interest in doing things in concert with their Protestant neighbours.

We tried to approach community relations by getting clergy together to discuss pastoral problems, and the problems of ministering in a divided society, and their own professional problems of communicating with young people in a rapidly changing society. But although a faithful few such as Canon Hugh Murphy and Father Sean Rogan participated, usually we would be told that it was Lent or Advent, or during a retreat, or just before one important feast or just after another one.

Another factor in the Catholic religious equation were the orders and the Christian Brothers. The Christian Brothers dominated education for boys in the working-class areas of Belfast and Derry. They had made a profound and important contribution to education and to Catholic embourgeoisement. They were dedicated men without whom most of the male Catholic community would not have received a secondary education, or even, very often, a good primary one. But there was a reverse side. The Christian Brothers tended to reinforce the values of a very narrow and introspective green flag-waving nationalism, a suspicion of the establishment and an antipathy to all things English. Most of the brothers came from rural areas in the south and west of Ireland, they entered the order in their early teens, were educated within it in an ethos committed to strong nationalistic values, and they were then sent north where, living in a monastery, generally in a Catholic enclave, they rarely made contact with people who would differ from them or who would promote an alternative set of values.

If, however peacefully, you are promoting a romantic view of history in which the heroes are always the hopeless rebels and the victors the militant revolutionaries, it is not surprising that every now and then some impressionable youth will decide to follow that path, especially in a religious tradition where martyrdom is a short cut to salvation. And if the culture is developed and reinforced by the belief that salvation lies within one true church and survival within a single community, it does not leave much space for cross-community work or for ecumenism.

Not that the Protestant churches were necessarily more enlightened. The Church of Ireland archbishop was a delightful man, George Otto Simms, a good man and a scholar, who was in my judgement one of the great men of his age. The Bishop of Down was George Quinn, a fine and helpful man and a very good friend, as was Bishop Butler in Connor, and Peacock in Derry. The Presbyterian Church was evenly balanced between evangelical and ecumenical wings (which were also somehow reflective of Presbyterian attitudes to political accommodation). As a result, the moderators alternated like the little figures in the weatherhouse, one with an umbrella to forecast rain, and the other with a parasol for the sun. They included, however, men of amazing quality and courage, such as John Barkley and Jimmy Haire. In all my dealings with the churches, I found the Methodists the most consistently open and fair-minded, and the ones most likely to take a chance to promote peace and understanding. The Quakers, too, were fine people although there was a distinction between the more urbane Belfast Friends and their country cousins in north Armagh who tended to take on the protective colouring of their unionist neighbours. I discovered this when I spoke about tolerance and the role of minorities at a Friends' School prize day in Lisburn. I was told afterwards that I had divided both the staff and the parents down the middle.

There were, of course, differences between the hierarchical churches and the others. In the Roman Catholic Church and the Church of Ireland, bishops were appointed for life (or latterly until retiring age) and retained status and prominence as spokesmen over a few years. The Presbyterian moderators and the Methodist presidents, on the other hand, were elected for a year and so had much less time to develop either a public persona or a leadership role within the church. Nevertheless there were men like Eric Gallagher and Jack Weir whose integrity stood out and who gave courageous and committed leadership over many years.

For the first year or so of the commission's life, Arthur Young was chief constable of the RUC. He was quite prepared to talk openly and to share his views with us. At that time I conceived the idea that policing would be made more acceptable and tolerable in rural areas where there was a strong tradition of Gaelic games if a few prominent footballers could be recruited to the police. In the same way as their counterparts in the Garda Síochána played for the local team and were a role model for young men in the community, I thought that it would be helpful to the RUC if it was to pursue such a course. In 1969 the Hunt Report had promised a new, reformed, depoliticised and unarmed police service. Arthur Young himself had made a good impression on Catholics. The GAA ban on RUC personnel becoming members remained in force (as was indeed the infamous 'ban' on members playing, watching or supporting 'foreign' games, though that was to go in 1971) but using my contacts in the GAA and along with Paddy O'Donoghue (then chairman of the Down County Board) and Gerry Arthurs (town clerk of Keady and secretary of the Ulster Council of the GAA) I was able to establish that the GAA in Ulster was prepared to accept the reformed police force as a new departure, and while the membership rule was unlikely to be changed for a time, it could well be quietly ignored. I passed this information on to the RUC chief constable and suggested that he might headhunt a few young footballers in his attempts to encourage Catholics to join the force. A few weeks later I had a phone call from a rather surly senior officer who opened by saying, 'I believe you are looking for jobs for Gaelic footballers.' At that point I gave up.

I had several discussions with the chief constable about the sensitivity of Orange parades, which tended to provoke a reaction in strongly Catholic areas. One day I met him in his office to discuss one such parade, and as he left to go to brief the Northern Ireland Cabinet he said ruefully, 'It's all right for you. Now I have to go to talk to a bunch of Orangemen.'

I had actually tried to speak to the Orange Order myself. On my appointment I wrote to them as a group committed in their articles of association to the defence of civil and political liberty, suggesting conversations, confidential if they wished. I also said I would not publicise the fact if they felt unable to meet me. They declined the invitation.

I tried too, in those early days, to encourage Catholics to join the Ulster Defence Regiment as a means of ensuring that it was representative of the whole community, and not seen, like the B Specials which it was replacing, as the tool of any particular political party. But Catholics were extremely unwilling to join. First, they thought that the B Specials should have been disbanded without any substitute, an attitude that was blind to political realities and to the real difficulty of keeping unionist hardliners on side. Then there were objections to the name, both 'Ulster' and 'Defence' being regarded as offensive. I tried to point out that if it were only an attempt to placate Protestants, they would get very fed up with the whole idea if hundreds of Catholics joined. On the other hand, the best way to stop the force becoming a stick to beat the Catholic community with was to ensure a large Catholic membership. There was little support for this policy. Many Catholics did join, but one of my Downpatrick councillors, a former serviceman prisoner of war and a member of the Alliance Party, told me of his disillusion at the failure of the regiment to promote Catholics. Subsequently, after internment, many Catholics withdrew, and many were intimidated out by an IRA campaign of murder; after the Ulster Workers' Council strike the regiment was extended and flooded with loyalists, after which it became incapable of making any contribution to community relations. Indeed, quite the reverse.

Shortly after my appointment, I had been asked to accompany a delegation from the Northern Ireland Girl Guides to the celebration of the seventy-fifth anniversary of the founding of the parent organisation in London. The ceremonies included a mass at Westminster Cathedral, at which Princess Margaret was to be present, and Lady Baden-Powell. Northern Ireland Girl Guides had very few Catholic members, and I supposed that they were trying to drum up such support as they could. In any case, it was a mark of the new ecumenism, and I was glad to go. The mass was presided over by Cardinal Heenan, and afterwards G.B. Newe suggested that I should meet the cardinal. The penny then dropped that G.B. had engineered the whole thing so that he could get to meet the cardinal. Anyhow, I agreed, and we were led along endless passages to meet the great man. He asked what he could do to help Northern Ireland. Rather at a loss for ideas, I suggested that he might pray for us. He seemed taken a little aback by this, a reaction that surprised me in a churchman.

Late in 1971, I was part of a group which was asked to participate in a think-in for the English Catholic Church on the subject of its response to unfolding events in Northern Ireland. The venue was a centre called The Grail in Pinner. On the first morning there was a painful debate about whether this professedly ecumenical group could take communion with their visitors from other churches, which I thought rather unpromising. I found the English Catholics fascinating, as for the first time I looked at a minority group from the outside. They included not only newly arrived lace-curtain Irish from Luton, but also the descendants of people whom our history books had described as 'Popish Recusants': they had been blamed for the Spanish Armada and for Guy Fawkes, and they were making sure that they would not be blamed for the Provos.

When rumours began to circulate late in 1970 that Arthur Young was going on transfer to the City of London police, I was visited by a young and earnest head constable in charge of the training depot, whom I had previously met at seminars about community relations training for policemen. He told me that if Arthur Young was replaced by a serving RUC officer, the reforms would go into reverse. He asked me to use whatever influence I had to argue for the appointment of another person from an outside force. I thought it was courageous of him to step out of the crowd and to adopt what must have been an unpopular line. His name was Jack Hermon, and I have retained a great affection and respect for him ever since.

What he said reflected the difficulty of changing the ethos of large traditional, hierarchical organisations simply by changing the man at the top, and that only for a short period. Values are too deep-seated, the culture too firmly established to be changed other than by crisis or by drastic surgery. I would have removed everybody above the rank of head constable and promoted from within to fill the vacancies. The resulting release of energy and drive from young people with a clear goal for change, and the energy and ambition to achieve it, would have transformed the organisation. It would, I believe, have accelerated the changes that have taken place in the RUC by ten years at least, and spared many lives and avoided much trouble in the interim.

Meantime, of course, all was not sweetness and light in the outside world. The IRA had split into two groups, but at this stage there was competition in ruthlessness between them, the difference, apart from ideology, being the difference between an Armalite and a Kalashnikov. Arthur Young had explained to the Community Relations Commission how a very small number of desperate people with a knowledge of traffic nodal points and a telephone could paralyse any modern city by hoax bomb warnings. They only had to let off a real bomb every now and again, and the police could not ignore their warnings. This the IRA did. They rapidly graduated to higher levels of terror, and invented the car bomb and the indiscriminate act of terror in a catalogue of outrages in the early part of 1971. On one occasion there was a bomb in the car park under the building which housed the commission offices, and my car was destroyed. There was nothing personal in this: we did not threaten anybody enough for that, but we were part of an attack on a large office block in the commercial centre of Belfast. John Darby told me afterwards that as he dragged me to my feet in an office showered with splintered glass, I had snarled that I had been blown twenty feet across the room by the bomb, and forty degrees to the political right.

As the violence escalated, internment was increasingly felt to be on the cards. Internment had been the stock response by unionism to republican violence in practically every generation since partition. In the 1920s internees had been held on the prison ship *Argenta* in Larne Lough, and during the early years of the Second World War another ship, the *Al Rawdah* could be seen from the golf course in Downpatrick, anchored in Strangford Lough just off Killyleagh, and when I was at St Malachy's College in Belfast I was conscious of the presence of republican prisoners and internees on the other side of the college wall in Crumlin Road jail. Internment had been used again in the fifties during an IRA bombing campaign (largely mounted from the South and aimed at police stations in border areas), when Brian Faulkner was Minister of Home Affairs, and Faulkner had attributed the failure of that campaign almost solely to internment. Internment had been used in the South too: of republican Irregulars in the 1920s, of IRA men in the 1930s, most notably by de Valera during the Second World War and again by a de Valera government in the late 1950s. The appointment of Brian Faulkner as prime minister in March 1971 to succeed Chichester-Clark, supported as he was by Bill Stout (the former permanent secretary at Home Affairs, and closely involved with Faulkner since the late fifties), made it more than likely that in a crisis resort would be had to the measures that had appeared to be so effective in the past.

The possibility of internment had personal implications for me. When I had joined the commission, I had worked out in my own mind a graduated series of steps I would have to take should my situation become difficult, culminating in resignation. I had always felt that the breaking point would be the introduction of internment. A government that set aside the rule of law in that way could not reasonably appeal to the general populace to use legal means and due process in their search for justice. It would also signal an attack by the government on the nationalist section of the community, which would then withdraw into itself, become even more disaffected, and spurn everybody with the slightest connection with the state. Community relations work would become impossible, and in such circumstances, I thought, I should resign, and probably sooner rather than later.

But at first Faulkner's appointment as prime minister seemed to herald the possibility of positive change, or at least of more decisive government. Chichester-Clark was a very limited and extremely wooden man who had been far out of his depth as a parliamentary secretary, and a cruel caricature as a prime minister. It had been quite clear that he was only there to keep Faulkner out, and as a symbol of the antipathy to Faulkner of the landed gentry who had dominated the senior ranks of unionism. In part it was the Tory despising the Whig, in part a matter of people who had inherited power and wealth feeling that they should continue to rule although power was challenged and wealth was dissipated; in part it was the gentry expressing superiority to those in trade, old money against the *nouveaux riches*, in part the Anglican establishment in opposition to the Presbyterian and to the more evangelical sects; in part it was privilege against the meritocracy; in part the people who had attached themselves to the Orange Order in order to capture the symbols (and the votes) of the masses against those who were really Orangemen; and in part it was a clash of personality between O'Neill and Faulkner. (Chichester-Clark, 'Chi-Chi', as he was dismissively labelled by Paisley, did not have enough personality to clash with anyone.) It was all these things, but the main reason for the antipathy of members of the gentry to Faulkner was that they were a military caste and they despised him for his lack of a war record; they did not trust him not only for what they now saw as political opportunism, but also because they were deeply suspicious that he had not only failed to join up but had also arranged his work in a reserved occupation (making shirts for soldiers) and his residence over the border in Donegal in order to avoid the draft should conscription be introduced.

Faulkner did try to move things forward on his appointment as prime minister. There was an amnesty for people to hand in guns, and some did. And he appointed David Bleakley from outside the Unionist Party as Minister of Community Relations (although that turned out to be a mixed blessing). Faulkner phoned me the night before the announcement was made and when I demurred, both because of the personality and because it still further diluted the effectiveness of the office to have a nonpolitician in it, he said that he had wanted to show openness to change, that the appointment would only be for six months anyhow, that he would appoint a Catholic next time round and would I be interested. I wasn't. I suspect that what he wanted to do was to balance the return to the cabinet of Harry West. Faulkner was attacked for illiberality by including West, then seen as a leader of hardline unionism, but the prime minister was essentially pragmatic with generally good political instincts, and it made sense from his point of view (and more generally) to prevent the sort of split in the party that was later to sink Sunningdale.

Faulkner also tried to find a way to involve the opposition members in parliamentary affairs. Opposition members had traditionally been treated as nonpersons by successive unionist governments and their backbench cohorts. There had never been any case of an opposition proposal for legislation being carried (except, it was said, the 1931 Wild Birds' Protection Act), the benches usually cleared when an opposition member was speaking, and the opposition members had no role on committees. Undoubtedly the noninvolvement on the part of nationalist members was contributed to by long periods of abstention on their part, and by ineptitude, lack of research and failure to do their homework when they were there, but it was a pity to see men of the calibre of Eddie McAteer, an intelligent, witty and articulate man, lose heart and purpose as he was diminished by the straits and slights of the parliamentary process. I had previously spoken to Chichester-Clark about the desirability of providing a more dignified role for the opposition – people without responsibility are bound to act irresponsibly from time to time – but he remained unconcerned.

One argument was that the opposition was simply a group of individuals and could not be accorded the courtesies available to official oppositions. I met Paddy Devlin one day and advised him very strongly that if the opposition was to get anywhere, the sooner they formed a party, the better. Paddy went off to think about it and to consult his colleagues and the SDLP was formed in August 1970. Faulkner, however, jumped well ahead of the field by proposing a series of additional parliamentary committees, two of which would be chaired by opposition members. Desmond Boal, on one of his visits as a Stormont MP, dismissed them cuttingly with the remark, 'Prime Minister, twice nothing is still nothing.' Paddy Devlin, however, with characteristic generosity, welcomed them effusively as 'Faulkner's finest hour'. Things seemed to be improving slightly. The possibility of internment seemed to have receded.

In the middle of June 1971 the Community Relations Commission had one of its periodic meetings with the GOC. By now Freeland had been succeeded by Harry Tuzo, an engagingly frank man who discussed things openly. He was forthright that there could be no military solution and that the best the army could do was to hold the ring while the politicians sorted things out. When pressed by one right-wing member (a Catholic) on why the government did not immediately introduce internment, the general took some time and in words of one syllable explained the futility of internment as a method of containing conflict, the likelihood that it would not work, the difficulty of getting the right people before they went into hiding or skipped over the border (if they were not already there), the likelihood that internment would be seen to be one-sided, and the likelihood that there would be an explosion of violence and his soldiers who had come to keep the peace would become targets. It was a very comprehensive demolition of a policy proposal, and one that seemed to have been well rehearsed. That, it seemed, was that. The relief was almost universal. Internment appeared to be off the agenda.

At the same time, on the parliamentary front, Faulkner's finest hours were fading fast. While the proposals for extra committees were on the table, two men called Cusack and Beattie were shot by the army in Derry, and both died of their wounds. The SDLP demanded an immediate sworn inquiry and withdrew from Stormont until this was granted. Not for the last time in the SDLP did Derry issues and the Derry view of things overwhelm all others. It was, of course, tragic that two young men had died, but given what had been happening, withdrawal from Stormont seemed to be an overreaction, and it certainly was in the light of what has happened since. It effect-ively ended nationalist parliamentary participation and the prospect of developing co-operation at this level. It may have been taken as an opportunity to end these by some who were not enamoured of Stormont, or who did not trust Faulkner. Incidentally, one of the men had died by bleeding to death from a wound in the thigh while being taken by car to a hospital across the border in Letterkenny. If he had been taken to the area hospital at Altnagelvin in the Waterside in Derry, or had a simple tourniquet been applied, he would most likely have survived and the course of history might well have been different.

Meantime things grumbled on during July with riots, bombs and street battles. Given the level of disturbance, the commission was on alert and I did not go on holidays – although why anyone should leave Strangford when the weather was good was another question. Here my next-door neighbour was Paddy Dougherty, a former Down All-Ireland captain, and one of the great Gaelic footballers of all time. He had been intimidated out of Willowfield in east Belfast, where a Catholic community had been decimated, and he was living with his father-in-law. His five-year-old daughter Patricia provided me with a symbol of the effects of the conflict on children. I heard her playing with my little daughter, Clodagh, one day, saying, 'Come on and play Protestants. I'll be the Protestant.' This was a bit much on the premises of the chairman of the Community Relations Commission, and anxious to take an opportunity to effect practical reconciliation I said, 'Why do you want to be a Protestant?'

'I want to put her off the swing.'

John Benn, as a member of the commission, discovered that he was entitled to consult with it without breach of confidentiality on matters arising from the discharge of his duties as Commissioner for Complaints. He used this freedom to take the commission's advice on a couple of general issues including the refusal to let public halls to groups on political grounds. This was a case that produced the rather bizarre result of banning all political meetings from public property. There was on the one hand the undesirability of giving racist and bigoted groups a platform from which to incite others to violence. On the other hand, there was the danger that even the most harmless or peace-seeking group could be prevented from meeting just out of fear that the bigots would cause a disturbance. The result was that there were virtually no neutral venues, and political parties (apart from Alliance which usually met in the better hotels) were driven to use church halls, or Orange halls, or venues that were in one way or another compromised or aligned. This decision exemplified the tension between rights such as free speech and free assembly and the desire to ensure that public venues were kept free from political contamination and that public bodies were prevented from acting in a discriminatory way. In this case, a complaint, essentially about censorship, resulted not in greater freedom of speech but in less, with everybody being censored. It also revealed a deep fault line in the commission between the establishment liberals who thought of all display as vulgar and wished to see Orange parades banned for ever, and those who were prepared to tolerate, even encourage, difference so long as violence, intimidation and oppressive behaviour were contained. I remember once expressing the hope that Orange marches could one day become colourful folk festivals with life and music and bands, festivals which shorn of the excesses of sectarian rhetoric could be enjoyed by the whole community, only to be told that, in an ideal world, Orange marches would not take place at all.

More interestingly, John Benn used his power of consultation with the commission to involve me in mediation in some of the cases he was dealing with. This was, I suspect, principally because of my background in local government. One such case involved Dungannon Urban District Council whose activities in the past had done so much to stoke the fires of the emerging civil rights movement. Not surprisingly, when the office of the Commissioner for Complaints was set up, there was a preponderance of complaints from Dungannon. The council was stalling on most of these, where it was not actually prevaricating, and John asked me to go with him to interview senior council members and officials with a view to at least expedite procedures. It was a fruitless exercise. They were full of righteous pomposity: not wanting to be seen to be giving in to the mob, not willing to admit any degree of culpability for past behaviour, Bourbons who had learnt nothing and forgotten nothing, who saw the tide of political change wash away their sandcastle, but who were prepared to stand on it to the last. Like so many in Northern Ireland politics at the time, they were frightened, stupid men with very little backbone, who saw themselves as bound to carry out the wishes of the majority of the council, without any duty to the other members or to the community at large, with no vision of a better future, and with growing insecurity as the council was challenged on an increasing number of fronts and life as they had known it was turned upside down. I was at that time president of the Town Clerks' Association and a sort of shop steward for the profession, and I tried to encourage the officials by explaining the need to stand for probity and integrity, to give the council consistent and sound advice – even if it was unwilling to take it – and to promote greater openness and better relations. I reminded them that changes were impending in local government, councils were likely to be swept away, and their time in purgatory was likely to be limited. None of which did much good.

This incident perhaps says something about the role of the permanent official in an elected democracy. The official tends to be in post longer than any of the elected members. He (there were no women in office at that time – very few since) could either be the tool of the majority or a force for conciliation. He could give the advice that was expected, welcomed and accepted, or he could when necessary stand out against injustice or plain folly. Committees tend to appoint people in their own image and likeness – very few job descriptions would provide a role for Cassandra – and the promotion of in-house candidates tended to reinforce the local culture, whatever that might be. Nevertheless, in most places where relationships were better than average, there tended also to be a type of senior official with rather more independence of mind, with the stature to discuss issues openly with the councillors (but not necessarily in public) and with a standing in the community that enabled him to maintain connections across a wide range of contacts. Of course the system of appointments did not help. Officials depended on councils for employment and advancement, councils were ruled by majorities, and majorities in Northern Ireland never changed. This is why several people in local government were arguing for a local appointments commission, as in the South, and something like the protection the county managers there enjoyed which would protect executive acts from political interference. This would have given the town clerk a degree of independence in that his progress would not depend on him currying favour with any particular group, or keeping his mouth shut when all professional and ethical standards required him to speak out.

In the emerging field of conflict studies, Northern Ireland had been quickly promoted to the status of a field laboratory; by now there were at times more sociologists in places like Ballymurphy than there were local people in gainful employment. Very many of these people came to the Community Relations Commission looking for a steer, for the voice of moderation and neutrality among the warring factions. Many of them were fine scholars who had been interested in the subject for years and stayed with it. Richard Rose comes to mind as the author of one magisterial book on Northern Ireland –

Governing without Consensus – which was published in the early days of the commission and quickly became a basic text.

Alfred McClung Lee, an American sociologist, was another caller who was to maintain an interest in Northern Ireland for many years. When I first read his book on race riots in Detroit in 1944, I somehow decided from his name that he was Chinese. It was only years later in the USA when I came to know him that I realised that McClung was good old Scots-Irish, and I slept in the bed in which great-great-great-granny McClung had slept as the Conestoga wagon trundled through the Cumberland Gap. My friend Paul Ylvisaker from Salzburg had now become Commissioner for Community Relations for the state of New Jersey, following the Newark Riots, and he was a constant source of support and advice on what was happening in America. John Burton was a constant visitor, as was an interesting American called Irving Goldaber, who had set up a consultancy on mediation and conflict resolution in Grand Rapids, Michigan, and yearned to get into the Northern Ireland situation. Not all academics were benign. Some were academic mercenaries, seeking only to get their next book out of the Northern Ireland situation, or to advance their academic reputations with quick-fix solutions for a conflict that was sexy, close at hand and had a high media profile, and a conflict in which all the protagonists spoke English, or a variety of it. Others came into the situation carrying more ideological baggage than the people they were supposed to be studying, and some saw it merely as a laboratory test-bed for testing social and psychological theories, and the people as little more than laboratory animals whose behaviour was to be observed and measured.

Another constant group of visitors were the Oxford Movement, or Buchmanites, who kept parading ex-communist coal miners from Durham, and Gandhi's grandson, and ex-Eoka men from Cyprus as a means of gaining a foothold in Northern Ireland for their movement. They repelled me as being slightly cultish, and more than a little sinister with their anti-communist hidden agenda. I'm afraid the ex-Eoka man slipped a cog or two as I mischievously got him engaged in a discussion of terrorist tactics. The courtship finally came to an end when, exasperated by their habit of calling unannounced in Strangford late of a Sunday evening, I told one of their chief emissaries that since I was obliged to be a professional moderate during the working week, I preferred to revert to my own bigoted self in my time off.

Late in 1970, I had been asked to the Directors' Lunch in the Northern Bank, late in 1970, to speak about community relations. This was my first contact with corporate business, and I decided to frighten them a bit. They were all talking about a return to 'normality', which was a bit galling after I had been explaining the social consequences of what had been regarded as normal behaviour by significant groups in Northern Ireland for the previous half century. I asked them to consider that conflict was now becoming the norm, that the genie had been let out of the bottle. I thought of the worst scenario I could, and then decided to multiply the figures by three.

'What would you say,' I asked, 'if I told you that this trouble might last for another nine or ten years?'

8
INTERNMENT

A S I CAME OUT OF THE HOUSE IN Strangford early on the morning of 9 August 1971, Paddy Dougherty told me that there had been a news flash that internment had been introduced. I groaned. Of all the stupid things that government could do this probably was the worst. Even if Brian Faulkner was correct in attributing the failure of the last IRA campaign almost solely to internment, circumstances in 1971 were very different. The 1956–62 IRA campaign had scarcely affected Belfast. It had been largely a rural guerrilla campaign aimed directly at police stations and military targets. It had been mounted mainly from outside Northern Ireland, and it failed to engage the active support of more than a minority of the Catholic population. There had also been internment in the South at the same time.

More significant was the upheaval in political attitudes that had taken place across the world in the 1960s and which had manifested itself in Northern Ireland in the civil rights campaign. People were aware of the power of protest, of a right not to be governed against their will. Everywhere the very legitimacy of governments was being questioned. Increasingly, too, police and armies were being seen as the agents if not the tools of oppressive majorities. Human rights were now an issue worldwide, extended to include the right to protest, the right to due process of law and a fair trial. There was a withdrawal of respect for authority. There was a feeling of excitement and stimulation in the air, reinforced and fuelled by the TV pictures from the USA and France, and latterly from Northern Ireland itself. The Catholic, or nationalist, population in Northern Ireland had become increasingly politicised over the previous five years, and anybody who thought that such population would submit meekly to internment was making an enormous political misjudgement.

Driving down the hill into Belfast, on a sunny summer morning, it looked, as ever, a sleepy and sinister giant waiting to erupt into action. But smoke was rising from fires and barricades in the Falls Road, Ardoyne, Short Strand, the Markets. Sporadic gunfire could be heard, and a periodic *whoom* as the tank of a burning vehicle exploded. There were no buses, few people on the streets, and a general air of fear and panic. By taking the Malone Road route down past the university, I managed to get to Bedford House without interference.

The commission staff struggled into work, each with his or her own horror story. It was clear that the city was in turmoil. Two meetings were rapidly convened, one of the field workers under Hywel Griffiths and one of the commission, or such members as could get there. The field workers reported confusion, distress and fear on all sides. Local people were erecting improvised barricades to seal off entry to Catholic areas, which were becoming increasingly isolated and cut off. Public transport had broken down, and there was increasingly a breakdown in services. Catholic anger was directed towards the police and the army, who had swooped in fairly heavy-handed snatch squads in the early hours. There was the ominous rattling of hundreds of bin-lids as communities sent out a call to arms and for defenders to man the ramparts. Buses were being hijacked on all sides, cars were dragged from burned-out showrooms, builders' skips, rubble, anything was being used to make barriers. Milk vans were being commandeered and the bottles used to make petrol bombs, pavements were being ripped up for missiles and to build barricades. Smoke, fire, disorder, noise and impending disaster were everywhere. In many Protestant districts too, similar if smaller barricades were being thrown up, out of fear of attack – unnecessary and unfounded, but none the less real for that – and at the ends of streets and at the entrance to housing estates groups of men with sticks who might be concerned citizens, or vigilantes, or worse, were standing an uneasy guard.

In all this confusion, there was a great dearth of information that was accurate and reliable and reasonably up to date, which might halt or dispel the damaging rumours that were spreading like wildfire. We decided, therefore, to withdraw workers from the field – the time for mediation and low-level peacekeeping having now passed – to set up an information centre in Bedford House which would be manned round the clock, and to respond to need, within our capabilities, as it emerged. This approach was endorsed by the commission and put in train immediately. In fairness to Billy Slinger, he gave very rapid financial cover for whatever we might need to do in this emergency.

The commission was in a very difficult position. The members were totally disheartened, as I would have been myself, had I had time to think. Internment, the derogation from the rule of law, was the negation of all that we stood for. We had been telling people that there was a better way than violence, that inequalities could be removed and justice achieved through the legal process and by peaceful means, and here was the state not only tearing up our fine words like confetti, but in the eyes of the Catholic people reverting to type, and doing no more than they had ever expected of it. With our fragile linkage with the Catholic community now shattered, we accepted that violence of unpredictable levels would ensue and that we should now concentrate on damage limitation. We also accepted that there was very little point in talking about community relations in the traditional sense while the city was on fire, and emotions were too. I conveyed our conclusions to Brian Faulkner by letter and per-sonally when he saw me later that day. These were: (a) internment was a profound mistake whose repercussions were likely to be dire and could not be predicted; (b) the deed had been done, therefore the immediate need was to limit damage and to take some of the heat out of the situation; (c) unpalatable as it was, internment might just be defensible if it were handled in a way that was seen to be effective and even-handed, which meant the internment of some Protestant paramilitaries also; (d) because political prisoners, almost by defi-nition, would claim ill-treatment, it was in everybody's interest to ensure that the conditions in which they were held were as tolerable and humane as possible, that families were not disadvantaged and could be helped through the social welfare system, and that the International Red Cross were invited to inspect conditions from time to time.

Meanwhile the commission's information centre cranked into action. The most immediate demand turned out to be for information about men who had been lifted in the early hours of the morning and taken off to where, nobody knew. Some of the families were out to make trouble, some were in great distress, and all were concerned about the fate of the men. And the degree of distress was directly proportional to the distance of the family and the arrestee from any paramilitary activity. Once news was flashed on radio and television that the commission had set up an information service with a telephone number, the calls began to come in. The names of those arrested began to be discovered through the telephone calls, and the field workers recoiled in anger and horror. They told me that those most likely to be involved in terrorism had skipped and that those caught in the net were of the superannuated class of '56, or even the class of '42, men who had once been active in the republican cause, but who had not been involved in any way for years. Worse still, from our point of view, many of them were voluntary community workers who had been encouraged by our intervention to put their heads above the parapet and point people towards new and peaceful paths. If we ever got out of this crisis, it was going to be increasingly difficult to get them, or people like them, to do anything of the sort in the future.

The problem that caused the families to phone was that the police would not, and Home Affairs and the Government Information Service said they could not, tell where individual prisoners were. Indeed it was difficult to establish where any of them were. After a lot of to-ing and fro-ing, we were generally able to establish that a particular man (a) had been arrested, (b) was in a holding centre at Ballykinlar, or Linwood on the Antrim Road, or Holywood, and (c) their families could not see them for a day or two. To my surprise, those arrested were not taken to Crumlin Road jail, but it was said that a wartime American camp at Long Kesh was being readied as an internment camp. I remember spending a great part of the day, in response to a request from his wife, trying to locate Michael Farrell, the chairman of People's Democracy, and being able to give her information late in the evening.

All over Belfast, the barricades were closing in. I sent Joe Campblisson, one of the field workers, up to Norglen Parade in west Belfast to get his wife, who was pregnant (and who had a serious kidney condition), in case an ambulance could not get through to her in an emergency, or she could not get to hospital when her time came. I managed to get him the loan of a house in Downpatrick for the duration. We began to take on extra volunteer staff to help with the phones. Louis Boyle came in from Newry, and Tony Gillespie, a priest from Ardoyne under the name of Father Marcellus. Tony was reputed to have the great advantage to the local community of night vision, and could give early warning of attack by loyalists. He was an enormous help to us in sorting out the deserving from the militant and those who were merely opportunistic. He was also the first person, in those lonely night watches, to tell me of the infinite talent and potential of Van Morrison.

Another caller was John Robb, a Downpatrick man, whose father had delivered me at birth. John was then a surgical registrar in the Royal Victoria Hospital. He called in the middle of the afternoon, distressed and angry. He told me that he would speak at corners, answer telephones, run messages, anything to be useful and relevant and to do something about the appalling situation. I said that he might be more usefully employed sewing up the victims, and I asked him what had annoyed him. He said he had just come from a medical staff meeting at the Royal, in the middle of a battle zone, with the city going up in flames all around, which had spent two hours debating whether or not to fly the Union flag on the Falls Road façade in honour of Princess Anne's birthday.

In the early evening, I went to see Brian Faulkner, who, as ever, received me graciously. He was an unfailingly courteous man who showed his feelings only slightly by a tightening of the mouth and a sharpness of tone. I reiterated the commission's, and my own, worries about internment as a policy, and then moved on to the issues of amelioration which I had mentioned in my letter. He said he had been acting on police intelligence, which he had been assured and believed was accurate and up to date. He said the situation had become so bad with continual bombings and shootings that the government had to take urgent and drastic action. He believed that they had got the ringleaders, that the day's violence on the streets was being orchestrated and indicated that they had hit the IRA where it hurt, and his expectation was that after a short period of turbulence, calm would be restored. On the subject of across-the-board intern-ment, he said he could act only on advice and he had no knowledge of Protestant candidates for internment. I asked him what about the people who had almost certainly blown up the Silent Valley reservoir to get rid of O'Neill, and several others. He said he would look into it.

In terms which reflected a *Realpolitik*, of which I am now a little ashamed, that would make the average civil rights lawyer's blood congeal, but which Machiavelli (a much-maligned man) would have approved, I suggested that the politics of the situation, and the need to restore some degree of calm, required the arrest of twenty or thirty loyalists and their detention, even for a minimal period, in order to show that the government was prepared to be impartial, and that internment was not simply a weapon to be directed only at the Catholic community.

I also explained the concern of the commission that internees should be well treated, both for humanitarian reasons and to prevent the community becoming even more disaffected, or to avoid the situation where Catholics disposed to take a moderate view and to give time for the reforms to work might be sucked into a general revulsion and protest that would negate all the work that had been done to improve community relations. I explained that our work was founded on respect for human rights and respect for the rule of law. Once government had derogated from that, it was very difficult to say that there was a role for a community relations commission as a government-appointed body. Brian Faulkner promised to write to the commission.

Even as we spoke, the commission's information service was gain-ing momentum; it worked round the clock as a relief organisation as well. While I had thought that internment would be a resigning mat-ter, I now had no time to think about that, and in any case it was no time to jump ship when so many people were in need of the services we could offer. Calls were coming in from all sides. People were being intimidated and burnt out of their homes, or were taking flight through fear. There was a government scheme to help people to move in these circumstances, but it was slow and cumbersome, and creaking badly. I arranged cover for expenditure by telephoning Bill Slinger, who responded most helpfully. Money was not going to be a problem, but there were others. Most of the removal firms either would not go into Catholic areas, or were afraid to let their vans approach districts where lorries were being hijacked to form barricades. Finally, Northern Ireland Carriers agreed to let us have some dilapidated, out-of-use lorries, provided we could supply drivers with the appropriate PSV licence. An appeal for drivers produced, among others, a volunteer from the Simon Community in Liverpool who came over on the next boat. I remember watching him load up a supply of baby food and disposable nappies for a community centre in Ballymurphy. It was about eleven at night, and I suggested that he should identify the lorry in some way so that we could let the army and the people in the community centre know that he was on his way. I discovered afterwards that he had cut up sheets of red paper and stuck them on the sides of the lorry in the shape of a crude cross. He got through without mishap, but I received a letter of protest from the Red Cross in Belfast about the use of their emblem. When I pointed out that if they had been doing their job, we would not have had to do it for them, this produced an even stronger letter threatening me with High Court proceedings and all sorts of sanctions for having contravened sections of the Geneva Conventions. I thought that Ballymurphy at midnight, caught in crossfire, was not the place for a volunteer driver to be overly concerned with the Geneva Conventions.

In a way, this incident exemplified the dual standards of the fur-coated charitable sector in Belfast at the time, which found it easier to cope with an earthquake in Nepal or floods in Bangladesh, or to respond to famine in the Horn of Africa, than to deal with the refugees or casualties of indigenous beastliness in Belfast. I have never subscribed to the Red Cross since.

The same sort of moral paralysis afflicted the Belfast Welfare Department, whose officers could not decide whether they could provide services in troubled areas while they wrestled with the ethical dilemma of the propriety or otherwise of providing succour to rebels in an insurrection. With an odd sense of historical relevance, one senior officer told me that there had been no welfare state in the French Revolution. He might have reflected that if the welfare state had operated effectively in Belfast there might not have been a revolution there either. I was surprised, on coming into the commission office one day, to find two new volunteer workers busily answering phones and giving advice. On asking where they were from, I discovered that they were full-time welfare workers with the Belfast Welfare Department, who finding themselves, in their own office around the corner, with nothing to do in the midst of catastrophe, came round to ours to volunteer what practical help they could. As trained personnel they were extremely useful.

One night when I had got home for a few hours to see the children and snatch an hour's sleep, I was telephoned at about 4.30 a.m. by Joe Mulvenna, ringing from the Ballymurphy Community Centre. He said the centre was caught in crossfire between the army and Provos, with loyalists chipping in on the side. He said if I could get the army to stop firing, those in the centre might be able to stop the others for long enough to get the mothers and children out, or to get supplies in. I could hear the bullets banging into the wall at the other end of the phone. I conducted the conversation watching dawn rise in glorious splendour over the Bar of Strangford, the river running full to meet the incoming tide and Portaferry in a bowl of light on the other side. The contrast with conditions at the other end of the line could not have been more striking.

Another great upheaval at this time was the burning of Farringdon Gardens, Farringdon Park and Velsheda Gardens, a largely Protestant enclave on the edge of old Ardoyne. With the onset of rioting, they had found themselves on the wrong side of the line. Some moved, no doubt from fear, some were undoubtedly intimidated, but it was also clear at the time that the main pressure came from loyalist paramilitaries, anxious to create a defensible area, who forced those people not already disposed to flight to move at the point of a gun. In order to keep the houses from being occupied by Catholics, they set fire to them as the tenants left. It was a spectacular scorched-earth tactic. The picture of torched houses burning in whole terraces, their burnt rafters and roof timbers stark against the evening sky, went round the world as a potent symbol of the Northern Ireland conflict.

Very soon, Catholic community workers came forward and offered to make the houses waterproof and weatherproof as a prelude to rehabilitation and reoccupation. It was an area where there was tremendous pressure on housing, where Catholics, intimidated from previously mixed areas, were seeking the relatively safe haven of their own kind in Ardoyne. But the offer presented a problem for the commission. While the idea was a good one and there were sufficient skilled building workers in the area to do the job, who could not get to work on sites in other parts of the city because of the disorders, we could not be sure of the bona fides of the spokesmen. Neither could we be sure that money advanced for repairs would be fully accounted for in the longer term, and that it would not be used for offensive purposes.

We came to an arrangement with the locals. They reckoned that £100 worth of materials would make a house weatherproof and they would provide voluntary labour. We then made an arrangement with a firm of builders' suppliers that allowed the workers to draw sufficient materials to repair three houses. When the three houses had been roofed, we would release an order form for materials for another three. As confidence grew we were able to raise the number to five and then to ten until all were completed. The community put people into the houses and raised money for further repairs. Eventually the whole scheme was taken over by the Housing Executive, which sorted out title, paid compensation to former owners and completed the rehabilitation.

The Belfast Corporation operated a scheme, on behalf of the government, to buy out any house whose owner had been intimidated or was in danger. A lady had come to live beside us in Strangford with her aged father. They had both fled from their house in Velsheda Park and wished the corporation to buy it. Unfortunately it had been squatted in and the corporation would only acquire with vacant possession. I sent a message up to Ardoyne saying that no further funds would be available until the house at Velsheda Park was cleared of squatters. The keys were left in that evening. The sale to the corporation was speedily completed, after which, I am sure, the squatters returned.

One of the commission's field workers, who was covering a nationalist area, came with a request for £100 to provide necessities for a children's centre over what looked like a difficult weekend. If there was rioting or shooting or barricades were erected or there were attacks by loyalists which would cut the area off from access to shops and pharmacies, families with young children might have to be brought to a centre. He had been asked for this help by a local doctor. I was surprised that the doctor could not simply issue a prescription for emergency supplies under the National Health Service, the NHS, but there was some convoluted reason why this could not be done. I advised the field worker that we would not pay money to individuals. If the doctor ordered emergency supplies for a creche we would pay the chemist who provided them. Next day, prompted by some suspicious instinct or other, I asked to see a copy of the note to the chemist and his invoice. The order was for a large supply of triangular bandages and wound dressings and drugs, and looking less like preparations for a children's party than somebody digging themselves in for a siege. He was as surprised and disappointed at these developments as I was and readily agreed to go immediately and repossess the supplies, take them back to the chemist, and replace them with milk, baby food and disposable nappies. The field worker, a kind man who took people at their face value, did this, apparently to the annoyance of the doctor, and of the locals who gave a very muted welcome to baby food and paper nappies.

During the period immediately after internment, the commission's research and publications officer John Darby set up an information office and also developed the research capacity of the commission to track what was happening. We were particularly anxious to quantify the extent of intimidation and population movement. This work was subsequently published as *Flight*. The first instalment, produced during my term as chairman, produced little stir and was not suppressed. The later version was suppressed by the commission under pressure from the ministry – and because of lack of courage by the commission and its new director – until it had been leaked and a bitter row had erupted between the commission and its staff. The trouble was that the second instalment showed the police in a poor light, and especially those at the Whiteabbey station as providing practically no protection at all to Catholics who were being intimidated. I had a relevant experience myself when a woman from Comber came into the office in Downpatrick looking for a house after having been threatened. I asked her whether she had reported the matter to the police. 'Yes,' she said. 'They said I would be better to go.'

The effect of such flights had been a huge population movement, described in hyperbole as 'the greatest population movement since the Second World War'; this cliché continued to be used even after

141

the break-up of the former Yugoslavia. However hackneyed, it concealed a real horror story, and one of the most damaging and corrosive series of events in the modern history of Northern Ireland. The effects were far-reaching and repercussive: one of those expelled from the Whiteabbey area, and launched thus into a career of republican activism, was a youth called Bobby Sands. It was reckoned that 80,000 people were affected in the Belfast area: one Catholic family in five, and one Protestant family in ten. What was happening was a great redrawing of boundaries as foreign bodies were expelled from mixed estates in which they were in the minority. Those who suffered most were the brave souls who had pioneered integration. They were now sent back to their ghettos with a bloody nose, or worse. Most vulnerable of all were those in mixed marriages who had few friends on either side and enemies on both, depending on how you looked at it. In terms of social structure and mobility, rungs of the housing ladder were knocked out, the normal progression was broken, and people were driven back to their own. There was a particular problem in Catholic areas, where there was already a housing shortage and severe overcrowding. Protestants had a choice of four-fifths of Belfast and many safe and hospitable surrounding towns to go to (although that did not justify their eviction). Catholics had only west Belfast, which was bursting at the seams, and Downpatrick.

This period burned deeply into the psyche of working-class Belfast, and drove young men into the swelling ranks of the paramilitaries as they sought revenge, or even mere defence for their community.

In the late autumn of 1971, with things getting increasingly out of hand, I was approached by Ian Paisley and Desmond Boal. Both said that they were appalled by what was happening, that the whole society seemed to be on the verge of disintegrating, that the government did not seem to be able to handle it, and that we were on the verge of a long and bloody civil war. Paisley said that he had got such a name for extremism, that if he could make peace, then anybody could do so. What they were proposing was some sort of a meeting of paramilitaries on both sides in an attempt to reach an accommodation. He asked me to consider chairing the proceedings, and assured me that the talks would be held in secret and that there would be no leaks.

This was on a Friday. I asked for time to consider. My initial reactions were negative. I would not be able to take the members of the Community Relations Commission into my confidence, I would be acting on my own, behind the back of, and not necessarily in the interests of, the government which had appointed me. If the whole thing blew up, it could seriously compromise me and the work of the commission. It might even bring Faulkner down. If it worked it was even more likely to do so. I was fairly convinced of the protagonists' desire for peace, but not completely sure of their political motivation. More seriously, I had deep reservations about negotiating with extremists and paramilitaries behind the backs of elected politicians in a way that was certain to undermine them, and perhaps even the political process.

Later I was sorry not to have been more enthusiastic. In the event there was a garbled reference to the process in the papers next morning. I grasped this, rather ingloriously, as a lifeline. I phoned Paisley and told him that as they clearly could not guarantee confidentiality even at this early stage, I did not wish to become involved. Des Boal rang later to say that the whole thing was off anyhow. In later years I often wondered what would have happened had the meeting taken place.

During the emergency period, all sorts of people had come to work for the commission, and every time I came into the office, at whatever time of the day or night, people were beavering away, manning phones, arranging transport, providing information or advice. Among them was a group of academics who, after a while, I converted into a think-tank and sent over to the Europa Hotel to brood. I asked them to consider what steps were necessary to get the society out of the hole it was in. The result of their labours, a few weeks later, was a short paper which suggested that there had been such a loss of faith in government by sizeable sections of the community that peace or stability were unlikely to be restored unless the current arrangements for government and policing were drastically revised. The paper indicated that there should be an intermission during which alternative forms of government could be worked out that would have the support of all sides. The word we used at the time was the rather mannered *caesura*, invoking the pause in the middle of a line that marked a change of pace or direction in some forms of Latin poetry. In cruder, more modern terms, this idea meant that the British government should exercise its role under Section 75 of the Government of Ireland Act, suspend the Northern Ireland Parliament, and take direct responsibility for the administration of Northern Ireland for an interim period of two or three years.

I sent a copy of the paper to Howard Smith, then the UK Government Representative at Laneside, who asked to discuss it with the authors. This led to a request for the group to go to London to speak to the Home Secretary. We all went along to the old Home Office in Whitehall, through high, double-leaf doors, with an inner door padded in leather, into the office in which Palmerston had sat, and Churchill and Lloyd George, and where Reggie Maudling now sprawled in a huge leather armchair at one side of a blazing open fire. The visit left my colleagues totally depressed at the apparent lack of information, poor understanding of the problem, and lack of strategic policy direction at the centre of the British government. Partly this was induced by the apparent torpor of Maudling who, having asked us over, appeared not to be totally engaged by the issue. However, the discussion lasted for about an hour, and on the way out the Home Secretary asked me to come back for a chat the next morning.

This I did, but I never had the heart to tell my colleagues the outcome – they were sufficiently depressed already. As before, I was shown into the inner sanctum. The Home Secretary was slumped in the same large leather armchair at one side of the open fire, his shoulder against one arm, his legs sprawled over the other. I sat in a similar chair on the other side of the fire, but more decorously. Coffee was brought in. The meeting did not last long. He opened with a question: 'What do we do? Arm the Protestants and get out?'

After the SDLP had withdrawn from Stormont in July, they had formed a grandly named Assembly of the Northern Irish People at Dungiven, much to the amusement of Gerry Fitt, who was going round offering unused and unnecessary assemblies for sale at giveaway prices. He treated the assembly with the sort of levity he reserved for any political activity outside the Belfast city limits. Shortly after internment there was a call for Catholics to resign from government-appointed bodies and from local councils. I attended a meeting one Sunday in a hotel on the outskirts of Lisburn, called, I think, by a few lawyers, local councillors and others. At it there was much confused discussion about withdrawal from office, but not much unity of purpose. I was not very good at following the crowd, especially if it did not know where the road it was taking was likely to lead, and in any case there was pressing work to be done to meet the various emergencies that were afflicting people.

I was not then, or at any time that I am aware of, pressurised to give up office. Neither was I intimidated or threatened. The only approach I remember was a rather mild one from John Hume: on the phone one day, on some other business, he said in Irish, 'Ba mhaith liom tú d'fheiscint in áit éigean eile' (I would like to see you in some other place). I was innocent enough at the time to think that he was asking me for a meeting outside the office; I told him that I would see him anywhere at any time, and the conversation lapsed. Perhaps if John's Irish had been more idiomatic, or my understanding of it less literal, it might have translated into pressure.

One outcome of the meetings I had been having with senior civil servants was a weekend get together in Cumberland Lodge in Windsor Great Park in which these civil servants were able to sit down with a group of people from the community whom most of them had never met. There were a couple of headmasters, one from Ballymurphy, the other from Glencairn, who did more to bring the reality of life on the streets home to the gathering than anything else. They expressed the fears and worries of ordinary people, they exposed the deep social and economic problems, and they argued the implausibility of dealing with the conflict purely as a matter of security. On the other hand, the community people were impressed, for the first time, almost, to find that there were senior civil servants, concerned and compassionate people, anxious to find a just outcome for the problems of society. The headmaster from St Thomas's said to me that if anyone had told him there were people in the unionist administration at Stormont who cared about what was happening in Ballymurphy, he would not have believed them.

The seminar included an economist, a sociologist and a couple of clergymen from Northern Ireland as well as the civil servants. There was an English component of a churchman, an academic and Dennis Trevelyan, then at the Home Office. He was to transfer to the Northern Ireland Office on its foundation, and to devote most of the rest of his official career to Northern Ireland policies. He was a sensitive, intelligent, concerned man who was to be a good colleague over the years. Douglas Hurd, who was then Heath's PPS, came down for dinner on the Friday evening. Another key figure was a hardy old warrior called Ned Dunnett, who was permanent secretary of the Ministry of Defence. The exchanges were tough and very open, but in the end we all felt we were getting somewhere, that there had been a real exchange, and that in particular we had opened Dunnett's eyes to the inappropriateness of the present security policies and the actions of the army in Northern Ireland. I remember Ken Bloomfield responding to criticism of internment by saying that of course they had expected a violent reaction. When pressed on how many deaths they had budgeted for – 3, 30, 300 – he would not be drawn.

One slightly jarring note, which showed the insensitivity of the civil servants, was on the Saturday evening after dinner when they all retired with a couple of bottles of whiskey to a private session in Dunnett's room leaving the lesser breeds to kick their heels in the common room.

On the plane back home, there was an air of something having been accomplished. We felt that we were getting there. Sean McKeown, headmaster of St Thomas's, thanked me for giving him the opportunity to speak up for Ballymurphy. Norman Dugdale told me that the civil servants had agreed to ask Faulkner to allow them to continue as a more formal co-ordinating committee. All agreed that we had made an impression on Dunnett, which would be reflect-ed in army behaviour, and on Hurd. The Community Relations Commission was beginning to justify its existence.

We stepped off the plane at Aldergrove on a damp, cold, January evening, to the news that the paras had shot twelve people at a demonstration in Derry that afternoon.

I resigned from the Community Relations Commission in the immediate aftermath of Bloody Sunday. I had held on through all the violence, disappointment and backsliding, through progressively more draconian security policies, and as the Catholic community, particularly in Belfast, lost all faith in the fairness of government. Then, just as we seemed to be turning the corner after internment, Bloody Sunday was the last straw. I could not be even vicariously the representative and defender of a government that shot its citizens on the streets. All the emotions I had bottled up since internment could be repressed no longer. I pondered Churchill's dictum 'Never resign!' but in the end I felt I could not continue.

I took a few days over it and tried to reason it out. Nobody's motives are ever entirely pure, or uncomplicated. Maybe it was emotion, maybe it was race memory or the result of cultural conditioning and programming, maybe it was physical and spiritual exhaustion, but it was my decision. It seemed to me that Stormont was finished, that no British government could allow the situation to continue. It is strange in retrospect how much blame was seen to attach to the unionist administration and not to the British government, which was actually responsible for the army. I thought there would be a period of chaos in which there would be no role for the men in the middle, but after which there might be a need for mediators, provided they had not been compromised. The metaphor I used was of a ship trying to make a landfall on a lee shore in a storm. Sometimes it is necessary to go out to sea and come in again safely when conditions have improved. Norman Dugdale, who was very supportive at this time, put it more elegantly when I explained my decision to him: *Reculer pour mieux sauter.* I thought I should get offside for a while and wait for better conditions for peacemaking. Another factor that influenced me was the safety of people working for the Community Relations Commission. I was afraid that there would be a public reaction to events in Derry and that the IRA in particular might declare commission workers to be legitimate targets as agents of the government. I wanted to make it clear how much the commission reprehended what had happened, and in the strongest terms that I could.

I phoned Brian Faulkner. As always, he was courteous and gentlemanly, even though he must have known that it was one small prop knocked from under his administration, a withdrawal of support that made it that much more unstable. I spoke also at length to G.B. Newe, that decent and upright man whom Faulkner had brought into the Cabinet. He was also understanding, but had decided that he should soldier on. The members of the commission were understanding too. Like me they were appalled by what had happened, but they preferred to stay and make the best of it. I put no pressure on them, neither did they on me.

I received great support from the commission staff and most of them remained friends for many years. I think perhaps I thought too much about the dangers to field workers in republican areas and not about the effect on workers in loyalist areas, many of whom had required considerable courage to make the commitment to work for the commission in the first place. Neither, in retrospect, am I sure that I would do it again. My motives at the time were certainly mixed and it was a time of great public emotion.

One reaction I still remember was a leader in the *Daily Telegraph*, which alleged that I had given in to intimidation. I can say categorically that not only was I not intimidated or threatened, I was never even approached by any person about my position. The only person to intimidate me was myself and my conscience, and that was quite sufficient to scare me.

One thing I did regret was leaving the team we had developed in the commission. I was replaced by Brian Rankin, a kindly man with a conservative, legalistic frame of mind, who was not going to rock many boats. Hywel Griffiths went too, to a Chair in Social Administration in Coleraine, and he was replaced by David Rowlands, a Quakerish sort of boy scout who had no perception at all of the nature and viciousness of inter-community conflict. Between them, they quickly reduced the commission to the tea-and-cakes level, blunted the enthusiasm of the staff, who were now much more radical than their masters, quarrelled with them, suffocated initiative and stifled every adventurous thought, and paved the way for the ultimate demise of the enterprise.

On resigning from the Community Relations Commission I returned to Downpatrick and took over my post there as town clerk full-time. Although I had made my public gesture of opposition to security policies, I maintained my connection in other ways at an official level. I was deeply involved in working parties that were considering the practical issues of local government reorganisation in parallel with the Macrory review, and I chaired a couple of working parties that were considering arrangements for the organisation of public health inspection and building control.

I also maintained my contacts with the Whitehall system through Howard Smith at Laneside and Philip Woodfield at the Home Office in London. On one visit to London, I was having a drink in the House of Commons with Maurice Foley and Gerry Fitt when Gerry got a message to go and see Willie Whitelaw – whom I had only heard about but had been advised to keep an eye on as a man of influence in the government. Gerry came back a few minutes later saying that Whitelaw wanted to meet me. We met in his room. He was a big man – very impressive. He broke the seal on a bottle of whisky, took down three glasses, and emptied the bottle on the second round. He was very interested in developments in Northern Ireland. I told him about the corrosive effects of continued internment. He said that Edward Heath, the prime minister, was anxious to establish a way forward and he asked me to talk to Michael Wolff, who was popularly regarded as Heath's principal adviser. Although neither of them said anything I was left with the clear impression that Heath was of a mind to take radical action, but was not sure yet exactly what to do. The visit confirmed my view that Stormont's days were numbered, and that the British government would no longer allow troops to be deployed, even in aid of the civil power, where somebody else was responsible for security policy.

In order to get away for a while, I availed of an open invitation from Paul Ylvisaker to visit the USA and to give some lectures. Paul eased my path to the Ford Foundation, which gave me a study grant to examine the extent to which the methodologies developed in race relations in the USA might be transferable to Northern Ireland. This enabled me to visit the American Arbitration Association in New York, Ron Haughton in Detroit, Andrew Greally in Chicago, Jim Laue in St Louis and Warren Bennis in Cincinnati, as well as Paul Ylvisaker who had taken up the Chair of Planning at Princeton. I remember talking to a group in Ron Haughton's home in Grosse Pointe and trying to explain some aspects of the Northern Ireland problem, when a black trade union official came up and said, 'Man, I didn't catch all the words, but I sure recognised the tune.' It was also satisfying that a lady came up claiming to be the niece of a senior RUC officer and thanked me for giving a fair analysis of the situation. It shows that you should never take chances on being far away from home.

I had at this time one of the few really graphic dreams that I remember. I was on my own in New York the night before I left for home. I dreamt that I had gone into the UK Rep's house at Laneside, along a narrow panelled corridor and down steps into a room panelled in brown wood. Sitting on a chair was Howard Smith, grey and drawn, on the sofa was Harry Tuzo, uncharacteristically unshaven and bedraggled. I danced around in imitation of Rex Harrison singing 'You did it! You did it! You just got up and did it!' And they looked at me in doleful unison and said, 'Yes, but we don't know whether it's going to work or not.' Next morning there was a note in the *New York Times* that Stormont had been prorogued and direct rule had been established with Whitelaw as Secretary of State.

By the time I got home there had been protest strikes against the proroguing of Stormont, and the march on Stormont itself. The Unionist cabinet had appeared on the balcony of Parliament Buildings and Bill Craig had threatened war. But by now things had begun to settle down. The civil service was working the new system, the police had not mutinied and life more or less went on. I was invited by Whitelaw to become a member of an advisory council he was setting up to help him administer direct rule. I asked to see him and I told him I felt that membership of the council, which had no clearly defined role and very little legitimacy, electoral or otherwise, and which might well attract hostility in several quarters, might well prevent me from participating at a later stage in administration. I wished him well in his efforts and offered him what advice I could give, saying that I hoped that the outcome of his work would be a new Northern Ireland administration in which all sections of the community could play a part and for which I wished to reserve my position.

Whitelaw fully understood. He then referred to my having mentioned internment at our earlier meeting in London. 'Do you know,' he said, 'the first day I came in here this chap came in with a bundle of papers for signing. What are these, I asked. He said they were internment orders. I said I had no intention of signing them. He said Mr Faulkner always did. I called Bill Nield. I said, I don't want to see that man again. And funny thing, I never did.'

Whitelaw was a big man by any standards. He had a gravitas which was lacking in Northern Ireland politicians, he was soft-hearted and compassionate, and he had a great way of jollying people along. I often thought that his most effective negotiating ploy was never to end a sentence. Each group would leave, having added their own predicate, and go out satisfied. Willie would splutter, 'Good gracious!

You don't think, do you, that her Majesty's Government, or I would . . .

As Margaret Thatcher used to say, 'Every government needs a Willie.'

9

WAITING FOR SOMETHING
TO TURN UP

DOWNPATRICK WAS DULL AFTER THE excitement of the Community Relations Commission. Apart from which, local government was winding down as people prepared themselves for change in the wake of the Macrory Report, the work of a review body, chaired by Sir Patrick Macrory, into the structure of local government in Northern Ireland, set up in response to the civil rights protests. I was still involved in working parties at official level developing strategies for implementing the changes. This work involved a meeting every six weeks or so with the grandees of the county councils and the barons of local government. These tended to be sumptuous and bibulous affairs as each local potentate sought to outdo the others in entertaining their friends at the expense of the ratepayers. They were also an interesting opportunity to watch from the sidelines the writhings of a system of privilege and patronage in its death throes. What was strange was that none of these potentates seemed to be aware of the magnitude of the changes that were about to happen. Perhaps more accurately, there was a sort of fatalism, a feeling that the world had been turned upside down, a recognition by some that things had not been right in the past, and a new feeling of impotence at no longer being in full command of their own affairs.

Seeing other town clerks jump ship and move on to better things, I feared that I would be left like Casabianca on the deck of a burning ship while others sailed off into the blue horizon. It seemed extremely likely that local government would be emasculated, and this became more likely when Callaghan had ordained the transfer of housing powers to a new housing authority. I had tried to join the Housing Trust a few years earlier, but those nice liberal people, who were prepared to ask me to lecture to them and to take my advice for free, apparently were not yet ready to appoint a Catholic to a senior position. The Community Relations Commission had given me a taste for wider things, a taste for action at the political level, and the confidence that I could hold my end up with senior people in the public service. Local government, in its diminished form, was unlikely to provide a satisfying platform. I sought advice from John Oliver, permanent secretary of the Ministry of Development, asking him where I might consider going. John's reply was a masterpiece of mandarin evasion. 'Well, you are a distinguished man, highly thought of, deservedly so, deservedly so. But very hard to fit into a department, you know.'

I knew I would probably be absorbed into the civil service, the problem was, at what level. I had no great desire to begin to battle my way up through the ranks, or to write off as valueless years of experience in local government and with the Community Relations Commission. I wanted to be where the action was, and where policy was being made and could be influenced. This was at assistant secretary level.

In the end, John Benn, the Ombudsman, came to the rescue, or so I believe. A job was advertised at assistant secretary level as Assistant Director in the Office of the Commissioner for Complaints. By the arrangements that had been agreed for transferring local government officers, the post was trawled rather than publicly advertised. I applied, was interviewed, and got the job. Interestingly enough, the interviewing panel, whose members were very friendly and open, seemed more worried about my ability to keep a low profile than about any other quality.

I often thought afterwards that John Benn had created the post in the hope that I might get it and that it would provide me with the means of entry to the senior civil service. For me, it was a wonderful gateway to the wider service. Dealing with complaints against a whole range of bodies meant having to research each in order to understand the allocation of powers and functions. It meant, too, meeting and beginning to understand the mentality of a whole range of public servants. It was a crash course in public administration and one that enabled me to move easily from local government to central administration. What I brought to the office was a smell of reality, the fact that I had actually performed the functions in local government that they were investigating, had experience of the political process, and some understanding of the pressures under which public officials in direct contact with the public had to work.

There were, of course, culture shocks too. I was surprised by the sense of hierarchy in the civil service and the deference to superiors that this created. I never became fully acclimatised to this – even as a recipient. I found civil servants, by and large, easy to work with, although they had different ideas about productivity and the use of time. I had been effectively my own boss, directly responsible to Downpatrick Council, which met monthly and did not care much about methodology so long as the job was done and results were achieved. I now had to work in a chain of command, which was especially difficult if your immediate superior worked at a different pace. I quickly learned a lesson that was to serve me well in my civil service career. I found that both he and the system could be satisfied by feeding him a couple of files a week which he could brood on and annotate in careful script while I got on with the real work, which increasingly involved direct discussions with the commissioner. The thing I found most irksome was not being free to speak my mind on a variety of topics, the feeling that it was improper for a civil servant to have ideas of his own about anything, or to comment on matters that fell within someone else's sphere of responsibility.

I remember going to the founding meeting of what became the Committee for the Administration of Justice, along with Alfie Donaldson, a remarkably talented official lawyer who was Director of the Office of Law Reform at Stormont. The following week I was chastised at the behest of the secretary of the Ministry of Community Relations because I had agreed to take office in the organisation. Since its funding was jeopardised as a result, I withdrew – something I have often regretted since.

The vulnerability of civil servants in this regard, and their paranoia, are illustrated by a story. After one of the local government deputations to Stormont in 1968, Albert Anderson, a Stormont MP and mayor of Londonderry, took a few of us to lunch in the Strangers'

Dining Room. Seeing John Oliver at another table, he launched into a vitriolic attack on him as the hidden hand behind restructuring, as a socialist centraliser.

'That damned Fabian, Oliver, that damned pink.' I was telling this story as a joke about a year later to Caldwell Hoey, a deputy secretary in charge of housing, when he blanched. He told me that he and John Oliver, as young administrative trainees, had attended the founding meeting of the Fabian Society in Belfast in 1936, but had never gone back. Nevertheless somebody in their social circle had thrown it up to his wife only a few weeks before.

I had had a fairly high profile as chairman of the Community Relations Commission, including interviews on radio and television. While I had to forgo this, I was able to maintain the contacts I had made, and I still remained a point of reference for academics and journalists of the more serious kind, like Nora Beloff and Margaret van Hattem. I was invited, through Dipak Nandy, to give the Runnymede Lecture in London. The lecture was chaired by Edward Boyle, then vice-chancellor of Leeds University, and one of the great men never to have led the Tory Party.

I was also involved at this time in the gestation and incubation of the British/Irish Association, and attended its first meeting at Magdalene College, Cambridge, along with John Benn, Jack Magee and Norman Gibson. The BIA was heavily infiltrated by titled members of the Guinness family, and booze was ad lib. The only difficulty was that the unionists did not come. Neither indeed had the Fianna Fáil government been enthusiastic about it, perhaps because of the involvement of Conor Cruise O'Brien and Garret FitzGerald. Fortuitously there was a change of government in the South shortly before the inaugural meeting, many of the new ministers came, including FitzGerald and O'Brien, and there was a full turnout from the Irish embassy of high-fliers such as Ted Smith (now a vice-president of the Heinz Corporation), and Dermot Gallagher (now the Republic's ambassador in Washington), who were to become long-time friends. Also present was a young lawyer, the Reid Professor at Trinity, Mary Robinson, and Declan Costello, the newly appointed Attorney-General, both of whom were very interested in the possibility of introducing the office of ombudsman in the Republic. Indeed John Benn and I were invited to visit the Department of Justice there shortly afterwards to talk about the concept to officials.

In the middle of the BIA conference, the news broke that Joe Cahill, a prominent republican, had been arrested on a gun-running ship, the *Claudia*, off the Waterford coast. For a brief moment Garret (who had attended Scoil na Leanbh in Ring) and I became world experts on the geography of Dungarvan, Helvick Head and Muggort's Bay. It was ironic that the ship was arrested within hailing distance of Ballynagoul, where the *Erin's Hope*, running arms for the Fenians, had been arrested in 1867.

Shortly before this, while attending a local government conference in Coleraine, I got an urgent message, relayed through the British embassy in Dublin to Stormont Castle, to go immediately to Dublin to see Gerry Fitt who was ill in St Vincent's Hospital. I dashed off, picking up a parcel in Belfast as had been requested, and drove straight to Dublin, arriving there at about 8 p.m. I believed that Gerry was on the point of death and that I was to be made the recipient of his political testament and whatever messages he wished to pass on to posterity.

When I got there, he was holding court in a private ward, having slipped at the airport and hurt his back. The parcel turned out to contain 400 Gallagher Greens, his favourite cigarette, and that appeared to be the main reason for my being summoned. Grouped around the bed were Conor Cruise O'Brien, Garret FitzGerald (both then still in opposition) and a man from the British embassy. Gerry was holding forth in fine style and there was a constantly changing retinue of visitors. The room was hung with rather garish oleographs in ornate frames, a reproduction of the Last Supper over the bed.

A month or so later, I went to see Gerry in a semi-public ward in the Westminster Hospital in London, where he was having further treatment for the recurrence of his back problem. He was deeply impressed at having been presented by the holy nuns with a bill for £700 for his few days' stay in St Vincent's, an X-ray and some physiotherapy: it impressed on him, as a good socialist, the high priority to be accorded to a free health service.

'Maurice, do you remember the photo over the bed?'

I said I did. It was the Last Supper.

'Well, they put the price of the meal on my bloody bill.'

It was shortly after this, in October 1973, that Ken Bloomfield asked me to call up to see him. In those days, Ken was under-secretary to the Northern Ireland Office. He had been speech-writer to three Stormont prime ministers, and for some years had been a rising star in the administration. He had been credited with a major role in formulating the more liberal policies of the 1960s, and he had been closely associated in the public mind with Terence O'Neill. Nevertheless he had survived not one, but several changes at the top, retaining his position in turn with James Chichester-Clark and Brian Faulkner. I had got to know him a few years earlier, first through John Oliver when I was in local government, and then during my period as chairman of the Community Relations Commission, when I had periodical meetings with senior people in the administration.

I was still working as a Deputy Director in the Office of the Commissioner for Complaints, in an ugly modern office block in the centre of Belfast. When Ken phoned I drove the six miles to see him. The mock-Gothic Scottish baronial pile, approached by an almost unnoticed path marked 'Castle' a foot above the grass off the back road from Dundonald House to the main Stormont building on the hill, was symbolic of much of the unionist administration: a poor copy of something else, unsure of itself, and poorly maintained. Once the centrepiece of the Stormont Estate, it had become dwarfed by the Parliament Buildings on the hill and been bypassed by the processional grand avenue flanked with double rows of limes that rose from ornate wrought-iron gates at the Newtownards Road up the hill to Carson's statue and the neoclassical pediments and porticoes of Parliament Buildings.

We moved outside, not out of fear of bugging (which was scarcely thought of in those days except by paranoid professors), or out of undue desire for privacy, but because the Castle was stuffy and depressing, as was Ken's office. So we walked in the bright sunshine around the sunken formal garden, where the ground was laid out in paths edged with low box hedges in a pattern of squares, triangles and quincunexes. The purpose of Ken's chat was to inform himself about the SDLP, then emerging as the main political force in the nationalist community, and looking increasingly forceful and articulate, if not always united or unanimous.

Ken said, 'We are beginning to negotiate with these people and we know nothing about them. I am anxious to learn.' I thought this was sad, a reflection of the sterility of political debate in Northern Ireland for generations, and of the social and political distance between government and opposition. Here were people, elected members of parliament, some of whom, like Gerry Fitt and Austin Currie, had been around for years, yet they had rarely, in the days of government at Stormont, met government ministers or senior civil servants, and never for any sort of meaningful exchange at a political or personal level. This might be said to reflect their failure as an opposition. More seriously it reflected the failure of successive governments to accommodate, much less encourage a responsible opposition. Politicians had been either in or out: there was no middle ground, and insider status was determined not by ability but by membership of the Unionist Party. The fact that the opposition could never become the government by the sorts of swings of electoral fortune typical of Western democracy, and that the government majority was massive and secure, had meant that senior civil servants had no great incentive to cultivate the acquaintance of opposition politicians, did not even have to get to know them. So here was Ken, a highly intelligent, sophisticated person, with well-developed political antennae, the confidant of prime ministers who had had a role near the centre of affairs for a decade at least, who did not know, except in the broadest terms, either the personalities or the political motivations of the leaders of one third of the population. And he was probably the best and the brightest.

We spent a couple of hours, I suppose, discussing the various strands of opinion in the Catholic community, their fears and their aspirations and the practical politics of accommodation. I also talked about the personalities who made up the SDLP, not mainly in terms of politics, but as an interesting and disparate group of human beings who had arrived in the party by different routes, and who had different emphases and styles, sharing both friendship and common purpose but with periodic tensions. They were, by and large, the most interesting, creative and stimulating group of people about. More important, they had gained the ear of the media and British ministers, they were seen as the spokesmen of an oppressed people, as the best bet to avoid a descent into anarchy and unbridled terror, and as men whose time had come.

It was now nearly eighteen months into the Whitelaw regime. Direct rule had resulted in the establishment of the Northern Ireland Office, the NIO, staffed mainly by Whitehall civil servants seconded from the Home Office. These innocents, thrust into the wastelands of Ulster politics, had grappled Ken to themselves, a trusty native guide, adept, articulate, witty, well-informed, experienced and game for the higher peaks. More than any other Northern Ireland civil servant at the time he had retained his place and his credibility with the new arrivals. His sapiental authority made him a formidable member of any team. Apart from that he possessed all the unwritten records, the race memory of an administration, the keys to unlock the written memories and the codes to interpret them. He was widely credited with having almost single-handedly written the discussion paper on future political structures that Whitelaw had used as a basis for policy development and to begin discussions with the separate parties. Now they were trying to get it all together. Ken was, in fact, preparing for what became known as the Sunningdale talks.

He told me that if the talks succeeded, the intention was that they should lead to the setting up of a Northern Ireland administration based on power-sharing principles. This would have a unionist majority, probably with Brian Faulkner at its head, with SDLP representation and probably somebody from Alliance. He expected that in whatever form it emerged there would still be the skeletal form of the old Stormont administration with six or seven ministries or departments and something reasonably like the old Cabinet Office. He clearly expected to become secretary to whatever executive emerged and he asked me to join him in it, mainly on the basis that a power-sharing executive would need to be served by a cross-cultural office in which staff were drawn from both the main Northern Ireland communities and were less introverted, inbred and claustrophobic than the Northern Ireland Civil Service. He asked me to join because of my experience in local government and with the Community Relations Commission, but mainly because I was a Catholic and came from a culture and background that had not previously been represented in the Cabinet Office, which had been the holy of holies of the old system, undefiled by any unanointed foot – or at least those anointed with the wrong brand of chrism.

I told him that I was not prepared to work in a setting where Catholic civil servants were allocated to work with Catholic ministers and Protestant ones with unionists. But if there was to be a service where everyone pulled their weight and work was allocated on the basis of who was available and able to do it, and there were no inner sanctums, no reserved pieces of work, no files hidden from unworthy eyes, then I was prepared to have a go. He quickly set my mind at rest about his own aspirations and values and about the sort of office he wanted to run. He agreed to arrange my transfer from John Benn's office to the Castle. That was the beginning of a long and pleasant working relationship which I think both of us enjoyed.

10
POWER SHARING

FOR THOSE INVOLVED IN IT, and perhaps more widely, the power-sharing Executive represented the bright spring of reforming liberalism in Northern Ireland politics. Adlai Stevenson talked about the 'liberal hour', the pregnant moment when all the institutions of society seem to be moving towards a more liberal stance. It may not have been actual bliss then to be alive – it was by no means a peaceful and trouble-free period – but there was at least hope. In many ways this short period was the most satisfying of my working life. There was the hope for the future engendered in seeing people who had been sworn and bitter political enemies sitting down together, getting to know each other, and growing in mutual respect. There was the stimulation of a joint venture, a shared sense of purpose and achievement. There was the feeling that a page had been turned, that a new history was being written that would overcome the conflict and animosity of centuries. An opportunity had been presented and grasped to end a tired old fight, to build a better future, and to harness the enthusiasm and ability of people from all parts of the community in a new society.

It was also a period of great disappointment as opposition grew, as support ebbed away and the whole edifice crumbled in the face of intimidation and open attack, the withdrawal of consent by large sections of the population, and the surprising lassitude and inaction of the sponsoring government,

I moved to the civil service proper in October 1973 to prepare for the incoming Executive. At this stage negotiations were still going on about the precise form of the arrangements and the size and shape of any future administration. There had been the Darlington conference, which the SDLP had not attended, and following that the White Paper on Future Government – largely credited to Ken Bloomfield as the main author.

The old Cabinet Office was still in place, an administration in internal exile, waiting for the prince to return from over the water, meshing uneasily with the embryonic Northern Ireland Office structures. Harold Black, the Cabinet Secretary, was still in office, but nearing retirement as Bloomfield took up more of the running and quite clearly commanded the respect and confidence of NIO officials and ministers. Black was a quiet, not very colourful man who epitomised for me, perhaps wrongly, the type of civil servant who had kept their heads down and allowed successive unionist administrations to govern as stupidly and as myopically as they had done. The others in the Castle, apart from Bloomfield, were mostly dull men, immersed in the minutiae of honours, protocol, when to fly the flag, whom to ask to functions, how to keep up appearances. There was no great sense of urgency – perhaps the result of shell shock caused by the collapse of their world with the fall of Stormont – and there was a lack of engagement with the new and more powerful motors that were revving up, a willingness to be bypassed.

Stormont Castle itself was an appalling place to work in. The only redeeming feature was its setting in the Stormont Estate and the view from the front across to the Castlereagh Hills. Unfortunately I was at the back and looked out over what had once been the walled garden and now housed the police alsatians, whose howling and snarling provided a threnody in the background that was not inappropriate to the setting.

Another occupational hazard was our proximity to the press office and the genial presence of Tommy Roberts. Tommy would surface about 11.30 in the morning declaring, 'It's going to be a fun day! I took Miss Bossy-boots [his dog] for a walk on the prom, and I said to Margaret, It's going to be a fun day today.' For the poor fools who had been grappling with the problems of perhaps a bloody awful day since 8 a.m., this was hard to take. Even more difficult, though, was escape in the evening past the open door of Tommy's den where he would be entertaining a foreign journalist (often a lunch-time guest) and where, because he was attracted by my facility for phrase-making, I was invited in to share a glass and to help the bemused visitor more clearly to understand the nuances of the Northern Ireland problem.

One thing that did impress me was the persistence of the government machine in trying to manage the news, and its relative failure to do so. I also saw the need for journalists to get behind the deliberate opacity of the press handout and the obscuring hospitality of the lunch. Many of my friends, readers of the quality broadsheets, had remarked on the difference in tone between the stories filed by journalists in the field and the editorial line enunciated in the leaders. I discovered that phone calls from the office to contacts in the editorial departments were apparently sufficient to convince them that the reporters were callow young Englishmen who, if they had not gone native, could not possibly understand the nuances of Ulster politics.

I was struck by the ease with which the civil service machine had adapted to direct rule. In part this was because ministries went on doing whatever it was they had been engaged in without too much interference from the Castle. The fact was, too, that ministers had so much to learn so quickly that they had to depend largely on the permanent secretaries, and in any case they were more interested in politics and security than in social and economic programmes. What did surprise me was that a couple of the permanent secretaries, whom I would have placed at the liberal end of that spectrum, seemed to be more affected by direct rule than some of their fellows. They were, in a way, shattered. I could only speculate that they had suppressed any ethical doubts they might have had under the old regime by the rationalisation that it was all for the greater good, and here was the Westminster Parliament, the ultimate custodian of the public interest, telling them that not only was this wrong, but that Stormont rule must stop immediately.

The first weeks were dominated by political manoeuvrings involved in agreeing the coalition that was to form the new Executive. In the elections to the new Assembly in June 1973, Faulkner had held on to just enough seats to remain the largest unionist grouping, whose members were known as the 'pledged' Unionists because they had undertaken to support the party line which had mustered a wafer-thin majority behind the leader. Faulkner had been pushed out of the official Unionist Party and he was doing his best to create a new bridgehead with Peter McLachlan as main organiser. This left Harry West with the rump of the Unionists, Bill Craig with Vanguard and Ian Paisley with the Democratic Unionist Party, the DUP.

The formal requirement in the Constitution Act was for an Executive of eleven members, and the opening proposal was for it to comprise six unionists, four SDLP and one Alliance, on the grounds that the Unionists must be seen to be in the majority. From the beginning, I argued that the SDLP could not agree to accept only four seats, on the simple pragmatic grounds that their main negotiating group had numbered six people and, given the fragile nature of their coalition, they could not afford to drop anybody, especially from a paid post, after years of struggle together and shared hardship. They argued the case less materialistically and more politically on the grounds that they had nearly as many members as Faulkner, and should have near-equality of seats. There was a lot of to-ing and fro-ing about who should have what cabinet posts and on what grounds. The SDLP was determined to get its hands on the high-profile spending departments, especially those that covered the fields where the discrimination that had sparked off the civil rights movement had operated: employment and the location of industry, housing, health and social services. Gerry Fitt was not particularly interested in administration, only in politics, but as party leader he could not be passed over for a senior post. Normally one would have expected the second-strongest partner in the coalition to take the Finance job, but Gerry was not attracted by this and would not have had the temperament or the background for it anyhow. John Hume seemed to be a natural for Finance, but perhaps he thought that there was more political mileage to be made out of opening factories than in enforcing the rigours of public expenditure controls on other departments, especially those in which his party colleagues were the main spenders.

In the end, in a sort of cliffhanger, the number of posts in the administration was increased to fifteen. This was achieved by the device of inventing four additional posts. The Executive would still have eleven members, but another four were designated ministers outside the Executive. In a way it was a division into ministers and junior ministers, although even this distinction was not clear cut.

The final outcome was a fairly shameless piece of pork-barrelling in a sort of Parkinsonian calculus. It was not a case of work expanding to fill the time available, but of posts being created to suit the number of ministers. Housing was separated from the Environment to create two departments out of the Ministry of Development. The Manpower and Training wing of the Department of Health and Social Services, the DHSS, was hived off to provide a Department of Manpower Services. Oliver Napier made life easier for everybody by insisting on a Department of Law Reform, and filling it himself in what seemed to be a cop-out from real politics.

The office of Deputy Chief Minister, with undefined functions, was created for Gerry Fitt. Still there were not enough jobs to go round. There were lurid stories of Frank Cooper, the permanent under-secretary at the Northern Ireland Office, coming out of the rooms asking, 'Can you split anything else? Can we find another department?' Eventually as time ran out the requests became more frantic. 'For God's sake find a name for something!' And so we ended up with a Minister for Information and a Minister for Executive Planning and Co-ordination – as near as dammit two ministers without portfolio.

It was a nonsense in a small group of highly political people, all with their own connections with the media, to appoint a Minister of Information, and that the most callow and inexperienced of them all, and one with no media personality whatsoever. As if highly political animals like John Hume and Roy Bradford, having brought a scheme to fruition, would be willing to pass the parcel to John Baxter so that he could announce the good news. Eddie McGrady's function as Minister of Executive Planning and Co-ordination was even more difficult to identify, and had not been fully defined by the time the Executive fell.

These first months were useful for meeting the members of the proposed Executive, for getting to know them and for building relationships. Gerry Fitt, at this stage, developed a great regard for my supposed ability to reason with Paddy Devlin, whom he at times found difficult. Once, when he asked me to make peace for him with Paddy, I refused on the grounds that this was a party matter, not suitable for a civil servant, and in any case he was the leader and should not shirk the task. I advised him to talk directly to Paddy.

'What will he do?' asked Gerry.

I replied that he could take it well or ill, but the thing to do was to speak to him.

Late in November 1973 I went on a management training course in Sunningdale. One day when we were having a lunchtime drink at the bar, I heard the head barman complain that they were having to install draught Guinness. We had been preparing for a joint meeting between the Executive designate and the British and Irish governments, but in the interests of security nobody would tell us where it was going to be held. Suddenly the penny dropped; I was not surprised to hear a week later that the meeting was being held in Sunningdale.

Sunningdale was an uneasy starting point for the Executive. In one sense it identified the opposition: everybody who was not there. This included the rump of non-Faulkner Unionists, Vanguard, Paisley, and the IRA. All of them had a vested interest subsequently in bringing it down. This was particularly marked on the unionist side. Some of us argued for some formulation that would enable the 'unpledged' Unionists at least not to be fully excluded. This might have been achieved by giving them an invitation at least to take part in the discussions. The Brits were not keen on this, the Irish much less so, and the SDLP not at all. The result of some indecision was a half-baked invitation to Paisley after the session had begun, which he made a meal out of refusing.

Another difficulty about Sunningdale was that while the Irish and British delegations formed coherent and separate entities, each with its own agenda, the parties to the Executive went separately. There was no single Executive view, and this had a significant effect on the outcome. In particular, while the SDLP more or less secured the support of the Irish government, Faulkner did not have the backing of the British when he most needed it. Faulkner himself was a naturally optimistic man, confident of his ability to make a deal, and also sure of his own ability to sell it afterwards. There is now plenty of evidence that he was pushed farther than he should have been, and beyond his power to deliver. It is also clear that on crucial issues, instead of backing Faulkner, Heath joined the others in putting pressure on him. From talking to those involved it is clear that the two people who most quickly realised Faulkner's difficulty and did try to help him were Paddy Devlin and Conor Cruise O'Brien. The general consensus now is that the nationalist side (Dublin/SDLP) overbid their hands – and won. It is also clear that Faulkner was saddled with a load which he could not carry and which eventually brought him down, and with him the whole power-sharing experiment.

Amid the euphoria, particularly in nationalist circles, which followed the announcement of the Sunningdale Agreement, setting up the political framework for the new Executive, there was one jarring note which should have been a warning. Two of the major players interpreted the outcome in diametrically opposed terms. Brian Faulkner hailed the agreement as the unionists' bulwark against being absorbed into a united Ireland, while Hugh Logue of the SDLP announced that Sunningdale was 'the vehicle which will trundle us into an Irish republic'. The trouble was that the Protestants believed Hugh Logue and the Catholics believed Faulkner. Meanwhile, the Provisionals maintained their campaign.

The Executive was sworn in at noon on 31 December 1973 in the old Cabinet Room in Stormont Castle. The ceremony was conducted by Sir Robert Lowry, the Lord Chief Justice. The first hiccup was the use of the same formula for swearing in full-blown ministers and those who were outside the Executive, and some had to be done again. Then Paddy Devlin, much to the alarm of his SDLP colleagues, declined to be sworn. Ken Bloomfield had asked me a few days earlier what I thought Paddy would do. I said that although I had never discussed religion with him, my impression was that Paddy would probably describe himself as an agnostic. Whatever he was he was not a hypocrite: he was a man of great integrity and it would be wise to have the alternative formulation of an affirmation ready. Ken took note, and was in a position to respond rapidly with a form of affirmation when Paddy made his stand.

On 1 January 1974, I came into work to be told that the Deputy Chief Minister wished to see me. I went to Fitt's office and was shown in by the private secretary, Alec Ireland. 'Well, Minister,' I temporised, to be greeted with the broadside, 'For Christ's sake, Maurice, you're not going to start that bloody nonsense.'

We spent the first half-hour or so arguing about what we should call each other. Then it struck me that here was a man who had fought at least existentially for power for two decades, and power, when achieved, was an empty desk. There were no great levers to pull, no great decisions to be taken, no in-tray loaded with documents to be disposed of, nothing requiring the smack of firm government or crisp decision.

Eventually we decided that he should phone somebody to announce that the show was on the road, so he phoned Maurice Foley, who had by now moved to the EEC in Brussels, to announce the safe delivery of the Executive.

In part our problem in finding an agenda arose from the failure to define the role of the Deputy Chief Executive. Part of the problem was that Brian Faulkner was a prodigious worker and a very efficient minister, who got through an enormous workload, whereas very little work did Gerry. In terms of having a man to 'mark' Faulkner, the SDLP would have done better to assign the post to John Hume, as well as his departmental brief. Gerry was more cut out for the House of Commons. It was scarcely fair to constrict him in the straitjacket of office. Files bored him and he would not carry a brief. He attached himself to me as his friendly sherpa and announced that I was to be his speech-maker, an empty occupation if ever there was one.

Gerry was a natural – put him up in front of a crowd and he would perform. He also had a good political sense, a wicked sense of humour, and a racy, allusive style honed on the election platforms of Belfast. None of this could be captured in a scripted speech. Furthermore, fidelity to theme or party line was not his strong point: he went where the spirit led him. He did not read prepared speeches easily and the wickedness of his own imagination kept wanting to break out. So the drafts were torn up. An attempt was then made to give him topic headings that would more or less align with the press release the Information Office would issue. Eventually I settled for talking to him in the car on the way to whatever official function he was attending about the line he might take. That was only a very small brake on the spate of colourful language that flowed from Gerry, which, to give them their due, most of the seasoned journalists enjoyed but did not print. Gerry had a great affection for the Downpatrick area. His mother had been evacuated to Bells Hill after the blitz, when he was sailing on the Archangel convoys, and his sisters had attended Inch School. This gave him something of a bond with me, and also with Brian Faulkner who was also an east Down man.

One of my lasting memories of the Executive is of the efforts that

Brian Faulkner (a staid man who never used bad language) made to pretend that he understood Gerry Fitt's jokes (which were invariably scabrous) and, even more difficult, to pretend that he was amused by them.

Gerry's greatest feats had been enacted 'on the marble' in Belfast City Hall, and in the corridors and bars of the House of Commons, where his friends and cronies were, and where he exerted considerable influence. With his rolling seaman's gait, cigarette in mouth, his 'How's about ya?', the story, the nudge, the wink, he conveyed the feeling of being inside or having the inside story as he laid the destructive little anti-personnel mine of character assassination. Gerry was more at home at Westminster than at Stormont, more respected as a character. It was on a bigger scale. Also there were more journalists to speak to. He would have run out of patience with the Executive role before very long.

The SDLP members of the Executive came into office with a degree of suspicion of the civil service; civil servants, for their part, were wary of this new breed of ministers who had been seen on television leading civil rights marches, sitting down in streets, squatting in houses, being batoned and hosed.

One of the first steps to break the ice was an all-day session involving all the members of the administration and all the permanent secretaries, in which each permanent secretary laid out his wares, deploying the policies the department had developed, describing its present activities and laying out the possibilities for progress. Most of them had picked up the messages in the Executive manifesto *Towards a Better Tomorrow*, which was largely an SDLP document since the SDLP members were the ones most capable of thinking for themselves and doing their homework. The Unionists, having been in government for years, had got into the habit of waiting for drafts to be prepared by officials and were rather lost when on their own.

The permanent secretaries were a mixed bunch, but included some formidable men: Jimmy Young in Agriculture, John Oliver in Housing and Planning, Norman Dugdale in Health, Ewart Bell in Commerce, and George Quigley, newly promoted into Manpower. These were men of great ability, capable of taking a broad strategic view. More important, especially in the eyes of the SDLP, they showed that they cared. They were not merely bureaucrats, they had thought long and hard about the problems of the society and they welcomed the opportunity to do something constructive about them.

This was one of the very good days in the Executive. Faulkner was at the top of his form. He was capable of mastering his own brief, but he was well clued up on the others as well. His previous experience had covered the ministries of Development and Commerce, and whilst he was happier in these more practical fields than in dealing with social legislation, he had a formidable ability to keep in touch with the details of what his colleagues were doing.

Arising out of the day, it was interesting to see the growth of respect between the new ministers and their permanent secretaries. Paddy Devlin very quickly formed a close rapport with Norman Dugdale, a reserved Lancastrian, a poet and a Greek scholar. What brought them together was their concern for the casualties of society and their love of literature. Another formidable combination was George Quigley and Bob Cooper, who quickly became immersed in the preparation of anti-discrimination legislation and in reviewing the industrial relations and training fields. John Oliver, who could have chosen to stay with the rump of Environment, interestingly enough elected to move to the new Department of Housing and Planning, with Austin Currie as his minister, towards whom his behaviour was almost paternalistic.

The SDLP ministers for the most part were very good indeed. They worked hard, mastered their briefs, argued strongly and passionately for their programmes and policies, and were able to go places and meet people where ministers had not gone before. Paddy Devlin was generally regarded in the DHSS as one of the best ministers they had ever had. Paddy generally got his own way. He complained a bit about obstruction by a senior officer in Supplementary Benefits whom he regarded as a reactionary bigot. He was right on both counts, but not precisely in the sense he meant. The man was reactionary in his addiction to rules and petty regulations, and bigoted in his belief that all claimants were impostors who should be unmasked and denied as much as possible. Apart from that, he treated them all alike.

In some ways, the new men were a bit of a disappointment in being less radical than might have been expected, but then they did not have much time. I remember talking to an old hand in

Commerce, whom I regarded as a staunch unionist, and asking what he thought of his new minister. He confessed to being disappointed with John Hume: 'I thought he would have been different from the last guy, but he was just the same.' In his way, John was rather conservative, but in fairness he had only been in office a matter of weeks. The civil servant had apparently expected instant action. Even at that stage of his career, however, Hume was a formidable man, able to analyse problems clearly, to formulate an argument and to present a case forcefully and succinctly. He was one of the best drafters I have come across, with a great capacity to envelop conflicting concepts in language of Delphic luminosity.

Early in the life of the Executive, Ken Bloomfield phoned me one evening to say that John Hume was going to America, and that Commerce had refused to draft a speech for him on the grounds that it was political and that civil servants should not be involved. He asked me to have a go at it. We both agreed that Commerce was taking a very puritanical view of what constituted a political speech. I was even more appalled than Ken, given the way the department had played the game with unionist ministers over the years. John Hume was going to America to explain how a coalition of previously opposed interests in Northern Ireland had come together in the Executive for the common good, to encourage support for the initiative, and incidentally to secure the support of an influential segment of US opinion for investment in Northern Ireland. It seemed to me that he was doing no more than his job as Minister of Commerce. I could not imagine a member of the British or any other government on a trade mission being told that he was on his own just because he was talking to other politicians, as John was in addressing a meeting of senators and congressmen.

As it was, even at that statge John Hume had an access to American politicians and the US media enjoyed by no other politician in Northern Ireland. It was an important speech and I sat up all night in order to have it ready for typing in the morning. Indeed it had to be cabled after him, and I had no chance to discuss it with him. He delivered it as drafted. It contained the first explicit statement that I am aware of, by a public representative speaking to public representatives in the USA, deploring fund raising for the IRA. 'Ask yourself whether you would throw a bomb or pull a trigger, for that is what your dollar will do.'

This episode meant that from time to time I was asked to draft speeches for Faulkner and others. Brian had a no-nonsense type of delivery, he liked the facts and he liked to tell it straight. He was also very good at telling you the sort of speech he wanted and the points he wished to stress.

The two loose cannon from an early stage were Roy Bradford and Paddy Devlin. Roy was fairly disenchanted by the whole exercise since he was not leading the band. He had a good mind, a brilliant academic record, a gift for languages and a feel for politics. One sensed, however, that he felt that Stormont was a bit below his capabilities. He was put out, too, by having to take Environment, the least glamorous of the departments and the one with the least opportunity for publicity – there is nothing very telegenic about a sewage disposal works. In order to make the job a bit more sexy, Roy had negotiated with Faulkner the post of EEC Co-ordinator. That at least would bring him to Brussels, if not round the capitals of the Nine. However, even here disaster struck. In February a Labour government took office with a mandate to renegotiate the UK terms of entry to the EEC, and all communication with Brussels by a subordinate regional administration was foreclosed for the rest of the Executive's period of office.

Roy was known to his Unionist Party colleagues as 'The Canary'. I asked one of them why, and he described how when coal miners were going into a mine where there was a danger of coal gas, they would carry a canary in a cage. At the first sniff of danger the canary would keel over. 'Roy', he said, 'is our canary'.

Paddy and Roy both appeared to have a standard letter of resignation in their pockets and be waiting for the appropriate moment to throw it on the table and walk out. Both were continually threatening to resign, Paddy in a roar, Roy in a mutter.

Towards a Better Tomorrow became an important document as plans were made to implement the manifesto's policy. All the ministers who had been at Sunningdale were convinced that the bounty of the British Treasury was endless in the search for peace. I have no doubt that Willie Whitelaw in his jollying way was likely to have said to people in corners, 'You don't think we'd spoil the ship for a few hundred million . . . ?' Whatever the reason, all the Executive's members, especially the SDLP, felt that their programmes would be under-written, that a splash of public spending would enable them to make a quick mark and would signal the reality of change to deprived, mostly Catholic areas. Even with a Labour government, the sums got increasingly difficult, and it became harder to believe that the Treasury was a party to whatever agreement had been made. At the start a figure of about £400 million was mentioned as a sort of a dowry. This got whittled down to £100 million as the public expenditure climate worsened; when the Executive fell, the money simply disappeared.

In the meantime, though, the task was to align the current programmes and what the new members wanted to do with the money likely to be available. From a programming point of view, the great advantage of the manifesto was that it did not have a time frame and that the programme could be extended over four years, or longer, to fit the money available. Apart from that, it was all good stuff, very much the nature of social policy in those Butskellite days when both Labour and Conservative governments resided in the middle ground, and there was little difference between them in their willingness to use public money for social engineering or to buy their way out of trouble, and nothing in the manifesto so radical as to cause a reaction.

I have mentioned the difficulty of defining a role for Eddie McGrady, the Minister of Executive Planning and Co-ordination, whom I was delegated to assist. However conceived, this title implied some capacity to encroach on the responsibility of other ministers, if not to overrule them. This most ministers were reluctant to allow, and none more so than McGrady's colleagues in the SDLP who, having fought for power together, were beginning to behave as ministers had always behaved, as barons defending their turf.

One possible task for McGrady was to be the steward or guardian of the manifesto. Each minister, and his department, was asked to prioritise his programme along the lines of the manifesto, and the Minister of Executive Planning and Co-ordination was required to conduct an audit with his individual colleagues in turn to assure this alignment and to check that agreed Executive policies were being progressed. I remember the day we went to the DHSS to check up on its performance. On the way up in the lift in Dundonald House, I noticed that my man was somewhat nervous. In mock fear he said, 'What will I do if he hits me?' We had a fairly robust meeting which ended up with Paddy and myself slugging it out verbally at one end

173

of the table with my minister, McGrady, and Paddy's permanent secretary, that decent man Norman Dugdale, in shocked silence at the other. This exchange cemented a long friendship with Paddy Devlin, an effective minister and one of the best-read that I have come across.

One of the jobs I got involved in at this time was to try to identify functions for the Council of Ireland. This, I thought, was a dead duck from the start: a piece of symbolic window dressing that was never going to amount to anything, and which would distract attention from the essential task of building trust in Northern Ireland. Ministers were political animals, and, having acquired power, they were not about to hand it over to somebody else. And civil servants in Dublin were not any better at divesting themselves of functions than civil servants in Belfast – or anywhere – and if they could not be persuaded to move to Athlone or Castlebar under their own decentralising proposals, were unlikely to want to move to Armagh, which was one of the places favoured for the Council of Ireland headquarters, and where the Archbishop's Palace had just become vacant.

One method we used to discover the possible range of functions for the Council of Ireland was to write to departments, North and South, asking them to nominate activities or blocks of work that might be transferred to the council, and to try to find a match. When the lists came in, they made sorry reading. It was evident that each department, intent on protecting its own core interests, had marshalled its smaller satellite bodies and lesser functions as sacrificial ewe lambs: the Nurses' and Midwives' Registration Board, the registration of opticians, the control of rabid dogs, and on and drearily on. Once I did get matching bids – on the protection of wild birds. The only common thread was the reopening of the Ballyconnell Canal from the Erne to the Shannon systems, which everyone agreed would rejuvenate tourism in the area and was a ready-made flagship project for the Council of Ireland. It is interesting to see this dream has at last been realised twenty years later through the bounty of the International Fund for Ireland and the EC Structural Fund.

The Council of Ireland, although I believe it was a threat to no one, became a stick to beat the Executive with. Some commentators argue that the Council of Ireland was the dead weight that brought the whole Sunningdale arrangement down. I do not really believe so. In the climate of the time it was less unfashionable and illiberal to oppose stronger links with Dublin than to be seen to oppose power-sharing. But even the most liberal unionist could be forgiven for bridling at the Council of Ireland. I believe that the fundamental, gut objection all along was to sharing power with Catholics, and that opposition to the Council of Ireland was a smokescreen to conceal a much deeper and atavistic historic antagonism which had not been put to rest. The Council of Ireland was also a distraction: it occupied the time of the Executive, it dominated the thinking of the SDLP ministers, and it obsessed their backbenchers. At times of crisis, when the whole enterprise was seen to be teetering on the edge, the SDLP appeared to be possessed of an almost theological urge to define and redefine the remit of the council. In the end, when they accepted a proposal to postpone its implementation until after the next Assembly election in four years' time, the Sunningdale enterprise was all over.

In February 1974 there was a mini-Sunningdale at Hillsborough, this time involving the Executive and the Irish government. It was brisk and workmanlike, reflecting the temperament (they were alike in many ways) of Brian Faulkner and Liam Cosgrave. They shared a passionate interest in hunting, and used hunting metaphors a lot. After the conference was over, I came upon the two leaders in the toilet. I delayed momentarily to hear what great affairs of state were to be discussed privately. Cosgrave waited for Faulkner, then said, 'Brian, I met a man in the County Meath the other day who told me he had sold a horse to your father.'

February brought the second of the hammer blows that were to weaken and eventually bring down the Executive. The first had been the removal in November 1973 of Whitelaw, who had been a tower of strength, and who exuded confidence and bonhomie in equal proportions. He had been drafted to England to deal with the miners and his replacement was Francis Pym, then a colourless figure with no experience in Northern Ireland, with no knowledge of the issues and the personalities, no contacts, little contribution to make, and completely out of his depth. The second blow was Heath's decision to call a general election in order to secure a mandate against the miners. He lost, which is another story. But the very fact that an election was held was immediately damaging to the Executive, since the parties had not been together long enough to present any kind of united front to the world. Each party fought on its own, in effect fighting each other and at the same time fighting the anti-Executive unionists who made the election a plebiscite on the Sunningdale Agreement. They were united only in opposition to Sunningdale. The election was not held under proportional representation, and in a first-past-the-post system the result was disastrous: eleven of the twelve seats were won by anti-Sunningdale unionists. Only Gerry Fitt in West Belfast held his seat.

The result immediately quantified the opposition to Sunningdale. Up to then it could be dismissed as a few dissidents in the Assembly. Now there was a measurable plurality of votes and, more significant, over 90 per cent of parliamentary representatives clearly against the Executive. Its legitimacy took a severe knock from which it never really recovered.

The election also brought a change of government. Heath, who had been the prime minister to take most interest in and the most decisive action about Northern Ireland since Lloyd George, and the one most likely to see the unionists off, had gone. Sunningdale was his baby. He had a commitment to it and was much more likely to back it than any successor.

In the event, although the new Labour government ritually announced no change in policy (bipartisanship can always accommodate changes in emphasis), it was never fully committed to Sunningdale. Wilson was a gnomic figure; Rees, the new secretary of state, was a haverer who found it hard to make up his mind on anything. From their point of view, Sunningdale had been designed to bring peace. It had not done so. The Provos were still active, and now the Protestants were up in arms. The new government's attitude was at best *laisser faire*: if the Executive survived, well and good, if not, there would be no great effort to provide a lifeline.

Sitting in at meetings of the Executive was both interesting and encouraging. Faulkner was a very good chairman, businesslike and brisk. He kept discussion going, gave people an opportunity to talk, and summed up succinctly and clearly. I don't remember a vote, and I don't think there ever was one. The two dominant personalities were Faulkner and Hume, mainly because they were on top of their briefs, and had the intellectual horsepower and the energy to range wider. Both argued clearly and articulately, and when it came down to business both presented a case forcefully and rationally. As a group the

SDLP ministers were the more impressive. They were also more interesting as individuals. Each had his own qualities: Currie, probably the brightest and the best political tactician, and Paddy Devlin, with a burning passion for what he was doing, a great commitment to justice, and an inability to keep his tongue out of other people's business, were clearly, with Faulkner and Hume, a cut above the rest. Gerry Fitt acted as a sort of court jester injecting levity even when it was not appropriate, but still adept at defusing heated situations or relaxing tension with a quip. Roy Bradford was at best a semi-attached member of the Executive, intellectually and politically, and in the collapse of the European dimension he was progressively disenchanted with the whole exercise. In fairness, he was probably better than most at picking up the vibes from the Protestant working class and the loyalist paramilitaries, and was aware before most of the strength of feeling in that community against Sunningdale, and the likelihood that feeling would progress to action before very long. Basil McIvor, now Minister of Education, beavered away manfully and laid the foundations for an interest he was to develop in integrated schools. Of the SDLP members, Ivan Cooper was the least popular, particularly with the Unionists, perhaps because they regarded him as something of a defector. The two Alliance members perhaps typically were less flamboyant than some of their fellows, and held a corner for moderation and decency in all things.

One thing that did light up the sky was the intense mutual dislike of Devlin and Bradford. Roy laced his remarks with asides which made him sound more right-wing and reactionary than he was, but which provoked Paddy to verbal retorts which were not always restrained and, on occasion, to threats of physical correction. When Paddy was speaking, Roy would sigh audibly and make some cutting remark not quite *sotto voce*, prompting Paddy to an even cruder expletive than usual, at which point his adversary would smirk and throw up his eyebrows. Roy was to write a thriller later based partly on life in a Unionist cabinet. It is called *The Last Ditch*. The title arose from a declaration by the hero that before he saw Ulster perish he would 'die in the last ditch'. It is by no means the best novel to come out of Northern Ireland politics, and ranks with an earlier effort by Roy about a young unionist hopeful who rose from obscurity to become prime minister. That is called *Excelsior*. Both books, if read carefully and with due regard for artistic licence, give a considerable insight into the author and his political ambitions. Paddy Devlin reviewed *The Last Ditch* for the *Irish Times*. He opened thus: 'Roy Bradford would not have seen his country die in the last ditch. He would have closed his eyes first.'

That apart, there was little acrimony in the Executive. Indeed, it was a warming experience to see men who had been bitter political enemies and highly suspicious of each other begin to develop trust and respect for each other's ability and integrity as they tackled common problems. This was particularly true of Faulkner and Hume, but it was true of others too. Faulkner had a particularly soft spot for Paddy Devlin, tempered with impatience at his verbal explosiveness, but based on the fact, I think, that Paddy, more than any of his fellows, empathised with Faulkner's difficulties with his own party, especially over Sunningdale, and was anxious that he should not be loaded with a burden of unnecessary political baggage that would bring him down, and with him the whole experiment.

If there was any noticeable division in the Executive, it tended to be on age grounds more than along the traditional fault lines of Ulster politics: allegiance and religion. There was increasingly a tendency for the younger members to see things in a different light from the older unionists. In this context, the SDLP were all young. For example, to people like Herbie Kirk, the unionist Minister of Finance, the traditional family firm or Harland and Wolff were sacred pieces of ancestral furniture, our heritage, part of the bedrock of the Ulster economy, to be preserved at all costs. The younger members were much more likely to question the yard's place in the order of things, to ask whether the firm was entitled to a blank cheque, no matter how low the productivity, how inefficient the management, how illusory the demand for the product they were making. There was the beginning of questioning too of the level of support for industries that were dying in preference to a restructuring of the industrial and employment base around new industries, new technologies and new skills.

If all was pleasant and constructive in the Cabinet Room, the Assembly was an unpleasant ordeal for those who had to endure it, and even for those paid to watch. It was a bear garden. The Speaker, Nat Minford, had been one of Faulkner's men: indeed, his appointment weakened the party. He had been a junior minister in previous unionist governments. A decent man of considerable integrity, he had a heart attack just after his appointment and did not have the force to carry through a very difficult job of maintaining order. Apart from which, standing orders seemed to be deficient in that nobody, it seemed, could be suspended or expelled for unparliamentary behaviour. The clerks, relics of the old regime, did not seem to be a great help.

The result was that ministers, and especially Faulkner, were abused verbally on every occasion, and sometimes even physically. Faulkner was spat upon, jostled, reviled and shouted down, as were the other ministers. He was well able for it, but it was sad to see him spat upon by lesser men, political pigmies and procedural bullies and wild men of the woods and the bogs. The most eccentric of these was Professor Kennedy Lindsay, who boasted a chair in a West African university and appeared once in Nigerian dress, who seized the mace once and swung it at Faulkner, and on another occasion chained himself to the table. It was on this occasion, I think, when Faulkner was being jostled that I saw the normally calm and sedate Basil McIvor land a telling punch on a member of the DUP. This kind of behaviour led ministers to avoid the house, to stay in their departments and to insulate themselves from the unpleasantness of the Assembly. Had they been more in circulation, they might have picked up the warning notes earlier. As it was, they were like passengers on a cruise ship. They had their own interests and timetable, their own deck games, that had little relevance to the storms that were brewing outside.

A more pleasant occasion, and one that I remember as a bench mark of another kind, was an afternoon when a group of schoolchildren from a Catholic secondary school in Crossgar was in the gallery, supervised by a teacher, Gerry MacNamara, who had been at school with me. Presiding as Deputy Speaker was Paddy O'Donoghue, another classmate. Speaking for the Executive was Eddie McGrady, whom I had taught at the same school. I happened to be the senior civil servant in the box on that occasion. Not bad for a group that had been excluded from the corridors of power for so long. It reflected a major shift in politics: the opening up of opportunities denied by religious or class barriers to a whole new generation of people. I hoped that the schoolchildren would be encouraged by this to play a full and responsible role in society.

Sadly, that was the high tide. The ebb set in rapidly thereafter.

One other aspect of the Executive arrangements was the failure to build linkages among the backbenchers. While good relationships and understanding were developing among the Executive members, their parties on the back benches rarely mixed and seldom made common cause. Faulkner's 'pledged' Unionists were the most vulnerable. Their numbers were shrinking daily, and the death of one of them in a car accident was a tragedy in the loss of a personable and reasonable man, David McCarthy, and in reducing the number of supporters still further. There was little margin. They were under constant and wearying attack and intimidation from the other unionists, and as previously mentioned, the latent divisions between Executive partners were accentuated by their having to fight the Westminster election as opponents. The SDLP members tended to huddle together in theological discussions about the role and remit of the Council of Ireland which they wished to expand, and with not a lot of interest in the real bread-and-butter issues that were of concern to the Executive, and little appreciation of, or sympathy for, the problems Faulkner was facing with the unionists, and his lack of room to manoeuvre. Eddie McGrady, probably the closest to these problems, and less absorbed in departmental work, told me one day that the SDLP had only assented to power sharing in order to get the Council of Ireland, which seemed to me an odd inversion of values and a retreat from reality.

One thing the SDLP did do during the Assembly period was to prepare the ground for the ultimate demise of the Community Relations Commission. Even at its best, the SDLP leadership had never been keen on the commission. As politicians, they wanted to be the sole channel of grace and goodies for Catholics. They resented any body that seemed to threaten their power base or which, by encouraging people to look across the barricades, might dilute the political cohesion of their constituency. I had had a reasonable relationship with the SDLP during my time as chairman of the Community Relations Commission, but no wholehearted support. After I left, things deteriorated.

The SDLP took the view that now it was in government there were no longer community relations problems, that it would speak for the Catholic population, and that the commission was superfluous. This played into the hands of the civil servants in the Department of

Community Relations, which had been jealous of the Commission. They quickly captured Ivan Cooper, the new minister. The commission had few friends, the commission staff even fewer, and so by the efforts of an SDLP minister committed to the improvement of community relations, it was closed down, although by the time this closure came into effect the Executive itself had fallen.

Working with the Executive was stimulating and, for the most part, pleasant. Faulkner appreciated clear advice and short papers. Executive papers were confined to two pages and you might sneak another couple in as appendices, but this was regarded as cheating. This was a great training in succinctness. It is surprising how much you can express the essence of a problem and the options available for action in two foolscap sheets. The very task of condensing the argument meant having to understand it, stripping out irrelevancies and embellishments and getting down to the bedrock of the problem. It also promoted a more focused discussion in the Executive as it produced fewer false trails to follow.

I was largely responsible for briefings on the social departments and on developments in the Republic. Robert Ramsey, a former private secretary to Faulkner, who had followed him from Commerce to Home Affairs to the Environment to the Prime Minister's Office, was recalled from Brussels where he had set up a Northern Ireland office. He looked after the economic departments and the EEC. Together with Ken Bloomfield, we were a fairly formidable team. Ken was easy to work with. He gave you your remit and let you get on with it. He was also easy to approach and unstuffy, so that a great deal of work could be cleared informally. You got to know how far you could go without referral, and policies tended to be developed over a period in discussions where views were welcomed and you felt you were contributing.

It was this period, I think, that confirmed my view of the need for the public service to be recruited on as broad a base as possible, and not merely as eunuchs observing the action but debarred from any active participation. It is important that the debate that takes place outside, however inchoately, should be reflected in the decision-making process. This is not to say that civil servants in particular should regard themselves as nominees of one or other political party, or as spokesmen for a pressure group or representatives of this or that faction. What it does mean is that if they are to be effective in developing policies that meet the current needs of society, they should retain some contact with the real world outside, they should be prepared to reflect differences in a constructive way, and they should not seek to camouflage their better feelings and apprehensions in the grey uniformity of the *apparatchik*. I have often thought that, in those days, my main contribution was to call attention to views that would not have been noticed if I had kept silent, to keep my foot in the door and shout through the aperture the otherwise unheard messages from those who had previously been unrepresented – whether because of their politics, class, religion or tradition.

I remember arguing with John Hume that power sharing was not necessarily the only approach to opening up the administration. I would accept that it was symbolically tremendously important for the SDLP and for Catholics generally that their people should be seen to be at the top table and that there should be parity of esteem for their tradition. But there was a downside in the constraints imposed by collective cabinet responsibility, which inevitably dulled the edge of public discussion, and the danger that public differences of opinion on major issues would bring the whole edifice tumbling down. These dangers were not fully exposed in the short life of the Executive, but they are inherent in the very nature of coalition, especially coalition framed on representational formulae rather than on common policies. It is also hard to change large organisations from the top, especially by people who have come in from outside the system, who are not aware of the ploys organisations use in self-preservation, and who are mainly dependent on the machine itself for information and research. For these reasons, I argued that if the object were to effect real social change, there might be more utility in twelve assistant secretaries strategically placed in departments than in two or three ministers in an Executive. In a perfect world, you would do both: in an ideal world there would be no need to do either.

There is a myth outside the civil service (and in some circles within it) that policy making is a discrete function with decisions taken rationally, or conspiratorially according to your preference. The common view is of decisions being taken at precise moments, probably in smoke-filled rooms. Margaret Thatcher has been quoted by Alan Clark as saying that you learn in politics never to take a decision before you have to.

I have been fascinated by this process for most of my working life, much of which has been a journey in search of the point of decision. First I tried to get into the smoke-filled rooms. When I got inside I discovered that they contained nothing but smoke. Decisions emerge from the culture, they are formed over a period from a range of inputs. This changed, of course, with the advent of Thatcherism when ideology became all, dogma determined argument, and policy meant simply forcing facts into the procrustean framework of monetarist theory. In this case you started with the answer and looked around for facts to justify it and for sums to make the equation come out.

We, however, lived in simpler, or perhaps more complicated times. Perhaps the smack of firm government was lacking, perhaps indecisiveness was induced, perhaps there was an over-dependence on the idea that the world could be altered by social engineering, that rational argument would in the end prevail, and an obsession with process at the expense of product. And in this milieu it was important to take part in the discussion and to ensure that all strands of opinion were represented. I found generally a receptiveness to alternative views – a broad ignorance of what was going on outside a small closed coterie, and surprise when it was brought to their attention. You had only to say, 'How do you think it will look in Monday's *Irish News*?' for people to hold hard and think again.

One of the effects of single-party government for seventy years, and a civil service that reflected the values and ethos of the dominant party, was a lack of challenge, a lack of intellectual rigour, and a willingness to accept traditional attitudes and procedures as immutable. There was also the myopia of a closed society. There were no political challenges from outside through the rotation of governments and ministers bringing with them new policies developed while in opposition, and no internal ferment either, partly because of the similarity in background and training of the civil service, but also because it paid, in career terms and otherwise, not to rock the boat. If there was corruption in the Northern Ireland Civil Service, it was not of the petty cash kind – its members were generally immune to that – but at the senior level in its members sometimes accepting that there was a limit to what the market would bear. Policies were sometimes not advanced because of fear of rejection by political masters on grounds of undue liberality, and because of fear of what association with doomed policy initiatives would do to official careers.

There were also dangers to competent decision making in the civil service's location in the rarefied atmosphere of Stormont, isolated in acres of parkland from the problems of the city and the daily experiences of the citizens, and also in the fact that so many senior civil servants lived on the edge of the estate or in the north Down corridor, met only people like themselves, read the same newspapers, and had a very poor appreciation of the facts of life outside their own limited circle.

This said, Ken Bloomfield and Robert Ramsey were interesting, witty and wholly delightful colleagues, with an easy manner and an iconoclastic approach to many of the pomposities that we encountered. Lunch in the Members' Dining Room, the great perk of office, was a variable pleasure. The food was consistently appalling, but the waitresses were extremely pleasant and friendly. There seemed to be a convention that civil servants sat at table together, which seemed to me to defeat the purpose of eating there in the first place. I was prepared to risk my digestion to make the acquaintance in a more relaxed atmosphere of some of the more difficult members, but not to make it worse by listening to the interchanges at the table shared by parliamentary officers and civil servants; these interchanges seemed to consist of two staple items of conversation: cricket, and who could remember the longest passages of *Winnie the Pooh* from beginning to end.

11
STRUCK DOWN

WHAT MOST PEOPLE REMEMBER ABOUT the Executive is its fall and the circumstances of the Ulster Workers' Council strike. There had been a sense of growing opposition, and the general election had been a hard blow, as was the withdrawal of Whitelaw and the change of government, but after that things had appeared to stabilise, and ministers like Hume, Currie and Devlin seemed to be gaining credibility and a degree of acceptability, although it was galling to have John Hume picketed in Harland and Wolff where the workers existed on the state's bounty to the extent that they did not even recover the cost of materials, making the shipyard the biggest occupational therapy workshop in Western Europe. The Assembly was a zoo, but that could be dismissed, perhaps, as a rump of irrationality. Resistance to the Council of Ireland was growing, but the council could be put on the long finger. The IRA kept up its attacks, and there were rumbles of discontent in Protestant working-class areas, but nothing, it seemed, that could not be survived.

Nobody, early in May, paid too much attention to an advertisement in the *News Letter* threatening action if the Assembly passed a motion confirming the Council of Ireland. There was concern at a theoretical level that it might constitute contempt of the Assembly by appearing to threaten members and improperly to influence their votes. The general air in the Executive was philosophical. In its view, the Assembly had brought itself into contempt by the boorish behaviour of the members. Since the people in it were unaffected by argument within the chamber, and were dominated by outside pressures anyhow, a newspaper announcement was not going to make things worse. The vote was seen as something to be got over: the worry was Faulkner's crumbling back benches, some with very faint hearts and little enthusiasm on the one hand, and on the other the efforts made by Peter McLachlan to keep the rest in line by downplaying the Irish dimension, which irritated the SDLP. It was felt that if the debate could be got safely out of the way, some sort of peace would be restored, the Assembly would relapse into quiescence, and the Executive could get on with its work. The situation was dire, but not dangerous.

So, when the vote was completed, late in the evening of 14 May, we left Stormont with something of a sigh of relief, and nothing presaging impending doom.

Next morning there was a desultory picket at Carryduff roundabout, at which point I turned round and went in by Saintfield and Ballygowan without trouble. Another picket at the main gate of Stormont was easily outflanked by a detour through Ballybeen and in by the Stoney Road entrance. Next day, things were much worse, the people manning the roadblocks were much more aggressive, kitted out in paramilitary gear, camouflage jackets, dark glasses and berets, and some carried clubs or sticks. There was much thumping of cars and intimidation of passengers. Many drivers gave up and turned for home. It was, however, possible to get by using country roads. The worry of course was that in north Down, and approaching east Belfast, these roads took one into unknown and increasingly hostile territory.

What amazed me was the extent to which the police and the army simply stood by, or were seen to fraternise and share jokes with those who were blocking the roads. This induced an enormous feeling of impotence, soon leading to fear, in the ordinary citizen, and a sense of having been betrayed by the authorities. There you were, trying to get to work, trying to use the highway, being stopped by bullies, while the people you relied on to keep the roads open stood by with their hands down, and gave no indication that they would intervene, even if you were assaulted, except perhaps to charge you with disorderly behaviour. This was hard to take for people who had been assailed over the years with rhetoric about the inviolability of the Queen's highway and the right to pass peacefully thereon. This 'right' had been exemplified time and again by the use of massive forces of police to keep roads clear for provocative Orange processions, whether in the Longstone, or Portadown or the Springfield Road. Now the very authority of the state was being challenged, and the state lay back and did nothing about it.

Oddly enough, reaction in Stormont was muted at first. Most civil servants had managed to struggle into work with tales of more or less harassment. An emergency committee of assistant secretaries which had operated briefly during the miners' strike late in 1973 was wheeled into dubious action in mid-afternoon of the second day. The general feeling was that the strikers would not run down the power stations, that management could run the system at a pinch, that a stoppage of tanker drivers could be coped with by plans already prepared for such an emergency, and that people would lose patience with the whole thing in a few days.

Nobody who was involved at the time believes that the strike could not have been halted by a couple of jeeps taking effective action patrolling up and down the Newtownards Road on those first couple of days. After that, a pattern had been set that could not be reversed. Some years later I was on a trip to Sweden with a group of youth and community workers that included Glenn Barr, who in 1974 had been the public relations officer for the Ulster Workers' Council, the UWC. We shared a room on a stopover in Copenhagen, and as the assembled Irish (who incidentally included Basil McIvor and Paddy O'Donoghue) gathered into our room for a nightcap of duty-free whiskey, the two of us conducted an impromptu seminar on the strike, I from the point of view of the Executive, Glennie as a leader of the strikers. One thing that became clear was the vulnerability of the whole enterprise to rapid and decisive – and not necessarily very extensive – action by the police or army on those first couple of days.

On day three, I found it hard to get to work. The barricades were bigger, the people manning them much more aggressive. They had adopted a new tactic, where there was sporadic police action to clear the roads, of forming a human barrier, dispersing, jumping into cars, and rushing off to re-form a mile or so down the road. This was extremely effective, and very hard to counteract without mass arrests.

I turned back to Downpatrick and hitched a lift with Eddie McGrady who was being driven in by police. By this stage, a procedure that was standard practice during lengthy transport stoppages or very bad weather was activated. This allowed civil servants who could not get to their normal place of work to check in at the nearest local office of any department and so avoid losing a day's pay. This device was widely availed of, and in part explains the uniformly high turnout of civil servants during the strike. Nevertheless, many civil servants endured severe threats and intimidation or long and worrying detours to get to work. Many in Belfast walked for miles to get to Stormont, which was in the middle of fairly hostile territory.

The strike was in its early days when, on passing through the lobby of Stormont Castle I encountered a dumpy, grizzled man in a rumpled suit of bright steel blue wandering about as if he were lost. It turned out to be Stan Orme, newly arrived from Westminster to be Minister of State, and he was indeed lost, or at least out of his depth. Orme was a trade-union-sponsored member of Parliament and he exemplified several of the difficulties that Labour ministers found themselves in. They would not admit that the action was a strike, because that would give it a degree of legitimacy and link it too closely with industrial action. At the same time, Orme believed that the trade unions could and would use their influence to end the strike. He put enormous and quite unwarranted faith in his own ability to talk to the trade union leaders, and in theirs to bring any influence to bear. We were all told on the Friday to do nothing because the TUC general secretary, Len Murray, was being brought over on the following Monday to lead a march back to work into the shipyard and aircraft factory in the Harbour Estate. Orme was later to change his view somewhat and to see the strike as an upsurge of populist activity which was going to produce a new form of political action in the unionist working classes, and this interpretation was to colour Northern Ireland Office policies in the aftermath of the strike. Another person affected by his trade union past was Paddy Devlin. While implacably opposed to the UWC strike (and resolutely refusing to call such action a strike in the first place) and totally committed to the values and processes of parliamentary democracy, Paddy was not going to be the one to attack strikers through their families, to starve them into submission through the wage packet or through the withdrawal of benefits. So, almost on the first day, the benefit system went on to emergency arrangements. These involved the payment of benefits at specified basic rates by employers on the promise of reimbursement by the state at a later date. This meant that the strike need never end – at least not in victory for the government. This was revolution on the rates, a state virtually subsidising its own subversion. Whilst the vast bulk of the strikers suffered the discomforts and privations of the rest of the population, there was no real hardship, no compulsion to draw back, no necessity to stop and count the cost.

At this time too, there began to be talk of bringing in the troops to run the power stations, which, we were assured, was quite feasible. I remember arguing with Brian Faulkner that no Labour government would allow troops to be brought in to any strike or stoppage, however motivated, in case it would be used as a precedent by a future Tory government during a dock strike or a miners' strike in England.

On the Friday too, the emergency committee became a bit more purposeful. An annoying feature was the continued police assertion that all roads were clear, despite the evidence of our own eyes, even at the gates of Stormont, and the difficulties people were experiencing in getting in to work. The police attitude at the time was very clearly to hear, speak and certainly to see no evil. There was a very impressive man from the Electricity Board who had a very clear picture of the operations of the power stations. Plans began to be made to bring in troops to man the stations. No difficulties were foreseen or indicated. Men were said to be available and standing by in Germany, Gibraltar, Hong Kong, Singapore, and on sundry submarines all over the place. We were assured that if you could run the systems of a nuclear submarine, the West Twin power station was child's play, that the army that had sorted out the Ruhr after crossing the Rhine would find no difficulty in Ballylumford. The Electricity Board man's only stipulation, I remember, was that military operation of the equipment would only be possible if middle management and supervisors remained at their posts. I remember thinking that this was a poor bet, given the tendency of hard-hat and promoted blue-collar workers in most industrialised countries to take fairly right-wing political attitudes, and given the hiring policies of the Electricity Board over the years, which had produced an unrelievedly Protestant, if not Orange, workforce, and given too that middle management lived in neat bungalows in Islandmagee and Larne and Whitehead with cars parked outside very open to damage, very prone to intimidation.

I took the papers home with me at the weekend to work up an Executive paper for the Monday. On the Monday morning I had a fairly fraught time in the Castlereagh Hills as one road after another turned out to be blocked. The police had promised on the Friday that the main commuter routes would be kept clear and that people would be able to get in to work. There was indeed a token police presence at some of the main intersections and at the Carryduff roundabout, but the protesters rapidly found a way of dealing with this by forming a human barrier across the road which was effective in stopping cars, and quite frightening in its members' attitudes to motorists, but which dissolved when the police appeared, only to re-form half a mile down the road. It was an infuriating game of cat and mouse which the police could not win, and after a while they gave up. It was possible, sometimes, to get through by showing a pass with the magical word 'Doctor' on it. On other occasions a better password was to say that you were going to work in a benefits branch of the DHSS whose staff they evidently had no desire to halt.

This was the morning too when poor Len Murray led his troops into the Harbour Estate – all twenty or thirty of them. Some courageous trade unionists did indeed join him, and some trade union leaders. But what had been overlooked was intimidation which prevented workers from getting that far. The strikers had simply shifted the locus of intimidation from the factory gates to the housing estates and commuter towns. A few crates thrown across the entrance to a housing estate, a few louts lounging ostentatiously with baseball bats at a street corner, ensured that the army of workers never got out of their billets, and General Murray was left stranded with no troops to lead.

Another thing that nobody connected with the period will forget is the voice of Hugo Patterson, the Electricity Board information officer, to whom the BBC turned for hourly bulletins on the state of the power supply. Patterson was an unheard-of junior official whose hobby had been to report the scores of local cricket games on the radio every Saturday in the season. He was now catapulted into prominence since it was necessary to listen continuously to the radio to receive warnings of power cuts. The rationing system operated by the power station workers meant that each area could only have power for four hours at a time, later reduced to two hours, and you had to be ready to take advantage of this for cooking, even in the middle of the night. Patterson had deeply sepulchral tones and a hearselike speed of delivery which made him a most appropriate Cassandra. As the news became more and more dire, his tones seemed to extinguish hope along with the lights, from day one holding out no prospect of alleviation or amelioration. Unlike Cassandra, who was fated not to be believed, his forecasts were taken as gospel.

Indeed the attitude of the BBC was another important and mystifying phenomenon and one that outraged the Executive. The BBC took the stance that it was entirely neutral in the process. If there was a struggle, it was there to give both sides of the story, and to give them equal status. This the members of the Executive and their staff found appalling. From their point of view, they were the legitimate government carrying out the policies of Parliament, and the BBC was an important social actor, operating under charter and spending public money. This, we thought, should cause it to include in its considerations a concern for the public interest and the interests of stability and good government. It was as if, at the first sign of revolution, an important institution of society immediately joined the rebels, or in the event of an invasion in wartime switched to broadcasting enemy propaganda. We could not understand how they could regard themselves merely as neutral agents seeking some higher truth which only they could discern. It was all the more galling for the SDLP, which had suffered from the BBC being in the pocket of the unionist government for years, that the BBC should seek this moment, to the great disadvantage of an administration of which the SDLP was a part, to proclaim its independence. Indeed the members of the Executive went further and said that the BBC in its presentation of the news, in its selection of people as spokesmen, and in dignifying louts was not even neutral. There is no doubt that the UWC had the better of the propaganda war, had the better speakers and produced the better stories. The BBC argued strenuously later (through its Controller, Dick Francis) that it broadcast what it got. If the Executive did not produce information, then too bad. What that did to the principle of balance is less clear. There is no doubt that the division of responsibility between the NIO Information Service and the Executive Information Office was a profoundly debilitating factor, and the two offices never really got their act together, probably because their basic policy assumptions were different. Indeed it was quite clear from an early stage that they were not singing off the same hymn sheet: Rees proceeded to distance the NIO from the Executive and prepared to cast it to the wolves.

On one evening, John Hume came down to Strangford as being preferable to a couch in Stormont or a hotel, or return home to Derry which was nearly impossible. We had the bizarre spectacle of the Minister for Light sitting in the dark waiting for the two hours of indulgence permitted by the strikers. John at this time, as Minister of Commerce, was pushing very hard for two initiatives: the introduction of army engineers to man the power stations and to increase power output, and the implementation of a plan whereby the government (using the army) would take over the distribution of petrol and fuel oil. As we went back to Belfast next morning in a police car and drove along Hawthornden Road where the UWC had its headquarters in a suburban villa, it was sickening to see the queue of people in business suits waiting for their permits to open their shops and to acquire fuel. This was when it struck me that there had been a transfer of allegiance from the legitimate government to a group of activists acting illegally. This represented the transference of the heart of the Protestant middle class once they saw where their personal advantage lay – and I despised them for it. On another occasion during the period, I spent a night in the office, and another in the Stormont Hotel, where there was no light or heat and, ultimately, no breakfast.

There were two main fields of activity: on the one hand, incessant meetings of the emergency committee and with the NIO (where, it turned out, there was at least one other emergency committee) in an attempt to generate action by the police, to get the troops into the power stations and to implement the fuel plan. At the other end of the scale, a real example of fiddling while Rome burnt, there were meetings about the terms of reference of the Council of Ireland. Here was the whole outfit going down like the *Titanic* and the SDLP backbenchers were obsessed by the arrangement of deckchairs on the deck. The Faulkner Unionists, led by Peter McLachlan, wanted the proposals diluted, or scrapped altogether. On one occasion Percy Sythes, an under-secretary colleague, and I worked late to produce a revised draft. There was no typist so I had to summon up my vestigial typing skills to get it typed out. There was not enough power to run the photocopier so we had to wait until morning for that, and no way to get home so I had to bed down. Brian Faulkner came in late in the evening and, a teetotaller, threw us the keys of his drinks cabinet.

As it happened, the SDLP backbenchers would not accept the compromise and there were frantic meetings in the committee room on the ground floor of Parliament Buildings, and rumours that they were going to pull out of the coalition. At one stage, Gerry Fitt rushed off to phone Rees to tell him what was happening and Stan Orme was despatched to read the riot act and tell them the likely consequences of the fall of the Executive and what would happen if they pushed Faulkner too far. Whatever happened in the confessional of the committee room, they reversed the vote, or at least enough of them did to get a different answer, and they adopted the amendment with an ill grace. By then, of course, it was too late.

In many ways, the situation came to resemble the last days of a regime. We ran out of petrol for the government cars, which reduced mobility enormously. I noticed that the typists in the NIO always seemed to have petrol, the more so if they were pretty. On asking about, I was told that the army had a petrol dump in the estate. A colleague and myself launched an attack on it and found a dozen or so jerry cans stacked in undergrowth at the end of an ill-defined path about fifty yards off the main road through the estate. We abstracted four of them and poured the contents into our own and other cars – with great difficulty as there was not a funnel, or as Joyce would have it a tundish, and we had to break a milk bottle and use the neck to improvise one. By some strange feat of public accounting, I received a bill for the petrol some months later. The world had cracked around us, but proper financial accountability still prevailed, and some little man was still looking after the books. I did not pay.

On another evening towards the end of the strike, in order to get home and having failed to get official transport or a taxi in Belfast, I phoned a taxi in Downpatrick. John Hume did not have a car either or a place to stay so I offered him a lift to Strangford and a bed there. The Downpatrick taxi driver was afraid to venture into Belfast, having heard appalling tales of attacks on Catholics and believing that the whole place was about to blow up at any time. After much coaxing, and on the strength of old friendship and a promise that I would get petrol for him, he agreed to come as far as Stormont. In the meantime, John had been spirited off to the BBC in an army jeep to do an interview, leaving word for me to pick him up there. The taxi man, when he arrived, was very reluctant to do so, but eventually agreed. We drove down the Newtownards Road, and he got tenser and more nervous as we approached the Holywood Arches. We avoided Dee Street and the headquarters of the Ulster Defence Association, the UDA, who were providing most of the muscle for the strike, by going down the Albertbridge Road and through the Markets area. The streets were almost deserted and there was absolutely no traffic. Ormeau Avenue was deserted too. I rang the bell at the BBC while the driver kept the engine running and the car doors locked. I rang for ten minutes without reply, by which time the driver had had enough and shouted that he would drive off on his own. Eventually I had to go with him, but persuaded him to stop at Rosetta, which had a sufficiently Catholic reputation to reassure him, so that I could phone the BBC to locate John. Every kiosk I tried had been vandalised.

The atmosphere was quite eerie. It was by this time about eight o'clock on a fine summer evening, but there was virtually nobody on the streets. Those who did appear scurried past furtively, not wanting to talk to anybody, fearful even to make eye contact. The doors in the quiet suburban area were tight shut, the blinds down. The sound of a car approaching was enough to make people look around. I tried asking two reserve policemen who came along for help. First I didn't know if I could trust them with the whereabouts of John Hume, and second, their radios were in danger of being listened to, so any message passed back to headquarters that he was at the BBC might, I feared, produce an attack on that building, or an ambush as he was coming out. In any case the taxi driver was threatening to take off and categorically refused to return to the BBC, so the problem was compounded by the need to find transport to bring him to meet us (if indeed he could himself be located). Finally, I stopped an old couple who seemed to be returning from church (it must have been a

Sunday) and asked to use their phone. They agreed, and I fell into step with them, expecting them to live nearby. Unfortunately they lived about half a mile down a side road and I in my nervousness, and conscious of the taxi driver's likeliness to bolt, walked rather quickly, until the old lady told me that her husband had a heart condition, so we had to sit on a garden wall and wait for him to recover his breath. In the end the phone calls to the BBC were void: nobody could locate John Hume, all was confusion and mess. I ran back to the car and the driver shot off. I learned later that John was rescued by Robert Ramsey who put him up for the night at his home in east Belfast.

One way in which the power failure affected us was that while the telephones worked on an emergency supply, the scrambler, which was plugged into the mains, did not. I remember having to phone Brian Faulkner at home in Seaforde to tell him that the army would not after all come in to the power stations as expected, and finding that I had to do it *en clair* on a line that was likely to be tapped. I asked him to tell Lucy that the boy scouts who had promised to help her with lighting for the church fête had refused to honour the booking. He got the message.

Through the week the dominant issues continued to be fuel, power, security and food. Many of the hospitals had emergency generators, but in others the lessons of the miners' strike had not fully sunk in. Generators were rushed from England, only to be held up at the docks. Others were flown in by the army, but it tended to hold on to them for itself. The interference with power supplies was beginning to affect water and sewerage. Shops were running out of perishable foods, the distribution of milk and bread was increasingly difficult. We were getting reports of alarm and confusion in west Belfast, where people felt themselves to be cut off and open to attack from loyalist paramilitaries. There was talk of lorries being sent to Newry and Dublin for food. Actually Catholics in west Belfast were probably safer then than at any other time, as the loyalist action was directed against the Executive.

The two great on–off sagas related to the oil plan and the power stations. From an early stage it was assumed that sooner or later the troops would take over the generating stations, and we were assured that they could do it. And then the difficulties developed. On the one hand, the Electricity Board people uncovered problem after problem –

very real ones, I believe, but they tended not to minimise them. First, it all depended on middle management, whose loyalty and commitment, as I had suspected, increasingly could not be assured, and who, as the strike went on, were clearly more in sympathy with the aims of the UWC. Then the question of sabotage loomed large. If there was not an orderly rundown before the strikers left, irreparable damage would be done. Just throwing a switch to stop the whole works would, apparently, shatter the machinery. Alternatively, a departing engineer throwing a spanner or a handful of nuts into the vanes of a revolving turbine could shatter the blades, do millions of pounds' worth of damage, and take months to repair. Then the problem shifted to the network. It was comparatively easy to produce electricity, and perhaps at a pinch the sappers could do that, but the distribution system was something else. It was argued that it would take a year at least to train a qualified electrical engineer in the intricacies of the switchboard and the vagaries of the Northern Ireland system, on the various flows and surges, peaks of demand and troughs, and several more years before he could be trusted to handle the console on his own. All of which produced a greater and greater reluctance to do anything, and dulled the enthusiasm of the army at the same time.

And yet the system was being managed and manipulated, played like a fiddle, by a group of men, none of whom, we were told, was of higher grade than a foreman.

An interesting phenomenon is the extent to which people working in these great enterprises fall in love with their machinery. Men who had spent years building up an electricity system in Northern Ireland could not bear to see it put at risk. For them the priority, emotionally and subliminally perhaps, but still the imperative, was to preserve the system, to avoid permanent damage, and to carry it through, machinery and men, to the quieter waters on the other side of the present turbulence. They were much less worried than we were by threats to democracy and the rule of the mob. In their sheer, studied refusal to contemplate the political consequences of their actions, they were the most political people about.

The same was true too of people in the Department of Commerce who had been involved in energy policy, and particularly with the Electricity Board over the years. They seemed to be much more interested in protecting the integrity of the system than in anything else, and were much less enthusiastic than their minister in pursuing the option of bringing in the troops. This whole question of the behaviour of individuals in self-defence or in defence of their agencies is a fascinating one. It is the same instinct that impels departments to refuse to contemplate cuts or the abandonment of any of their services. They develop a sort of love relationship with them, and will fight to protect them. At other times, departments begin to identify more with the recipients of their services than with central policies: the DHSS with the poor, Agriculture with the farmers and so on. There was evidence of at least a difference of emphasis between departments and the Executive, certainly at official level, which surfaced in the emergency committee. Departments were more concerned with keeping the place going, with delivering benefits, and subsidies and power or whatever. We were more concerned about keeping the Executive going, with issues of legitimacy, of refusal to bow to the dictates of the mob. No doubt ministers shared this view, but officials in departments were less committed politically (or more committed to somebody else) and did not see commitment to the Executive as such as part of their role.

There was a sort of witch-hunt afterwards about which department broke ranks first to do business with the UWC. Whether wittingly or not, the first to do real damage was the DHSS, I am sure from the best of motives, by enabling the payment of benefits. But most blame attached to Agriculture who were suspected of having done a deal with the UWC to keep the refrigerators in the semen banks connected with the artificial insemination service working. They had built up substantial stocks of semen from a variety of prize pedigree Ulster bulls – Herefords, Ayrshires, Charollais, Friesian, Dexter and Simmenthal – and it was said that the cattle, meat and dairy businesses would collapse and the breeding programmes would be put back for years if these invaluable genes were lost. I often thought that it was ironic that the country should be allowed to go down the tubes instead. Some years later, I suggested to Robert Fisk as an alternative title for his excellent and informed study of the strike *Fucked Up to Save a Semen Bank*.

As the strike progressed, the most worrying, and in many ways the most frightening feature was the transfer of allegiance by middle-class unionists, now more overt, from the elected authority to the strike committee. Every day the queues outside the house in Hawthornden Avenue became longer and better dressed. This reminded many of us of the Weimar Republic, where the fear of inflation, of anarchy and of communism drove the German middle classes to embrace Hitler and enabled the worst excesses of the Nazi regime. There were still gangs of roughnecks on the streets, becoming more prettified as they adopted a sort of uniform, but even more menacing. Appalling threats were made at barricades to people trying to get through, with assurances that people persisting in getting to work would be 'dealt with'. There were also lurid rumours of lists being prepared of people who had been associated with the Executive who would get their come-uppance once the demands of the activists had been conceded. The general atmosphere too, especially in Catholic areas, was even more tense than before. Apart from one drunken foray by a busload of braves from Newtownabbey shooting up pubs in mid-Antrim, which resulted in two Catholic brothers being murdered in a roadside pub, the expected attacks on Catholic areas by loyalist gangs did not happen, but the fear was still palpable. There were bombs in Dublin and Monaghan too, with a high death toll, which added to the feeling of panic. It was noticeable at church that people did not sit near the door and dispersed quietly afterwards, and people who had spent the previous couple of years denigrating the IRA began to wonder who the friendly local neighbourhood Provo was. He might be a useful defender when the attack came.

In working-class unionist areas you passed through, aside from the threatening behaviour at the roadblocks, there was almost an air of carnival, which increased as the action took hold. People, especially young people, were actually doing something, and they were enjoying themselves. There was a frantic, purposeful activity as people manned roadblocks, and the even greater thrill of the mobile human barriers. Deliveries were being arranged of milk and bread, people were queuing for permits, and there was no aggressive police or army activity. One morning, going across the dual carriageway from the Supermac shopping centre to Stormont, I saw a teenage boy thumbing a lift. Thinking that he might be a civil servant walking to work, I stopped and gave him a lift. He turned out to be a lad from Bally-been who had been manning an all-night picket on the motorway slip road at Lisburn. We had a pleasant conversation on the basis that I too was helping the cause by paying out benefits.

The sight of heavily subsidised and expensive farm machinery, bought largely out of public funds, being used to block the roads was hard to stomach. At this time a variant of the roadblock was for a long line of farm machinery to proceed at a snail's pace along main roads, letting no other vehicle past, and producing long queues. These were not the poor looking for a break, or the unskilled worker who feared for his job, or the unlettered fearful for his heritage: these were the rich, comfortable farmers of north Down, the backbone of conservative unionism, who were concerned to retain the power and privilege they had enjoyed for generations. Their final act of demonstration was a cavalcade of farm machinery, led by muck-spreaders loaded with ripe manure, to lay siege to the main building at Stormont.

Faulkner, Fitt and Napier flew to London on Friday 24 May, and this brought an immediate sense of relief. We were assured that the troops would come in and that the oil plan would be activated. On the Saturday morning I was given a copy of the speech that Wilson was to make on television that evening. I was amazed: there was nothing in it. I could not imagine why any prime minister would want to go on TV to say so little. That evening, sitting in the gloom (it was one of our powerless spells in Strangford), we had no TV but heard him on the battery radio. When he made his reference to 'spongers' I knew this would cause outrage and bring the whole unionist population in behind the strikers, and would not please most of the others either. I was extremely surprised because this reference had not been included in the version I had seen in the morning. If it had, it would have struck me immediately and I would have expected somebody to advise that it be cut out.

In any case, it provided no great illumination for us. The oil plan did go into effect. Amy Thomas, a principal in the Castle, was helicoptered into the refinery at Sydenham at dawn with a requisition order, and troops moved in to a number of selected filling stations. Junior civil servants had been delegated to each station to look after the money. The oil plan was a general mess. One of the first tankers had been left full of paraffin oil, perhaps deliberately, and this led to numerous claims for damage to engines by aggrieved drivers who had claimed their ration. The other main effect of the implementation

199

was to so annoy the strikers that they intensified action in the power stations and threatened a total closedown.

Meanwhile, the sepulchral voice of Hugo Patterson, every hour, on the hour, intoned messages of gloom and doom. In the Executive, we were outraged. Nobody seemed conscious that he was a junior official employed by the Electricity Board who could have been silenced simply by the department telling them to withdraw him, or by John Hume issuing an instruction to that effect. As it was, Patterson had now reached the point of predicting the irreversible collapse of the electricity system, which he described as the 'point of no return'.

This phrase was used by Bob Fisk as the title for his book on the strike, which generally records the course of the action in a very telling and generally dependable way. I took exception to one passage in which he describes a conversation with an unnamed senior official to the Executive who happened to be a Catholic, in which I am portrayed as gibbering with terror at the prospect of Armageddon. I remember the conversation well. It took place on the path between the car park and the side door of Stormont Castle. I had been comparing the development of the strike, and particularly the transfer of allegiance of the unionist middle classes, to the later days of the Weimar Republic. I was predicting that they had allied themselves to dark forces over which they had no control and which would lead the society God knows where. We discussed the fear in the Catholic community, the rumoured threats to people working for the Executive, the reputed hit lists and the possibility of total anarchy. I do remember referring to the possibility of perhaps myself being put up against a wall. I don't remember being the shaking mass of jelly that he portrays – but then I was not looking at myself.

In the meantime, the life of the Executive was drawing to its close. The SDLP was still worrying about the remit of the Council of Ireland. Paddy Devlin and Ivan Cooper had gone to Dublin (as the SDLP always seemed to the Unionists to do in times of stress) and we were getting messages that they couldn't get back. The permanent secretaries had a meeting that put the frighteners on Faulkner. There is a good deal of controversy about this. Paddy Devlin recounts it as *trahison des clercs*, Faulkner as a chance meeting in the corridor with John Oliver who simply asked him in to hear the news. I had been bearing some of these warnings in my briefings, but not to such dire effect. I believe Faulkner was sent for and presented with an extremely gloomy picture of sewage rising in the streets, of the risk of an epidemic, of rats and plague and cholera, of total anarchy and the breakdown of civil society. However the message was couched, and however motivated, it was sufficient to induce him to pack it in.

I remember going up to Sir David Holden, the head of the Northern Ireland Civil Service, secretary to the Department of Finance and, I suppose, my boss to tell him of the impending collapse of the Executive. He was, in his meticulous way, correcting the draft minutes of the last Executive meeting, in pencil. He heard my news without remark and went on with his task – I had just thought he would like to know.

The remainder of the day was funereal. There was a momentary attempt at a farcical *coup d'état* by some of the SDLP led by Austin Currie who refused to resign and said they would carry on without the unionists. This was quickly snuffed out by Rees.

That afternoon, Faulkner gave us all a drink. Ken Bloomfield was in tears: he had invested a great deal in the Executive, he had virtually written the White Paper, and he had worked hard to bring the policy into effect and to make it succeed. Probably, too, he had the prescience to see that this was the nearest we would come to an accommodation for a long time, that if the unionist population could not wear Sunningdale, there was very little hope for stability in the future. Later on, John Hume came in, picked up a bottle of whiskey and said, 'There's always drink at a wake.' Faulkner told me that the memory he took away was of one of Her Majesty's principal secretaries of state being told (by Gerry Fitt) that he was 'a spineless coward'. It appears that at a meeting in the Castle, Rees had been maintaining that all the roads were open, when Faulkner and Fitt took him over to the window of his own office and showed him the crowds blocking the main gate to the estate. Brian spoke feelingly of the way in which the Executive had worked together and of the satisfaction he had got out of seeing something hopeful develop: it was an idea a little before its time. We all expressed the hope that its time would soon come. I remember suggesting to Brian that his country might yet need him, after a period of chaos, and that he should retire to his farm, like Fabius, or like de Gaulle (who had Seaforde connections) to *Seaforde des trois églises* to wait for the moment. All of which was an elegant version of the common formula at County Down wakes: 'I'm sorry for your trouble.' It was a depressed and disconsolate little band who gathered our traps and slunk off, avoiding the exultant crowds in the main avenue and the dancing groups on the roads.

With the 20/20 vision of hindsight, there are many explanations of the fall of the Executive. I believe it was the nearest we came to a resolution of the problem of governing Northern Ireland, and possibly the nearest in my lifetime. Any foreseeable outcome of the present peace process is not likely to differ markedly from Sunningdale. Those of us who had advocated a caesura, a cessation of Stormont in order to break the mould, have been reproached by those who would have followed a more evolutionary pattern, who believe that the fracture of the Stormont parliament led only to confusion and disarray and destroyed the appetite for parliamentary democracy for some time ahead. Better, they say, to have stuck with Stormont with all its faults, and built on the committee system proposed by Faulkner and initially welcomed by the SDLP and on the climate of tolerance promoted by Terence O'Neill. Sadly, that was not to be. Outside events forced the pace. Internment had intervened, removing an important prop of legitimacy, respect for the rule of law, and Bloody Sunday brought final alienation and political disaffection. In particular, too, after Sunningdale the IRA did not let up, the expectations of the Catholic community after the Callaghan communiqué raced far ahead of any possibility of satisfying them completely or in any acceptable time scale, and the fears of working-class and middle-class Protestants grew in proportion.

My own belief is that the break was too short. There was no time given for new attitudes to develop. Whitelaw made his move in setting up the Executive too quickly – pushed inexorably by the time frames imposed by the electoral cycle. Heath was anxious to get Northern Ireland off the agenda once and for all. There is such a thing as taking advantage of a favourable tide which leads on to fortune, but the discussions in this case involved only political leaders. There was no time to involve followers, no time to build a solid base of support across the community, and the classic dilemma of producing simultaneously a sense of total loss on one side and of insufficient gain on the other. The agreement reached was the minimum possible to secure a sufficient number of votes in an assembly. It left a large group of dissidents outside, far above the critical mass that was capable of destabilising the whole, and it left Faulkner particularly vulnerable to defections and loss of support. The removal of Whitelaw was a blow, the change of government an even bigger one. True, the Council of Ireland was a distraction, but it was a symbol rather than a cause of opposition.

The real opposition was from people who had held on to power because they had been taught that that was the only way to preserve identity. They had been force-fed on a variety of democracy in which heads had to be counted and the winners took all, in which any dilution of power was seen to be the beginning of catastrophe, in which Catholics could not be trusted not to drag them into a united Ireland in which their values would be submerged and ultimately extinguished. On the other hand, I believe that they would have given a great deal for peace, for an end to bombing and shooting and indiscriminate terror. And peace is what they did not get. Not only did the IRA not stop, it intensified its campaign. And the SDLP, having got more, probably, than it bargained for at Sunningdale, could not yet bring itself to give unequivocal backing to the RUC. The most difficult questions about the administration of justice were avoided by having the Law Commissioners discuss extradition and common courts. This did very little to reassure either those who had suffered internment or who had been exposed to the day-to-day activities of patriots who were bombing in the name of, and purportedly to achieve, a united Ireland.

Nevertheless, it is worth noting, twenty years later, how many of those who combined to bring down the Sunningdale arrangements would now settle for something like it, and how many would ask whether the history of the intervening years justified the passion spent in demolishing the one real opportunity we had. What the UWC strike did was to establish a double stalemate. It showed that if the Catholics could bring down Stormont by refusal to be governed, the Protestants held an effective veto over any proposed alternative. This double veto is with us still, with each side more conscious of the weakness than the strength of its own position.

One of the benefits of the Executive was that it showed that Protestants and Catholics, unionists and nationalists, could work together, even if on a narrow range of social and economic issues.

Trust could be built – which had infinite possibilities. People who had been sworn enemies could begin to admire the accomplishments of each other. It is a pity that the young SDLP ministers who showed so much promise had such a short period on the ministerial stage. It is a pity too that Faulkner, whose life had been a preparation for the highest office, should have enjoyed it so briefly and in such difficult times. He was unquestionably the most effective minister in Northern Ireland, he had filled post after post with ability and distinction, he had adapted to changing times, he had built strong personal relationships, and he was not given time to build the stable and fair society to which he was finally committed.

12
IN SEARCH OF A STATE

IN THE PERIOD AFTER THE EXECUTIVE, we were an administration in search of a state, a government in internal exile. The old order had gone, the new one had collapsed and the direct rule regime, having concentrated all attempts at administrative level for over a year in getting the Executive set up, was at a bit of a loss too. It took some time for responsibility to be sorted out between the NIO, which was quite a small office supporting the secretary of state, and the departments of executive government. There was a need to develop a nexus where the two machines intermeshed. So Ken and I spent some time developing the Central Secretariat as the exchange between Whitehall and Stormont. The fact that we were quasi-unemployed meant that we were a couple of extra pairs of hands who could be given odd jobs to do. And in the fluid arrangements of the time it was possible to drift in and out of topics, to attend meetings and to watch the development of policy.

We had time too to amuse ourselves with a rather wicked game. The NIO people had brought with them from Whitehall a whole range of clichés: things had to be done 'before close of play' or 'before stumps drawn on Friday', and worse. We began to wonder how long it took for a phrase to become common currency, and we experimented by inventing new clichés – 'discrete', 'window of opportunity', and so – and releasing them into the bloodstream and watching how long it took for the bread thus cast on the waters to return. Par for the course was about two weeks, unless, of course, rain stopped play. Another innovation by the NIO was the custom of multiple copying of documents. I believe that photocopiers are a menace to individual responsibility. What you saw was people trying to disperse not information but personal responsibility. If your name was hidden however low on one of hundreds of circulated papers, you could never deny knowing about it, and the sender could say that he had told everybody who mattered.

The changes meant that we saw more of the secretary of state and his ministers. Merlyn Rees as secretary of state was an irritating man to work for, especially after Faulkner. He was pleasant and courteous at a personal level, but he could not get far enough away from the detail to take the broad view. On one occasion, as a result of the Macrory changes, the Department of the Environment, the DoE, had been trying to devolve power to agencies (years before their time) and especially to the local representatives of the roads and water services. Rees nearly cut himself shaving one morning when he heard the local roads manager in Craigavon being interviewed on local radio about gritting the roads in a cold spell. The secretary of state was outraged that a civil servant was making pronouncements on policy, which was the prerogative of ministers. He was also an academic *manqué* who conducted meetings like tutorials and could not come down on the side of any argument.

'I don't mind him wrestling with his conscience,' Ken Bloomfield said once, 'but does it always have to be a draw?' On another occasion when Rees had left the room several times during a discussion, and also broken off the conversation to take or make telephone calls, Ken said, 'Secretary of State, up to now I didn't really know the meaning of coitus interruptus.'

There was an odd assortment of junior ministers too. Stan Orme, having backed a loser with Len Murray, now decided that the UWC marked a new birth of Protestant populism that would sweep away the established political parties in Northern Ireland. He also wasted a lot of time establishing worker directors in Harland and Wolff and Shorts. At the other end of the scale was Lord Donaldson. Once, when I was to have lunch with Rees, Donaldson was late, having been despatched to investigate and report on some stories of ill-treatment of prisoners. Eventually we went ahead without him. When he turned up, at the cheese course, he insisted on ploughing through his own meal before reporting. Eventually, chivvied by an impatient Rees, he described his entry to the guardroom in the prison. 'There was a soldier sitting there in front of an enlarged picture of a male nude with his balls hanging down. Rather low, I thought!' I regret that I didn't have the courage to ask whether that was a moral judgement or an aesthetic or a physiological observation.

One rather buccaneering figure at this time whom I did respect greatly was Frank Cooper, the permanent under-secretary of the Northern Ireland Office. Frank was a larger-than-life character who went on to become head of the Ministry of Defence during the Falklands War and who, many thought, should have become head of the UK Civil Service. It was a poorer organisation in failing to have given him this role. He was a refreshing man to work with, if unpredictable. He was likely to give the same task to several people, unknown to each other. What he did with the answers he got, you seldom knew. I remember passing a remark at a general discussion one day about the possibility of developing community policing. Frank rang me that evening and asked me to work up the idea in a short paper and to mufax it to him in London first thing in the morning. This I did, staying up all night to get it finished. I never heard him mention the subject again.

I believed that there was some possibility of providing an acceptable police force by dividing the responsibilities both horizontally and vertically. If you could have traffic wardens and litter wardens and dog wardens employed by district councils, it was a short step to having housing estate wardens and local constables with no more than citizen's powers of arrest to deal with the broad generality of minor crime. There was, of course, the danger that they might become vigilantes, or be taken over as a front by some paramilitary group, but this could be faced. Indeed, since one of the problems was what to do in the future with superannuated gunmen, one answer might have been to make them policemen. They had all the attributes: a sense of discipline, a strong code of values, ideologically based, and a strong desire to impose them on other people. However, although the idea was discussed for a time, it was shot down by the RUC which was strongly committed to a single police force, and that was the end of that.

With not much to do and plenty of time to do it in, I began to develop an interest in the problems of poverty and in the inner city. This involved using the data that was beginning to emerge from the 1971 census and using it to map various forms of deprivation. It also involved groups of civil servants going out to meet community groups and local activists in a range of locations around Belfast, in schools, community halls and other venues, in Ballymurphy, Bally-been, the Docks, Dee Street, Ardoyne, the Shankill and the Markets. It was a great opportunity to get to know Belfast, its people and their problems, and for the civil servants concerned it proved a novel, broadening and exciting experience.

One of the sad things, I found, was how low people's expectations really were. If you asked them to think of measures and programmes that would alleviate their problems, they tended to refer to very local problems such as the absence of a pedestrian crossing or the lack of a play area. There was a fatalistic acceptance of their lot. It was almost as if unemployment was such an oppressive problem that it was held to be insoluble. There was little demand for better educational facilities for example, or better public transport, and a high degree of cynicism – the result of having been promised things before by politicians without visible effect.

At many of the meetings I went to I was shadowed by two groups: the Stickies, now going political, and the Catholic Church (generally in the person of Canon Padraig Murphy). Both advocated the establishment of a huge factory in west Belfast employing 8,000– 10,000 men. Talk of community enterprise or of a large number of small undertakings that would be less vulnerable to recession were dismissed contemptuously as Mickey Mouse stuff. What they wanted was a branch of Harland and Wolff on the Springfield Road. It was difficult to explain in public that the main problem for government at the time was not how to expand employment in Harland and Wolff but how to improve productivity by getting about two thirds of those who were there out of it without actually causing a riot.

The competing rationales, too, were interesting. The Catholic Church was advocating large-scale manufacturing in order to get rid of the scourge of unemployment, which they saw as a proximate cause of the violence, and to take a breeding ground away from the Stickies. The Stickies, in a dogmatic Marxist analysis, reasoned that a large factory would lead to worker solidarity and class warfare, the destruction of capitalism and the defeat of the Catholic Church. All roads apparently led in the same direction: the problem was to read the signpost, whether for Rome or Moscow.

It was not long before there were stirrings in the undergrowth and Rees got the sort of glazed look secretaries of state get when they have an initiative in mind. Most locals thought the dust of Sunningdale should be allowed to settle and that there should be a prolonged break before any new approach was tried. Policies havered between regarding direct rule as a temporary expedient and something that had come to stay, between making it tolerable and making it work. I once suggested to Rees that instead of trying for benign direct rule, he should aim for bloody awful direct rule, so dire indeed that politicians on all sides would clamour for the return of a local administration. The danger, of course, was that they already had bloody awful rule, but not as a matter of policy.

It has to be said that very few Northern Ireland civil servants contemplated prolonged direct rule, and most of them instinctively rejected moves towards further integration. There was a desire to preserve separate Northern Ireland policies in functional areas, and to maintain the identity of separate Northern Ireland legislation; none of the Whitehall people showed much enthusiasm for integration either. At times the two groups contemplated each other with some unease. This was most true of the more traditional Northern Ireland civil servants, who sometimes thought the newcomers patronising and brash, as some of them, particularly at the less senior levels, undoubtedly were. Ironically, from a nationalist background, I found it easier to get on with the 'Brits' as they were derogatorily called, than some of my colleagues did, to take them as they came, and not to feel put upon.

Most of the newcomers were extremely fine people whom it was a pleasure to work with and who worked extremely long hours in difficult conditions. Some of them, it must be said, were quite hard to take. They were the people who would have been running India if the Raj had still existed. Some indeed had transferred back from colonial Africa as the flag was hauled down in one outpost after another. They talked about coming 'out' to Northern Ireland and of being 'posted back home'. They had special allowances, special houses in north Down, and special cars to bring them in and out, all of which caused a good deal of feeling.

We began to get drawn into the drafting of a new set of discussion documents. This time there were to be three, one on possible forms of government, one on power sharing, and one on the Irish dimension. I remember beginning a draft on power sharing by saying that although the concept was new to British constitutional thinking, it 'could be shown to have worked in Cyprus and the Lebanon'. Luckily that draft never saw the light of day. Neither did the other paper on the Irish dimension. This I tried to define to my own satisfaction, but I eventually came to the conclusion that the relationships between Britain and Ireland, and their peoples, were so complex and had so developed over the centuries that there was now no direct linear relationship that could be plotted, but a melange of genes, attitudes and historical interactions such as to defy any attempt at simple explanation. Indeed the Irish dimension seemed more like a trapezoid figure with the base running from Luton to Slough. The interesting feature was that although there were strong linkages on most indicators between Northern Ireland and parts of Britain, as between the Republic and Britain, there were very weak linkages in Ireland on a North–South axis.

One bizarre episode that I came across in my researches concerned the relationships between the security forces, North and South. In Northern Ireland, the army was in the driving seat at the time, whatever the constitutional niceties. (This was not long after the case of wrongful arrest, *Hume and others*, the upshot of the judgement by Lord Lowry in the Northern Ireland Court of Appeal being that a law had had to be rushed through both houses of Parliament in about an hour and a half legitimating retrospectively the acts of the military when acting in civil conflict.) In the Republic the army acted only in support of the civil power, the Garda Síochána. The gardaí would not speak to the British Army, as being constitutionally incorrect, only to their counterpart police force, the RUC, the Irish Army would not talk to anybody but the gardaí. There was one ludicrous episode along the border after a land mine had been laid in Northern Ireland with a command wire stretching a couple of hundred yards to a firing point on an eminence in the South, and a firing mechanism there. The scenario is of a British Army ATO trying to immobilise the bomb at one end, and an Irish Army bomb disposal officer a couple of hundred yards away at the other end of the wire trying to understand his bit of the device. They could not communicate directly, but only by messages, passed back to Monaghan on the one hand and Armagh on the other, back to Garda headquarters, up to RUC headquarters, out to Armagh, and thence to the other end of the line, and to the unfortunate ATO patiently waiting for vital information.

In July 1974, a little over one month after the collapse of the Executive, the British government announced that it would be setting up an elected convention which would enable Northern Ireland parties to debate forms of government and to agree on a constitution. I was never sure whether this was intended to be a constructive contribution to a solution or a process of *reductio ad absurdum* which would legitimise direct rule, or just another hurdle placed there in the hope and belief that Northern Ireland politicians would fail to clear it. Frank Cooper kept making cracks about setting exam papers for Northern Ireland politicians which they failed, and though the questions were made progressively easier, they continued to fail.

13

CONSTITUTIONAL CONVENTION

N OTHING STANDS STILL FOR LONG. For some politicians activity is all, and Rees felt that he had to do something. He was particularly conscious that one of the Ulster Workers' Council demands had been for a new election. But to what? There was little point in having an election simply to restore the old Stormont. Neither, in the current climate of triumphalism, was there any prospect of an election providing anything other than a victory for reactionary unionism. Faulkner would be routed, Alliance was holding on by its teeth, and SDLP members were totally demoralised. Still, unionist politicians were demanding some action, and it was desirable to keep the others engaged in some sort of political activity, or at least on the payroll. There was a feeling too in some parts of the NIO that the UWC strike heralded an upsurge in Protestant populism and a turning away from politicians, and that maybe something of the same would happen on the Catholic side too. The answer found was the Constitutional Convention: this would put the constitutional question on the back burner for a year or so, even if it did not produce a result. If it did, so much the better: if not, the wider world would see the problem faced by the government in dealing with two groups of intransigents. So, late in 1974, it was back to the treadmill again.

I was asked to join the staff of the convention as adviser to the chairman, along with John Oliver who was standing down as permanent secretary of the DoE. It was only later I discovered that the first choice recommendation by the Parliamentary Clerks and by the Northern Ireland system had been a fairly traditional civil servant, which showed how little the Stormont establishment had learned over the years. Its members could not understand even then that a monolithic secretariat from a unionist background was no longer possible. I was included, I believe, at the insistence of Frank Cooper. This was to give me the opportunity to work closely with John Oliver for an extended period, which I enjoyed very much, and with a very interesting man, Robert Lowry.

In the preliminary discussions about the convention, I had been very doubtful about the advisability of appointing a judge as chairman, and particularly the Lord Chief Justice, Robert Lowry, who was being mentioned as a likely candidate. My reasoning was that you needed a wheeler-dealer who would get people into back rooms and twist arms and broker a deal of some sort. I suggested Arnold Goodman, who had emerged as a sort of fixer for Harold Wilson. I was aware that a judge was likely to adopt a legalistic approach, and that he would be conscious of having to protect the integrity of the judiciary and of the legal system and would be unlikely to take chances. When in the event Robert Lowry was appointed, I thought that it should have been on the basis that he retired from the Court, on the understanding that he would go to the House of Lords when the convention was over. But Rees was insistent on a judge. His main concern was that the convention should be well managed and disciplined. He had been appalled by the spectacle of the unionists' disgraceful treatment of Faulkner in the Assembly, which had got a very bad press in Britain, and he did not wish to see a recurrence.

There was a very strange meeting, in the spring of 1975, preparatory to the convention, to deal with fairly humdrum things such as the date and form of the announcement that the secretary of state would make. I remember it well because there were sixteen people in the room on the ground floor of Parliament Buildings, all of them prominent in the Northern Ireland administration and including the head of the Civil Service, the Clerk of Parliament, the Lord Chief Justice, the permanent secretary of the DoE and his predecessor, the Chief Parliamentary Draughtsman, the head of the Information Service, the private secretary to the chairman, and the future private secretary to the secretary of state, and I was almost the only person among the Northern Ireland officials in the room who had not been educated at Inst, the Royal Belfast Academical Institution. After leaving the Community Relations Commission I had been tempted by John Pinder to take up a fellowship with Political and Economic Planning to produce an anatomy of Northern Ireland, on the lines of Anthony Sampson's *Anatomy of Britain*. Here laid before me was the very physiology of Northern Ireland, the networks of the Presbyterian meritocracy that had permeated the public service and the professions. To emphasise the point, John Oliver was the chairman of the board at Inst, Robert Lowry was a former head boy, and Ken Bloomfield was one of its star pupils. Some months later, Lowry, who did not like trendy legal concepts, asked me rather peevishly what was meant by institutional violence, which all the fashionable sociologists were talking about. I suggested, jokingly, that it was a condition that prevailed when half the judiciary and half the civil service had been educated at Inst.

One bizarre sequence just after this meeting involved Merlyn Rees. We all met in his room in Stormont Castle on a Thursday or Friday afternoon to discuss the date of the announcement of the convention and the form of his statement to the House of Commons. There were, I remember, seventeen people at the meeting, all very senior. He arrived late, and when there was about ten minutes' work left to clear up the details, he stood up and said that he would have to go, and that we would reconvene on the following Tuesday. I was a bit cross at not having finished the business and at having to drag down to the Castle on the Tuesday. But worse was to follow. It turned out that the meeting was to take place in his room in the House of Commons at 10 a.m. Since an early plane would not guarantee attendance, we had all to trail over to London and spend the night there, all seventeen of us (except the NIO people, who would probably have been in London, or some of them). As it was, the meeting kept getting postponed and did not eventually take place until 6.30 in the evening; the group of us had had to kick our heels around the NIO all day. In the end, the business took less than an hour – but just long enough to prevent us getting a plane home that evening. So we had the expense of two nights in London, and the time wasted of some very expensive people, just to satisfy some whim of the secretary of state, or his inability to make up his mind.

I remember that Rees seemed to have a fixation about the day on which he wished to make the announcement. 'Maundy Thursday,' he kept muttering, 'I want to announce it on Maundy Thursday.' I had never heard the name mentioned like that, and I wondered whether he had met a soothsayer on his way to the Commons who had grasped his wrist and cackled, 'Maundy Thursday'. Other people thought it was not a very good idea either. Michael Cudlipp, who had been brought in by Rees from the *Daily Express* to head up the NIO press office, kept jumping up and saying, 'There are only two bad days in the year for making an announcement: Christmas Eve and Maundy Thursday because there are no papers on Good Friday or Christmas Day.' But Rees kept coming back to Maundy Thursday and kept muttering the two words like a mantra. In the end, he was pushed off it. For all I know, he might attribute the failure of the convention to his not having been allowed to announce it on an auspicious day.

The Clerks of Parliament were to run the Constitutional Convention as a mini-parliament, and John Oliver and I were deputed to advise the chairman on political and administrative matters, to test out possible models of government, and to help to develop – or to demolish – ideas brought forward by the parties.

I had serious misgivings about holding the Constitutional Convention in the Stormont building, but there was no other readily available, and the symbolism of Stormont was too great to risk offending the unionists by not going there. Equally, of course, the same symbolism was likely to discourage SDLP participation. I was concerned that the shape and the history of the building would produce its own dynamic – would encourage confrontation rather than compromise. The only concession to new thinking was the creation of a tier of slightly curved cross-benches to try to bridge the cleavage between the two sides of the chamber.

Briefing the chairman for his role was a slightly unusual sort of task. We had virtually to give him a crash course in Northern Ireland administration and politics, and in the personalities involved and the nature of the issues. Since he was still involved full-time in the courts – in hearing cases, in courts administration and in the preparation of a new judicature bill – our business had to be inserted in the interstices of a very full schedule. We decided to avoid burdening him with paper and to play to his strength, which was the capacity to absorb briefings rapidly. Discussions were usually held in Hillsborough Castle, where the chairman would call on his way home from the courts. It was not too far out of my way either, quite convenient and quiet. At that time the secretary of state had not gone into residence in the great house, the governor had gone with direct rule, and the virtually deserted house had an eerie feeling about it. Entering it was like going on board the *Marie Céleste*. The gate would open and you would be checked through without a word. The front door was open, and a snack meal was set out on a sideboard in a small room, with a bottle of wine and a table set for four. In all our time there, I don't think I saw anybody but ourselves.

John Oliver was in his element: slightly pedagogical and rational, sorting everything out into objective categories, preparing written briefing notes in a fine italic hand. He had a slightly portentous delivery, structured in triads, which tended to elevate the subject under discussion to importance, only to demolish it on the down beat. 'The Housing Executive, chairman, fine people, concerned, energetic, far-seeing: but somehow not just building the houses, you know.' John exemplified two aspects of the Stormont bureaucracy that fascinated me: they had not worked at close quarters with elected people and did not know the dynamics of party politics (Stormont ministers had been isolated from the rigours of the democratic process by single-party rule) and they were not used to working in public. They were also smitten by a condition, common to civil servants everywhere, of wanting to order everything from the top and believing that people would be prepared to fall in without question with their neat plans and programmes.

In an early discussion, John had mapped out a draft programme which would complete the business of the Constitutional Convention in the required six months, beginning in May: two days to draw up standing orders and set up committees, one week to draft reports, two weeks to debate, a fortnight to pull the whole thing together, two more weeks to finalise the report, a few days for printing, and so on in a fine mechanical sequence. There was to be a few days' break about the Twelfth of July and no other recess. It all sounded fine. 'What will you do if they don't agree?' I asked. John was shocked at the thought. It struck me that here was the expert in local

216

government, the drafter of schemes of reorganisation and the real author of the Macrory Report, who had never sat at a meeting of district councillors, who did not understand them or how they went about their business. In the event, the convention got bogged down in the business committee for weeks on end as its members argued about the minutiae of standing orders.

John Oliver and I had to learn new tricks in dealing with the chairman. Robert Lowry was a lawyer with a lawyer's metabolism, and his day was differently organised from ours. We were used to a steady nine-to-five, with an amount of after-hours work too, but basically an ordered day. The chairman did most of his work at night, when he wrote prodigiously. The day was taken up in routine and he really did not get revved up intellectually until after dinner. We were also used to sending drafts up to ministers for comment or change. It was quite a culture shock to have to deal with drafts emanating from above.

The most amusing early example of his night-time style of working occurred on the opening day of the Constitutional Convention, 8 May 1975. We had discussed the content of the chairman's address with him several times without commitment, without instructions to prepare a draft, and without a written response from him. It was also quite difficult to get drafts back from him. He tended to work best against deadlines which were more his than ours. As it happened, we had a final briefing the day before the opening, but still no speech. We were very conscious that there would be great media interest in the occasion, and we were accustomed to having press releases prepared and cleared and copies of speeches ready to be handed out before the event. The chairman had a judge's contempt for the press. He would rather not have been mentioned in the media at all and he saw no need for elaborate preparations to cater for them.

In the end, he agreed to take our notes home and work on them. I was to call at his house in Crossgar at eight in the morning to take the text up for typing. John and I would meet the chairman at ten o'clock and the speech would be released to the press at eleven.

Sure enough, when I called at eight o'clock, Lowry was in his shirtsleeves in the kitchen with a sheaf of papers which I collected and dashed off. When they were typed up, the problems in them were apparent. The content was first-class, but the style was Ciceronian: beautifully balanced phrases, long sentences built up of subordinate clause upon subordinate clause, reflexive verbs, references back to a subject long since forgotten. I shuddered to think what the hacks in the tabloids would make of the speech. I sat down with a pencil and chopped it into short sentences, substituting short, Anglo-Saxon words for long Latinate ones, and reshaped it while keeping the excellent sense and the sincerity of the message. At 10 a.m., John and I went to the chairman's room. The pair of us had discussed the problem and he took it in his stride.

'Wonderful speech, chairman. Excellent. Makes all the right points. Can't fail to impress the solemnity of the occasion. Congratulations... There are just a few little stylistic points and now Maurice will take you through them.'

I suppose John would regard that as giving one of his young men his chance. When it was all over, he said to me, 'You know, it's quite difficult telling these chaps who have been earning a quarter of a million at the Bar that their grammar isn't quite up to scratch.'

Lowry was a wholly delightful man to work with, a classical scholar and a fine lawyer with a great interest in showjumping. Very often when we were working late and his wife was on safari with his daughters round the various horse shows, we used to stop off for dinner together on the way home. He had an absolutely total recall of every case he had been involved in, and he could recount stories at great length – often with the disarming introduction: 'I must tell you a story of which I am myself the hero.' One of his great cases was in defence of the Lough Neagh eel fishermen who took to the House of Lords their claim for fishing rights based on the proposition that the seventeenth-century conveyance of these rights to Henry, Lord Chichester, was faulty. They won their case, and the fishermen paid him in instalments over the years, generally at Christmas, until he told them they had done enough.

The unionists in the convention were fairly rampant, and in no mood to compromise. They saw the convention as a means of winning back control in a Stormont-type parliament, they had the numbers, and they were determined to use them. They fell into three broad groups. First, there were the rump of the old 'unpledged' Unionists who had rejected Faulkner. They were led by Harry West, and looked upon themselves as the elder statesmen. Then there were those whom O'Neill had expelled, led by Bill Craig in Vanguard but

218

strengthened by various paramilitary outriders and those who had been prominent in pursuing the protest voters: Glenn Barr, David Trimble, Dougie Hutchinson, Ernie Baird and Reg Empey. And then there was the DUP, Paisley's party, the eternal outsiders but now inside, half of them clerics in the Free Presbyterian Church. The three parties worked together in a loose alliance, the United Ulster Unionist Council, the UUUC or Treble UC for short. They did not always trust each other, and neither did the followers trust the leaders.

To make up for the lack of trust, there was a series of monitoring devices. The leaders met together: Paisley, West and Craig. To ensure that they did not stray out of line, there was a committee of second-rank people – Martin Smyth, Willie Beattie, Ernie Baird, about ten or twelve in all. They came and sat behind the leaders when they were in discussions with other parties. And because the backbenchers did not really trust the others, a rota of backbenchers was selected from the three parties to sit in watch on the other two tiers. At its most ridiculous, this process resulted in David Bleakley conducting his discussions like Daniel in the lion's den, confronted by seventeen assorted unionists sitting in three tiers on the other side of the amphitheatre. What was disappointing about these exchanges was that the new intake of unionist representatives was even more hardline than the oldsters. There was no generational mellowing – but instead a belligerence and inability to compromise that boded ill for the success of the convention.

The Unionist Party had a recent history of electing leaders to be strong and uncompromising, and getting rid of them as soon as they showed any sign of mellowing. The party rank and file had an abhorrence of secret diplomacy such as Sunningdale; they were suspicious that leaders would go down the path of betrayal, and wanted open agreements openly arrived at. Leaders were afraid of sharing the fate of their predecessors. So there was an insistence on both sides that nothing should be done except in the full glare of publicity.

There is also, I believe, an inevitable and real problem in any negotiations in Northern Ireland arising both from the evangelical Protestant tradition of commitment to the Word, to revealed truth, and from the Presbyterian suspicion of rulers and hierarchies. That, and a more relaxed attitude among Catholics to broad moral principles, made any meeting of minds highly unlikely, and made negotiations in any real sense almost impossible.

I remember going round the parties after they had settled in saying, 'I have read your manifesto, and I know what it says, but what is your fall-back position?' They were horrified and outraged. It was obscene and wicked to suggest that they would not stand firm on the manifesto, that they could even think of retreating from the high ground of principle enunciated therein.

There was an interesting clash of cultures too between John Oliver and myself on the one hand and the Parliamentary Clerks on the other. Coming from an administrative background, John and I wanted to see the convention produce a tangible result, and our instincts were to push the members in that direction. The clerks on the other hand thought it almost indecent to discuss politics with the parties, and confined themselves to procedure. We thought of them as the original slaves of the lamp. They kept the procedures polished and serviceable: so long as the machine was in working order, they did not care what it produced, or whether it produced anything at all. They did not look kindly on our attempts to fraternise with politicians, whom they generally despised. We tried to build linkages at official level, and invited the party secretaries in for coffee from time to time, but it was hard work.

As if to show that they meant business, the UUUC turned the discussions on the draft standing orders of the convention into the battle of the Somme. The Parliamentary Clerks had produced a draft based on parliamentary procedures, and it was expected that they would go through on the nod. Not so. A committee was appointed to scrutinise every line and phrase, and every word was fought over. At one stage it was clear that the unionists believed that Parliament would accept whatever report the convention made, whether on a majority vote or not, and that the secretary of state would have to put the report to Parliament. The unionists' strategy appeared to be to push through very rapidly a unionist proposal based on the former Stormont parliament, to vote on it *en bloc*, and to suppress all opposition. They went further, in an Orwellian direction, in proposing that the acceptance by the convention of the final draft report would have the effect of automatically expunging from the record all the other drafts that might have been considered. The purpose of this tactic was apparently to ensure that the other proposals, even though voted down, would not even be alluded to in the final document. This was revisionism on the grand scale: what had not been endorsed by the vote of the majority would be regarded as never having been proposed at all.

This triumphalism nearly wrecked the convention before it got started. The SDLP in particular, and Alliance, complained to the chairman and sought his protection. Brian Faulkner was less exercised, since he saw little point in the whole operation, which he was involved in only out of a sense of loyalty to his few followers. He never had any hopes of the convention, he was in no way committed to it; he did the decent thing – but no more.

When finally the chairman asked to meet the business committee, a draft of standing orders was produced, which, thanks mainly to the Parliamentary Clerks, was shorn of the more aggressive provisions that the UUUC had put forward. Lowry, having skimmed through them, said that they seemed broadly acceptable. He issued a mild warning that if some of the clauses of which he had heard rumours had been included, then he would have had to object.

Early on in the preparations for the convention, John Oliver and I went to Dublin to see the arrangements that had been made to adapt Dublin Castle as a venue for the European Summit. We wanted to see whether we could learn anything that would be helpful in organising the work of the convention, and in particular to see the use Dublin was making of new technology in recording debates and servicing committees, in data and information retrieval and in preparing reports. It was tempting too to think of the utility of simultaneous translation for some of our more idiosyncratic speakers.

I was able to make use of old contacts, of Dermot Nally with whom I had taken part in many courses in the Institute of Public Administration (IPA) under Tom Barrington, when Nally was in the Republic's Department of Local Government and I was town clerk. By now, Dermot was secretary to the government and Noel Whelan, another IPA regular, was deputy secretary to the Department of the Taoiseach. I had got to know Sean Donlon when he was doing legwork in the North for the Department of Foreign Affairs in the early 1970s. He used to call with me in the Community Relations Commission for an update on the situation and spent the odd night in Strangford. He was now back on the Northern Ireland desk in the department and was subsequently to make his name as the ambassador in Washington, head groom to the Four Horsemen, and later secretary of the Department of Foreign Affairs.

We agreed to keep lines of communication open. I was afraid that a situation might arise in which the convention parties might have reached a delicate stage in their negotiations, might even, however improbably, be on the edge of an agreement, when the whole thing could be spoiled for ever by an incautious remark or a stupid or belligerent statement by a minister in the South. Equally, if somebody in Dublin was going to make a speech or do something that might alarm or upset any of the parties, we would like to have some advance warning. We saw ourselves, on both sides, not in any way as trading secrets or sensitive information, but as trying to keep everybody on side in a very difficult and hotly contested match.

In the event, the hotline (of which the chairman was made aware) did not have to be used, mainly because the convention proceeded so predictably that the whole world knew where it was heading without inside information and it never (except briefly on one occasion) got near enough to an agreement for any danger of spoliation to arise. On the other hand, Northern Ireland had receded as a subject of interest on the Republic's political agenda, and ministers, especially Cosgrave, were not impelled to make many pronouncements about it. Nevertheless it was good to know that the line was there, and the friendships with the people at the other end survived several changes of government on both sides.

We had tried from the beginning to ensure that parties to the convention would be properly serviced, that they would have some research back-up and that they would be encouraged to develop position papers and have the capacity to analyse those of others. There was also a provision, wrung with difficulty from the NIO, whereby we could advance money to parties to enable them to commission research or to employ academic or expert advisers on short-term contracts. This was all part of an attempt to professionalise their approach to the convention, and to help them towards a more sophisticated consideration of the issues. Remarkably, or perhaps not, it was difficult to get them to spend the money. The SDLP did get some help in drafting from Donal Barrington and Rory O'Hanlon, both then senior counsel who later became judges. The UUUC tried to employ a Colonel Hezlet, who had written a history of the B Specials, to write a paper on security. This we disallowed because security did not fall within the purview of the convention and also because of Hezlet's lack of academic (and indeed current military) standing.

The UUUC employed the academic Bernard Crick to advise it on its proposals for a committee system. What it really wanted was not so much research as confirmation, not expert advice but public endorsement of its proposals from an objective source. Crick, who was active in the Hansard Society and an active proponent of parliamentary reform through the introduction of committees, was superficially attracted by the notion of committees as suggested by the UUUC and had said so in passing in a newspaper article. Crick was brought over at the instigation of Bill Craig, and the UUUC public relations machine made arrangements for him to appear on local TV just after the six o'clock news one evening in order to endorse the product. However, the main news had to be extended because of some major bomb outrage, and by the time his interview came, Crick was in a slightly detached and whimsical mood. Whether it was the delay, or the fact that he had spent the time in the BBC hospitality room, or the fact that he had done so in the company of John Hume, or some combination of these factors, Bernard now took a much cooler view of the committee proposals. When, having been introduced as the great authority on parliamentary politics, he was asked for his view of the UUUC proposals, he said, 'They won't do at all, you know. The SDLP would be mad to think of accepting anything like that!'

Lowry was initially rather suspicious of the SDLP members and they of him. He was particularly wary of John Hume until he discovered that John had an interest in cricket and had understudied Scott Huey as left-arm spin bowler for the City of Derry club. After that, John was viewed in a new light. The chairman had a passion for cricket, and could recall test matches and recite score sheets from another era in amazing detail and, as far as I was aware, with total accuracy. The SDLP members, for their part, discovered that on sitting days the chairman used to relax with his staff over a drink at about 5.30, when we re-capped the events of the day. Subsequently, meetings with the SDLP often began in the very late afternoon and went on into the early evening. There was a definite improvement in the atmosphere, and better communication as trust was established, but at some unquantified cost to our livers.

There was in fact very little real communication at the convention, and very little contact between the groups. In part this was a carry-over from the UWC strike. Another factor, as I had feared, was the shape and history of the chamber, which imposed its own dynamic, and cast one group in the role of a government and the other of an opposition, with all the overtones that had for Northern Ireland politicians, especially when they occupied the very seats in the chamber they had been accustomed to in the past. It was hard not to believe that not only had the set been replicated, but the lines had been scripted as well.

There was little mixing outside the chamber either. You would never meet the DUP in the bar, which was the most likely place to meet the SDLP. This led me, as a joke, to promote the notion of temporal power sharing, whereby the DUP would run the place during the day and the SDLP at night, with the pubs open on Sunday. They would never need to meet and there would be a minimum of friction.

One of the great buzzwords of the Constitutional Convention was 'magnanimity'. Unfortunately the concept did not exist except as a rhetorical flourish, or as something to be demanded from the other side without cost to oneself. More seriously, what might have helped the convention members, given them some stimulus and some form of shared interest, would have been to facilitate their role as public representatives. This role was being forced on them anyway. The average Ulster elector, on both sides, educated in the Irish tradition of representative politics, saw the elected member of anything as a representative, a broker and an agent, and was not prepared to distinguish between the role of the convention member in fashioning constitutional forms of government and his traditional task, which was to act as a messenger and an intermediary in any problems constituents had with government departments. The members could not escape this: they were assailed at church gates and in markets, at fairs and in the streets, and with an eye to future electoral good health they were not prepared to ignore or rebuff the requests.

At the time, John Oliver and I acted as an unofficial Citizens' Advice Bureau and tried to get answers for them and to smooth the paths to departments. We argued strongly with the NIO that the convention members should be given some minor facilities and some entrée to departments, but Rees was adamant, as was Frank Cooper.

Rees in particular, although he had set up the convention, seemed to want to humiliate its members. He was certainly not going to allow them to take on any of the trappings of representation. It is of course true that their main responsibility, indeed their only statutory duty, was to come up with recommendations for an agreed form of government, but the other roles were being thrust on them and were a distraction anyhow. I suspected that Rees was being encouraged by the Northern Ireland Westminster MPs, especially Powell, Molyneaux, Fitt and Paisley, who did not wish to see any encroachment on their own territory and influence, which they guarded jealously.

Lowry, as chairman of the Constitutional Convention, was particularly good at putting members at ease. They were quite unused to the courtesy with which he would despatch a handwritten note to one who had made a good speech. He also hosted lunches to which a cross-section of members was invited in turn. He was mystified by Hugh Smyth's description as a 'welfare worker' until I explained that he was a welfare officer for the UVF. Then he wondered whether or not to make a citizen's arrest. On one occasion Frankie Millar, a former shipyard worker, failed to sit down when the chairman called him to order. Despite repeated requests he still did not sit down, and the chairman was about to name him when I rushed up a note with a brief message of explanation: 'boilermaker's ear', the popular name given to a well-known and extremely disabling occupational disease of shipyard workers. The chairman was most anxious to repair hurt feelings, and he asked me to apologise to Frankie. I did so and added that he could probably sue Harland and Wolff. The word must have gone round the yard, because there was a flood of cases. That bit of free advice must have cost Harland and Wolff millions.

In this first phase of the convention there was an idea floating about, with something approaching tacit approval in some NIO circles, of involving voluntary bodies and community groups in the work of the convention, perhaps through taking evidence from them or getting them into some kind of informal second chamber. I did a paper for the chairman along these lines, and added that this might be a means of giving paramilitaries on both sides a surrogate voice. John Hume got hold of a copy and said this was the most disgraceful document ever to emanate from a civil service office, and that it was totally subversive of elected members and of democracy itself. I suppose that is the nearest I came to being impeached.

On one occasion, just before the summer break, Austin Ardill came in to say that they were on the verge of a breakthrough. The SDLP had been very favourably impressed by a unionist document and had promised a response to it by 12 August when it would meet the UUUC leaders. When I read the document, I told John Oliver that I couldn't see the SDLP spending more than five minutes before deciding to reject it. By this time, the SDLP leadership had gone off on holiday, and as July progressed there was no word from them. In order to prevent misunderstandings I set off with Joan and the boys in search of the SDLP main leadership, which I found in Bunbeg, being guarded by half the gardaí in County Donegal. These gardaí, having been on this not entirely disagreeable duty for most of a month, had amassed large sums in overtime and threw a party in honour of their guardees in the Radharc Airigeal hotel. They very hospitably invited Joan and myself to join them, we having booked in to a nearby bed-and-breakfast where the children were well looked after. On the next evening, the politicians returned the compliment and threw their own end-of-term party to which we were also invited. It was a wonderful evening, dampened by news in the early hours of the murder of the Miami Showband near Newry. On the way home, we had to stop for petrol at a filling station at Moygashel. As I went in, conscious of having only Irish money, which was then acceptable currency but betrayed where you had been, Joan asked me where the so-called 'Murder Triangle' was. This was the name that had come to be given to an area of County Armagh and east Tyrone that had experienced an exceptionally large number of sectarian murders committed by loyalist paramilitaries, of which the Miami Showband massacre was a culmination. I didn't frighten her by saying that we were then in the middle of it, but I have rarely exited a filling station with such alacrity and so much relief.

As I had expected, the SDLP leaders were not aware of any obligation to respond to the UUUC on 12 August. However, they were quite anxious to avoid misunderstandings and John Hume agreed to phone Harry West to clear up any problems about the meeting. They also agreed to expedite production of their own submission so that they would have a paper to present to the convention when it reconvened after the recess.

There was one occasion when, against all the odds, the convention looked like producing a result. The UUUC had decided to have bilateral talks with the other parties and had formed subcommittees in order to do so. The group holding talks with the SDLP was headed by Bill Craig (Paisley having avoided such a politically problematic enterprise) and included Willie Beattie of the DUP; Beattie at this stage was regarded as Paisley's closest aide, always a dangerous position since Paisley, like the Turk, could 'bear no rival near the throne'.

Surprisingly, Craig and the SDLP began to move closer together. Partly this was due to the relationship between Craig and Paddy Devlin. Paddy, for a belligerent man himself, was a remarkable empathiser in negotiation. He let the opposition see that he understood their difficulties and reciprocated their point of view. Hume and Craig too were political realists with great belief in their ability to carry their constituencies with them and a facility for working with formulae and drafts. Probably, however, the main catalyst was the state of affairs outside the convention, with the IRA continuing their campaign and loyalist paramilitaries responding with sectarian murders. Both Hume and Craig looked over the parapet and saw anarchy, civil war and disaster. Craig wanted agreement on a strong government that would restore order and stability. The SDLP believed that a period of stability would induce economic growth which would help to remove Catholic disabilities. Its leadership also believed that if the power-sharing Executive had been allowed another couple of years, the political climate would have been changed irreversibly. Having been at the top table, even for a few months, they were not going to settle for less, especially as the alternative of direct rule was not nearly so detrimental to Catholics as a restoration of Stormont-type unionism. They were, however, wary of Craig. They were more afraid of being used to disarm the IRA and then being discarded. The main debate, therefore, centred on the duration of the arrangement, how long it could be held in place until normal party politics was allowed to return.

Craig, while still implacably opposed to imposed power sharing, found the concept of voluntary coalition quite acceptable. Periods of great crisis for Britain had seen the emergence of wartime coalitions under Lloyd George and Churchill, and Craig was prepared to look on the situation in Northern Ireland as a national, or at least a regional crisis, requiring the temporary combination of the efforts of all con-stitutional politicians to restore order and stability. There is little doubt that Craig saw himself heading this government of all the talents, which could not have endeared him to his fellow leaders in the UUUC, or made it easier for them to swallow any agreement.

The great phrase at the time was the need to 'copper fasten' the arrangements. Craig's proposal was for the parties to agree to maintain the arrangement for the life of a parliament. The SDLP was arguing for two parliaments: in theory up to ten years, but more likely to be seven or eight, and possibly even less.

The sub-group came to the chairman on a Friday evening to report progress and I remember being excited at the possibility of a break-through. I tried to encourage Bill Craig to keep at it by suggesting to him that Catholics might now trust him as a strong man who could deliver. He replied rather grimly that that would be a change, which made me regret my overture as rather silly.

Nevertheless, talking to the chairman afterwards we were quite sure that we were on the edge of something (John Oliver was off on leave). I took the proposals of both parties home to study them, and, setting them out in two columns like a profit-and-loss account, there seemed to me to be nothing between them that could not be bridged by negotiation and careful drafting, and I phoned the chairman to tell him so. When I came in on the Monday morning, I discovered that he had engaged in a similar exercise and had gone further, to block out the heads of an agreement, chapter headings for a draft report, and instructions to the Parliamentary Draftsman for a bill that would give effect to the arrangements.

But it was not to be. During the morning, Maurice Williamson, the chairman's private secretary, who always had his ear close to the ground, and the Parliamentary Clerks brought news that Paisley was in a wrecking mood and would destroy the agreement.

There was a great deal of speculation about why Paisley intervened in this way. The general impression was that he did not want a settle-ment, particularly not one engineered by Bill Craig which would leave him in the driving seat. There is also a view that Paisley had been visited by his Armagh elders over the weekend and told to have no truck with reconciliation. On this theory, it was more a case of Paisley listening to the voice of his Church than of him dominating it. By whatever means, his opposition was implacable, and Craig's support ebbed away rapidly. He was left with a few faithfuls, Glenn Barr and Reg Empey among them, but the bulk went over to Paisley or back to the UUP. Craig pushed the matter to a discussion, but was ignominiously beaten, and that was his end as a force in Ulster politics.

The convention staggered on to its sadly predictable end, with the UUUC stolidly voting their report through, and the others giving up the ghost. It finished on the last day of its six-month term with a report that the secretary of state declined to submit to Parliament. Instead, after a bit of havering, he decided to recall the convention on 3 February 1976 in the hope of its finding agreement, but again to no avail. In the meantime the IRA had perpetrated an atrocity at Kingsmills in County Armagh, stopping a workers' bus on a Friday evening, ordering the Catholics to step aside and murdering the Protestants. It was hard to make peace in this atmosphere. After one short meeting there was at last a consensus. The parties agreed that they could agree on virtually nothing. The recalled convention dragged on acrimoniously for a month, debating security and other things that were none of their business. In the end Rees seemed to be consumed by a fear that the loyalists would occupy Stormont and stage some sort of symbolic *coup d'état*: some heavyhanded bureaucrat in the NIO ordered in the troops, and I looked out the window to see armoured cars lumbering up the drive and soldiers unrolling coils of barbed wire in front of the building. Luckily Ronnie Blackburn, the clerk, intervened, and the forces were deployed more discreetly behind the building. In the end, the convention members went quietly and decently when they had gathered up their papers, the restaurant closed and the heating went off.

After this, we spent some time tidying up the papers. We were anxious to preserve them for future researchers, but did not want them to fall into the hands of whatever establishment was about in the meantime. In particular, I had made copious notes of the chairman's meetings with party leaders, and on other encounters of interest. These discussions had taken place in confidence. Some of the leaders had said things which might weaken a subsequent negotiating position, and we did not want this to be used against them. Eventually the papers were placed in the Public Record Office under the personal seal of the chairman, closed for a period of thirty years and only to be opened in the interim by the express direction of himself or his successor as Lord Chief Justice.

In retrospect, this was probably a lot of fuss about very little. In the long term, the Constitutional Convention was an entirely insignificant and ineffective interlude. Nobody except a few politicians, and those mainly in the UUUC, was in the least interested, and the papers could have been scattered to the winds without the least loss to scholarship or danger to public or private security.

During this time too I received an offer, on the recommendation of Richard Rose (who was very generous in these matters), of a one- or two-year fellowship at the Smithsonian Institute in Washington. The project was a study of federal/local relationships in government in the United States. It had been chaired by Hubert Humphrey, the former US vice-president, and was now being carried on by Elliot Richardson, the former Attorney-General. They were looking for a European Fellow after somebody had pulled out, and Richard had suggested my name. I was sitting beside Ken Shimeld, then head of personnel, at a lecture as he extolled the value of outside experience to the civil service. I told him that I might have a proposition and he seemed very interested. Later, when we got down to cases, he was much less enthusiastic. He took off to consult and came back saying that I could go if I liked, but at the expense of promotion prospects, and not to expect them to be there when I came back. I never quite forgave the civil service management for that. I thought it was a great opportunity lost, both for them and for me. Later when I was in a position to do so, I tried to facilitate people in the Department who had an opportunity to study abroad.

We also spent some time in reading files that were being considered for release under the thirty-year rule. These gave a fascinating insight into the concerns and attitudes of the Stormont administration in the twenties, thirties and early forties. But reading files soon palled, and instead of driving into the office to read books, I thought it would be more fuel-efficient to stay at home and read. So I told Ken Shimeld that I would stay there until he had found work for me to do. A week or so later, George Quigley phoned to say that I had been promoted to senior assistant secretary, and that I was to go to the Department of Manpower Services for a few months to provide a pair of extra hands while he was chairing a committee to review the economy. After that, I was to go to the Department of Health and Social Services to head up Social Policy and Health Services Personnel.

14
MAKING THE BEST OF THINGS

I N MY FEW MONTHS IN THE Department of Manpower Services, the
DMS, in the summer of 1976, I developed the guidelines to be
used by the Fair Employment Agency, then being set up,
prepared instructions for draftsmen on health and safety at work
legislation, and did some cleaning-up work on industrial tribunals.
This was my first job in a real government department and I found
it interesting to see how departments took on much of the colour and
attitudes of the client or interest groups they dealt with and became
their voice within government. In this context, DMS was the voice
of organised labour and the trade unions, with which it maintained
very close connections. The civil servants in the Department of
Commerce, on the other hand, spoke for the employers and were
capitalists and anti-union to a man. The DHSS was, as Norman
Dugdale liked to say, the 'caring department', and Environment
understood perhaps too well the attitude of the district councils.
Agriculture was even more symbiotic. I could never discover
whether the farmers' union was an arm of the Department of
Agriculture, DANI, or more likely, whether DANI was an agency of
the farmers' union. There was an even more unhealthy arrangement
in that DANI owned the Faculty of Agriculture at Queen's, and that
all the professors there were officers of the department. What that
did for independent criticism of policies and academic objectivity I
often wondered.

The DMS was the centre of all expertise within government on industrial relations. What was ironic was that its own internal relationships were very poor. There was a deep division between the top of the department, where policy was developed, and the working level. In part this resulted from the way the department had been put together and from the fact that most of the middle-grade officers had joined as clerks and come up through the local office system where they had served for years in the local labour exchange or 'buroo' during periods of endemic high employment. This produced an air of weary cynicism and a scepticism about the value of change or new policies. This division was accentuated by the physical arrangements. The top of the office was housed in a sumptuously restored and carpeted Victorian mansion (so lush that it was not thought advisable to invite trade unionists into it) while the foot soldiers occupied a nasty modern annexe some distance away. Between them there was a glass-walled passage which alternately boiled or froze depending on the weather, and an imposing oak door which was always closed. The 'golden door' symbolised the division in the department. It also symbolised the sense of separateness which enabled the two parts to operate almost without friction, each with its own agenda.

Here I faced for the first time the really hierarchic nature of the civil service and the tendency of people to take cover from unpleasant and difficult discussions or to find someone else to carry the can. Soon after I arrived, the other senior staff took off on leave and I found myself, although the new boy, the senior person there and the point of reference for all sorts of problems I knew nothing or very little about. Generally I was able to support or confirm people in the conclusions their own experience had led them to. On one occasion, however, I was asked by Commerce to sort out a problem. The man-made textile manufacturer Enkalon, then the main employer in the Antrim area, wished to expand production and to introduce a night shift. Since the workforce affected was largely female, it had fallen foul of the Chief Factory Inspector who, relying on a nineteenth-century act which prevented the employment of women at night, refused to sanction the practice. Here was an opportunity to provide jobs being frustrated by another government department despite the agreement of management and trade unions, and despite the firm's proposals to provide taxis and other amenities, and the fact that women worked at night in the local hospitals, and the further fact that it was the twentieth century and women were seeking equality in the workplace. Nothing would move the inspector. I pointed out the extent to which social conditions and the role of women had changed in the century since the legislation was passed, how the evil the legislation was directed against had now gone, the changing role of women in society and the new thrust for equality (which the department was spearheading) but to no avail. Every time I asked why something or other could not be done, he replied, 'That's a policy decision.' At last the penny dropped, and I said, 'Does that mean you want me to decide?' He said, 'Yes', so I rapidly made my first ever policy decision – though until then I would not have recognised it as such. The waiver was issued, he went off satisfied, and peace and production were restored.

I suppose there was a touch of myopia in my own reaction in that it never occurred to me to seek a ministerial direction. However, I was fairly sure that the creation of jobs was an important priority of ministerial policy, and I had been told by a senior officer, whom I trusted, to get on with the business and get it sorted out.

This division between 'policy' and professional judgement I found to be debilitating and entirely artificial, and often a refuge for people who did not want to take responsibility. All that was ten years after the Fulton Report which was supposed to have led to the breaking down of barriers between the administrative and professional cadres in the civil service. Some people, of course, when offered freedom, preferred the comfort of their chains.

On another occasion I was informed, first thing in the morning, of a fatal accident in Harland and Wolff in which a sheet of plate steel had fallen, killing a teenaged worker. I was told that the factory inspector was carrying out an immediate investigation and I was asked to authorise the employment of an outside expert on welding. I had no reason not to do so, but I asked whether they had thought of also taking expert advice on the quality of the steel being used. He was surprised that I should raise it, but he agreed that it might be a sensible thing to do. What my informant did not know was that I had already had a much more graphic account of the incident, supplied by a Harland and Wolff worker from Downpatrick who had thumbed a lift home with me the previous evening. 'Terrible day in the yard. Wee fellow killed. Might have been a bloody dozen. It's that rotten fucking Polish steel.' A week or two later, my colleague came back to me and said, 'How the hell did you know to ask about the steel?'

When the expert's report finally came in from an eminent professor of metallurgy in Sheffield, it contained a description of some of the ludicrous goings-on in Harland and Wolff. Apparently best practice required that the welding medium being used should be brought to a certain temperature, and then retained at another temperature until ready for use. In order to enable this to be done, an extremely costly battery of electric ovens had been installed along one wall of a huge engineering shed. 'However,' the inspector noted drily, 'these procedures appeared not to be invariably followed. Every oven I opened contained a pie cooking for the lunch.' It must have been the most expensive fast food installation in Western Europe.

Roy Mason as secretary of state did not particularly like dealing with civil servants. He had the insecurity of many small men, the over-compensating aggressiveness and the ignorance of the truly uneducated. He was a small man in every respect, probably the worst secretary of state in my time (apart of course from the totally invisible and lazy Humphrey Atkins). Mason had been Minister for Defence. He was a little boy playing with toy soldiers and tanks and he was completely in the pocket of the army. He greatly endeared himself to the unionist and middle-class business establishment by appearing to be tough on terrorism and to promote security policies above all others. He had the disagreeable habit of periodically claiming total victory over the IRA, which merely provoked them to worse excesses, and he disdained local politicians. He had no interest in or desire to promote political activity. When local politicians complained that this left a vacuum which would be filled by the men of violence, he would ask in his strangulated accent, 'What vacuum? I see only a vortex.' Unlike Rees, however, he did take decisive action to keep the roads clear during the next loyalist strike in 1977 and prevented any repetition of 1974.

He had no particular interest in social or economic issues either and he left his junior ministers a great deal of scope to run the departments allocated to them. This was the beginning of a pattern in Northern Ireland whereby junior ministers began to be known popularly in the media as the minister of this or that. This of course was a misnomer and a constitutional nonsense. The secretary of state was minister for everything and the heads of Northern Ireland departments (who were legally the permanent secretaries) worked under his direction. Junior ministers were there to help the secretary of state, but gradually identified with individual departments, and some of them behaved as if they were ministers. For junior ministers, Northern Ireland was a paradise in comparison to Westminster and Whitehall where they were a lower form of political life. Parliamentary secretaries hardly rated at all. In contrast, in Northern Ireland they were dealing with real business, with policy matters on behalf of the secretary of state, with a range of day-to-day decisions, with representations and delegations on a wide variety of topics. The better ones worked hard, put in a long day on top of their parliamentary and constituency duties, took a duty weekend once a month, and bore the brunt of heavy personal security and endless travel at highly unsocial hours. The best of them also enjoyed it and thrived on the additional work and an exposure to experience that they would not have had in years in a Whitehall department. Among these was Peter Melchett, a dynamic young Labour peer who appeared as a parliamentary secretary in the latter months of 1976, during my first stint in the DHSS.

We first heard that our new minister was an old Etonian hereditary peer in his early twenties. We were not cheered up by the news that he was on holiday on a remote Greek island, and could not be contacted to be given the good news or to be called back to duty. Norman Dugdale, always the literary gentleman, was able to recall some lines from T.S. Eliot regarding the foundation of the chemical giant ICI by Sir Alfred Mond on a transatlantic liner:

> I shall not want capital in heaven
> For I shall meet Sir Alfred Mond.
> We two shall lie together, lapt
> In a five-per-cent Exchequer Bond.

Sir Alfred was the minister's grandfather, the first Lord Melchett, and his father, the chairman of British Steel and a prominent Labour peer, had died suddenly shortly before, projecting the young man into the House of Lords, and into control of what we regarded as a large and serious Northern Ireland department, one that was not to be used as a plaything by the dilettante products of the public school system.

Our minds were not eased when the new minister turned up for his first interview in casual clothes, denim jeans, an open-necked shirt and loafers. I remember asking Norman what we would have done if he had presented himself in the same garb for interview for an appointment to a junior post in the civil service. We agreed that he was unlikely to get past the first stage.

How wrong we were. He turned out to be a thoroughbred, with a good Cambridge degree in sociology, who had done postgraduate research at the London School of Economics (LSE) on a drugs-related topic. Here at last was a minister who spoke our language and did not have to have everything spelled out or interpreted for him. More important, he related to the young people around, he was mobile, accessible, and very attractive to large numbers of people. He also had a lot of courage in fighting for issues that did not fall within his brief, but which involved some aspect of human rights or discrimination or criminal justice. One such was the case of a young woman who had been convicted and sentenced to a long term of imprisonment for killing her father with a bread knife. This became a celebrated issue for Northern Ireland feminists because the father had virtually killed the mother, had abused and sexually assaulted the oldest daughter, and was turning his attentions on her younger sister when she killed him. This was one of the first cases where domestic rape, incest and abuse by a parent was pleaded in justification of manslaughter, and while the court did not take it in the first instance, Melchett kept raising the matter with the secretary of state and the law-and-order people until he had secured a pardon and a release for the unfortunate victim of circumstances.

Melchett's success and popularity severely strained his relations with the secretary of state. Robert Ramsey, by now principal private secretary to Roy Mason, told me an amusing story about how Mason boarded the plane one Monday morning on his way back to Belfast and was immediately cheered up by a headline across the bottom part of the front page of the *Guardian*: 'The man who brings new hope to Ulster'. The story was by Anne McHardy, and Mason sank back in his seat to bask in self-congratulation. There was an explosion as he got to the end of the first column and threw the paper down in disgust at finding that the article was a eulogy of Peter Melchett.

Melchett chafed at the constraints that were put on him in the name of security or convention and on his ability to travel to any part of Northern Ireland. He went out as often as he could and on whatever pretext, to what were regarded as 'difficult areas' – generally places that no minister had ever visited before, or any representative of government more exalted or benign than a policeman or a summons server – and found that people were always glad to see him. He was also restrained by his other department, Education, whose officials were keen to ensure that he met only 'safe' people, those who were within the education system, and not the radical voices shouting in the wings. Melchett wanted to meet as wide a spectrum of opinion as possible, and in particular to hear those who were critical of established policies or who had an alternative analysis to offer. He soon devised a means of engineering these encounters by asking Joan and me to invite him to dinner in my home in Downpatrick when people like Des Wilson or Jackie Redpath or Paddy Doherty just happened to be about.

Melchett gave me one of my more pleasurable tasks as a civil servant, and the one in which, in retrospect, I almost take the greatest pride. He came in one Monday morning and announced that he wanted to set up a Northern Ireland trust fund on the lines of Rowntree or Cadbury. He had been concerned at the lack of money available locally to help voluntary groups that were trying to get started. They would, if they succeeded and proved viability, become entitled to a range of statutory and other grants: the problem was survival until they reached that point. The dilemma is classically stated by Dr Johnson in the prefatory letter to his great dictionary addressed to the Earl of Chesterfield: 'Is not a patron, my Lord, not one who having failed to throw a rope to a swimmer struggling in the water, encumbers him with help when he has safely reached the shore by his own efforts?' We agreed that such a fund would need a minimum initial fund of £500,000, must be seen to be totally independent of government, and must be in the hands of a group of independent trustees who would have the respect and confidence not only of the voluntary sector and the communities in Northern Ireland, but also of the businessmen and financial institutions they would be largely depending on for money in the future. He agreed to secure political support for the idea, and I was to take it through the official machine.

I assembled a small informal group of sympathetic and imaginative officials to plot a way through the maze. The most innovative, and by far the most helpful, was Max Reid, then solicitor to the Department of Finance. We learned to avoid the Charities Branch of the Department of Finance and all the people with an official track record in the field, all of whom tended to be hidebound by tradition and dismissive if not openly scornful of the idea.

We needed somebody to head the idea publicly and to be chairman of trustees. He or she had to be acceptable to most of the parties in the voluntary and charitable sector, to have sufficient standing and prestige to impress ministers, senior civil servants and the banks, to have political sense and judgement without being too politically identified, to have experience of business, a reputation for integrity and a slight raffishness when it came to public policy. Luckily there was such a paragon. David Cook had just been elected as the first (and sadly the only) non-unionist Lord Mayor of Belfast and was engaged in opening a few windows in that musty office and making it more relevant to the whole city, to both communities and to the twentieth century. He was a practising solicitor, son of a former headmaster of Campbell College, and a prominent member of the Alliance Party (a sort of guarantee of political neutrality). He was very taken by the idea and threw his whole weight behind it. Soon our informal meetings were held in the comparative luxury of the Lord Mayor's Parlour and enjoyed the civic hospitality which, without being Lucullan, was a good deal better than the departmental coffee and biscuits. I think of David every time I visit Belfast City Hall and see hanging in the midst of Maurice Craig's 'eyetalian marbles', among the serried ranks of stodgy official portraits of previous worthies who have held the office of Lord Mayor (merging in the end into blown-up colour photographs), the witty, iconoclastic portrait of Cook by Neil Shawcross. Among all the pomp and false finery, cocking a cheerful and irreverent snook at all the others, here is a good painting of a little man with his legs not quite reaching the ground, dwarfed by the office and by the huge ceremonial chair in which he is ensconced.

Thanks mainly to Melchett's support, but also through adroit negotiation of the system, we managed to get the approval of the Department of Finance to the payment of £500,000 out of DHSS funds into a special trust, with a commitment to match every pound

239

the trust raised up to the limit of another £250,000. So, the trust could start off with a capital fund of about £1 million, good money at the time.

The Northern Ireland Voluntary Trust had the great good fortune to appoint Hugh Frazer, a socially committed and visionary young man with a hard streak of practicality, as its first director. He was succeeded by Paul Sweeney, a young graduate from Derry with a burning passion for justice, and, like Hugh, a deep sense of compassion. Between them, and with a succession of enlightened trustees under the leadership of David Cook, they earned support from all sides, attracted money from other larger trusts and financial institutions outside Northern Ireland, and built up an enviable record for innovation and creative thinking in the field of social policy.

During this time too I picked up the threads of the old Areas of Special Social Needs Programme which I had initiated a couple of years earlier in Central Secretariat, and which with Melchett's backing developed into a programme for the Belfast inner city under the title BAN (Belfast Areas of Need). This led on to the formation of a Co-ordinating Committee on Social Problems (CCOSP) which I chaired. It was an under-secretary-level committee designed to complement the Economic Steering Group which had been dominating policy formulation up to that time. This chairmanship gave me access to the Policy Co-ordinating Committee (the committee of permanent secretaries) to which I reported directly. It also gave the DHSS an opportunity to intervene in problems that crossed departmental boundaries or that appeared to have a social content, and to stir up a bit of trouble in other people's backyards.

In all this we had the backing of the permanent secretary at the DHSS, Norman Dugdale, a wonderful man to work for and one deeply committed to producing a fairer and more equal society. As well as that he was a poet of some quality, a widely and deeply read man, and the translator of the modern Greek poet C.P. Cavafy. The chemistry between himself and Melchett was excellent, as it had been with Paddy Devlin in the Executive. At about this time, Dugdale published a poem reflecting on the transience of Northern Ireland secretaries of state. It also reflected his own deep love for the place,

and his exasperation with manifestations of intolerance. The poem is
called 'Provincia Deserta':

> Well, here it is: not Botany Bay
> But a penal settlement all the same,
> The sentence life without remission – saving,
> Of course, Sir, such as yourself, gentlemen newly come
> To live here at the Governor's Lodge. Two years from now
> You will be safely home again and dining out
> On your bizarre experiences, which cannot fail
> To please your hostess and amuse the company.

Despite the troubles, this was an exciting period with many gifted
and dedicated people working at community level, many of them
former colleagues from the Community Relations Commission or
stimulated by the work we had started then. One of the most stimulating of these was Paddy Doherty in Derry, one of the greatest lateral
thinkers I have come across, unsurpassed in his grasp of the dynamics
of community and of urban development and regeneration. Also
inspiring, in Belfast particularly, were nuns in pairs or individually
who had come out of the large convents to live and work in the
community. They were a tremendous resource for the communities
and they had no political or other agenda. They were not particularly
appreciated by the Church, which would have preferred them to
work within parish structures performing traditionally feminine roles
under the control of the clergy. Among them, doing remarkable
work in Unity Flats for years, was the daughter of my old friend and
mentor Paddy O'Keeffe. In order to give them some support, I asked
Kate Kelly, a social worker in the department, to meet them as a
group once a month. Out of this came many important initiatives
involving women, who were to play an increasingly important part
in community development.

Another small aspect of policy that gave me pleasure at this time
was the development of a policy on travellers. There had been little
in the way of such a policy up to that time, despite an excellent report
commissioned from Sam Girvan of the Northern Ireland Labour
Party in the 1950s. It is true to say also that there was no universal
demand for such a policy initiative, and that I took a flier as chairman
of the CCOSP, aided by a very dedicated deputy principal called

Jimmy Kearney. Between us we extracted sufficient agreement for a policy that went beyond mere law-and-order issues, moving travellers along, and closing off possible camping sites. Belfast City Council had spent more money fencing off sites than would have built a proper facility. I remembered that during the sixties the only issue that had united Catholic and Protestant in Ardoyne had been opposition to the provision of a serviced site for travellers, and yet when Ardoyne was in flames and Farringdon Gardens burned down, the first people to come along offering help to move burned-out or intimidated families were the travellers. They had been through it all before themselves. The study was the first to get departments to see travellers as a group with characteristics or traditions of their own, and a separate, wandering lifestyle which they wished to preserve (we had not yet discovered 'ethnicity' or 'nomadism'). It also encouraged departments and agencies to look at the needs of the travellers in a multidisciplinary way involving housing, health, training and education. My earlier contact with the McDonaghs and Joyces in my Downpatrick days came in handy, as did my education from Bryan MacMahon on long drives across Ireland as he researched his book for Longmans, *Here's Ireland*, which he subsequently dedicated to me. This interest in travellers has remained with me. I have many good friends among them and I am glad to see them beginning to speak up for themselves and to assert the validity of their culture and their right to their own traditional way of life. It is also a joy to see educated travellers like Michael McDonagh and Ellen Mongan emerge as dignified, articulate and effective leaders of their own people.

Another interesting policy development was the Black Report, the work of an interdepartmental group set up to review the Children's Acts and the juvenile justice system. The chairman was Sir Harold Black, who had been Cabinet Secretary in the old Stormont and who had retired at the onset of the new regime. He had spent all his years in the civil service, having entered as a boy clerk and progressed steadily up every rung of the ladder. He had no particular expertise in the field, but he had been given the job of chairing the committee and he did it earnestly if a little doggedly and with a little too much inclination to accept the traditional wisdom. The committee also suffered from being composed entirely of civil servants (from three departments, the NIO, the DHSS and the Department of Education for Northern Ireland, DENI).

The committee had been floundering for a year or more and it was time to draw its work to a conclusion. There were, however, real difficulties. The NIO team included an impressive principal called Ronnie Sterling (whom we were later to headhunt for the DHSS) who had a good grasp of what was needed and very good relationships with the main players in the field, particularly the training schools. The Department of Education was not really interested. Its personnel took the view that Northern Ireland had the best schools in the world and that any child who was not totally aware of this, or who did not take full advantage of it, was somehow eccentric and not worth bothering about. At this critical moment, however, there emerged from DENI as an assistant secretary one of the most creative and thoughtful civil servants, Ernie Martin, who had the wit to get out and talk to people. Together, the three of us decided to take control of the Black Committee and make a job of it.

Another part of the problem was the outside vested interests in schools, especially the training schools, the educational psychologists, the social workers, the children's lay magistrates and the police. There was a great deal of friction between them. The schools simply wanted unruly children excluded and provided for by somebody else, the training schools (mainly run by religious orders and by boards of governors dominated by clergymen) wanted to extend their interests and staff, the social workers wanted all juvenile offenders let out, the lay magistrates (caring and compassionate souls that they were) wanted them all locked up. I spent a good deal of time in the juvenile courts getting a feel for the system, and I was appalled. I decided that if any of my children got into trouble, they should opt for trial in the ordinary criminal court where there would be some respect for what constituted evidence and where nobody would be trying to do good to them. Another factor: there was very little money to be made in legal practice in the children's courts and no great incentive to specialise in that area. I thought the level of advocacy and legal defence was very poor indeed. I watched one day when a young boy, having pleaded guilty on the advice of a callow young junior barrister to a not very serious charge, which might have merited probation in an older offender, was given a training school order which would keep him inside for two and a half years, after which his counsel thanked the court for its clemency to his client.

In the end, amid all the conflicting submissions, we carved out a report. When Harold Black was away on an extended visit to the USA, I found out from Ronnie and Ernie what the policy market would bear, and crafted a proposal in two pages. We speedily got Melchett's endorsement and proceeded to prod the committee (and the reluctant Sir Harold) to reach the same set of conclusions. I could not, however, persuade them to include as an epigraph Philip Larkin's lines: 'They fuck you up your mum and dad,/They do not mean to but they do.'

The Black Report stands examination today as a significant document in its field. It was based on the proposition that much juvenile crime or deviance was an aspect of puberty, especially among young boys, a rite of passage which most children grew out of except those who had been trapped by being caught or imprisoned, and that most children could be diverted by an effective early-warning system operating through the schools, which would pick up signs of incipient deviance and enable effective avoiding action to be taken. There were also, it was accepted, some children who were simply bad and who were a danger to themselves and others. For these there should be criminal proceedings and a range of options for the courts to ensure the most effective form of treatment (not excluding custody in proper conditions, but excluding physical punishment). This outcome of the report disappointed both the main camps: the social workers because it was not a Scottish children's panel system, and the training schools because it spelt their virtual demise as residential establishments.

I had spent some time during the incubation of the report trying to sow the seeds of change in the minds of the training school people. Visits to the training schools, particularly the Catholic ones, were always fraught with danger to health or sobriety. The more senior the official, the more likely he was to be 'parloured', a device much favoured by religious orders to deflect attention from what was going on in their institutions. The programme for ministerial visits therefore involved a short briefing session over welcoming drinks in the parlour, a huge, long and bibulous lunch, after which, with winter evenings drawing in, it was really too late to do the rounds, and in any case the children could be seen through the window, at a distance, playing happily, and the minister would return to the department extolling the work of the school and the good fortune of the children to have been sent there.

I had worked with a religious order for whose work in this field I had considerable respect and admiration, but I knew the form. I therefore called at about nine o'clock in the morning, generally unannounced. As a result of these visits, I came to the conclusion that most of the boys would have been better served by some form of day care. I knew many of the brothers personally, some as former colleagues in teaching. They were generally hard-working, dedicated men who really had the interests of the children at heart, but they were not very receptive to new ideas, and neither were the boards of governors, which consisted mainly of elderly clerics. It is fair to say that there were not many liberal figures among these, and there were some who believed in punitive measures for their own sake.

I tried to persuade the brothers to switch to day care on a wider basis. St Patrick's, the training school for Catholic boys, was situated between Ballymurphy and Andersonstown, on top of some of the most deprived urban areas in Western Europe, and with superb facilities, which you had to be an offender to be allowed to use. I suggested that they turn it into a family support unit for the area, with provision for remedial education, for the elderly and handicapped, and as a resource for young mothers. I offered to persuade the government to continue to commit funds at the rate of £1 million a year, but they would have none of it. The Protestant training schools (properly, the state-run ones – they were both 100 per cent financed) were no better. Indeed the regime in them was probably less enlightened, although they did not have to face the close proximity of terrorist violence and intimidation that bedevilled St Patrick's. The only bright light in the whole scene was a nun called Sister Carina Muldoon who ran a training school for girls at Middletown, on the border, to whom I would cheerfully have handed the whole childcare programme to run.

Just when the report was about to go to the printer, there was another huge hiccup in the form of a change of government. Callaghan, having called an election at the wrong time, was beaten, and so we said goodbye to Melchett.

I remember, in the last days of the Callaghan administration, late in 1978, being concerned that people seemed to think that the Provos were beaten. This was induced by the sorts of things Roy Mason was saying, and I took the unusual route for a civil servant of making my own representations to the top through an academic network. Through David Donnison, I went to see Bernard Donoughue, formerly of the LSE and now political adviser to Callaghan. I told him that the present lull was cyclical, that violence would increase, and viciously, and that government should be addressing itself to the politics of the situation. I said I did not expect anyone to do anything in the run-up to an election, but I would be consoled if I knew that somewhere in the bowels of 10 Downing Street there were people working on a position paper that could be used as a first-day briefing for a new prime minister (or a re-elected one). This would analyse the Northern Ireland problem and point out the policy options. The option taken – coercion, conciliation, or political initiative – would colour the selection of the most suitable person to carry out the policy as secretary of state.

Donoughue told me that this government had time only to deal with those issues that were included in the first three items on the national news on any day. Furthermore, he said, if he were to draw up a list of the thirty issues causing most concern to government, Northern Ireland would not figure on it. At that point I gave up. I also spoke to Tom McNally, Callaghan's press secretary, who was passionately interested in the fortunes of Blackpool football club, and to Joe Haines at the *Daily Mirror*, whom I had met formerly with Wilson. Haines could only talk about his own book, which he thought explained everything, and the 'troops out' line he was propagating in the *Daily Mirror*.

Mason was replaced by Humphrey Atkins, universally referred to as 'Humphrey who?', and Michael Alison, a decent, worthy man, was appointed to look after the DHSS. What was a bigger problem in relation to the Black Report was that the new government had been returned on a stiff law-and-order ticket, which it took as a mandate to crack down on offenders. Melchett had not really liked the criminal justice element in Black. He would have preferred a child-centred, care-based system. We were able to persuade him that that was what he was getting, that 85–90 per cent of the children would remain in the care system, and that it would be a pity to allow the 10 per cent of young tearaways who beat up and robbed old ladies and who would generally be in the 16–18 age group to contaminate that care system. Better, therefore, to screen them out into the criminal justice system.

For Alison we had to stand that argument on its head. There were a number of really bad boys, perhaps 15–20 per cent of the total, who deserved to be dealt with severely. It would be a pity to dilute the rigour required there by mixing them with what were essentially and clearly care cases. Better therefore to screen these out into a welfare system. So Alison bought our approach too, and the Black Report was published and adopted as government policy.

Unfortunately, and this exemplified the dangers to progress in the civil service system, at this stage, all three of the senior civil servants who had thrown their energy and abilities into getting it adopted moved on to other things; for whatever reason, the subject slipped down the political agenda, and the forces of reaction were given time to regroup. The most persistent lobbyists against the report were the training schools. No secretary of state was anxious, given all the troubles he faced, to provoke a row with the churches, and certainly not with all of them together, and not in the interests of a few hundred little boys. And so the training schools still hang on today, not quite withering on the vine, but ensuring that a couple of hundred young boys are locked up in order to ensure the continuance of institutions and in order to keep staff gainfully employed,

One shameful effect of the change of government was the attempt to vet voluntary bodies for docility or political acceptability. (This was not the political vetting that was to become an issue in future years but it was perhaps the forerunner of it and showed the way people's minds were working.) We had made a grant to NICVA, the Northern Ireland Council for Voluntary Action (in Hugh Frazer's time) to run a magazine called *Scope*. Supported almost totally from government funds, this journal showed a healthy propensity to bite the hand that fed it, and it was often critical of aspects of government policy. Now we were made to feel that this was not allowable, and it required some doggedness, especially by Norman Dugdale, to keep the grant alive.

Another example of the change in attitudes arose in relation to a small group called CARA/Friend, which ran an information and advice service for gays. We had had some doubt about supporting them in the beginning, and checked them out with more than usual care. We also imposed conditions that they should not counsel children and that each young person should be counselled jointly by two counsellors. They kept all the rules, gave us no trouble, kept proper accounts and did good work in their own field. On the change of government we were advised by our contacts in Whitehall that a grant to the Albany Trust, a similar body in England, had been withdrawn for no good reason in a fit of homophobic pique. The civil servants in Whitehall apparently thought the whole thing rather shabby. I declined to take any action and the grant was recommended in the usual way.

The new minister picked up a reference to it and asked to see Norman and myself. He was an entirely conscientious man, no ideologue, but concerned about exposing young people to moral danger. We explained the conditions that had been imposed, and observed that we were not in the business of funding a dating agency for gays but that there had seemed to be a need for information in an accessible form, and that this responsible organisation seemed to be best placed to meet it. Alison seemed about to be satisfied with this when in burst the strangest figure, Dr Gerald Vaughan, a health minister in England, who was on a short visit. Alison invited him to listen to the discussion and I began a most long-winded and obscure explanation of what CARA/Friend was about. At this a private secretary who was travelling with Vaughan piped up, 'Minister, it sounds just like the Albany Trust.' 'Yes,' said Vaughan, 'and we took the grant off them.'

After this there was an awkward bit of sparring after which Alison agreed to look at the issue again. Eventually, more by default than otherwise, the grant was preserved (it was only a few thousand pounds a year anyhow), and some years later, when the AIDS scare arose, some people were very glad that there was an organisation in existence like CARA/Friend which could be used to run an AIDS helpline, and be given even more money to do so.

One amusing side issue was that the British government, in defending a case brought by Jeffrey Dudgeon in the European Court of Human Rights because of Britain's failure to change the Northern

Ireland law on homosexuality, found the grant to CARA/Friend cited as an example of inconsistency. Incidentally, Dudgeon was an employee of the DHSS. He won his case, and effected the change whereby the law in Northern Ireland was brought into line with the rest of the United Kingdom.

Another development of these years was in the field of policy for the mentally handicapped. Since 1948 Northern Ireland had had a pioneering special care service for mentally handicapped people. This involved a range of special care schools and workshops, and a few large hospitals devoted to mentally handicapped people. Although those in charge were all devoted people and much appreciated, they worked from a philosophy of total dependence and continuing total care, and they operated on the basis of withdrawing the handicapped from the community, both in the schools, and in the large, and very crowded, hospitals, and in which so many people spent so long that they became institutionalised.

The problem was to nudge the service along into a more modern concept of care, which would recognise and respect the dignity of the individual, which would place no limits on expectations and impose no arbitrary barriers on performance or participation. The existing system smothered the children with care, and in doing so almost suffocated them. I reminded myself of the legend that appears on the Parnell monument in Dublin, *No man has a right to put a bound to the onward march of a nation*, and applied it as a warning not to underestimate the potential of *any* human being.

At this time, I met an amazing man called Joe Hughes from Ballymurphy, who despite severe disabilities, virtually no speech, and being confined to a wheelchair, had raised large sums of money for charity. This he did by sponsored wheelchair circuits of the City Hall, or by a sponsored wheelchair trek to Dublin. He propelled his wheelchair backwards, which created difficulty from time to time. Once a group of soldiers, seeing him halfway up a hill, jumped out and assisted him by pushing him in the direction he was facing, to the bottom. He was unable to explain to them quickly or forcefully enough that he was actually trying to go in the opposite direction and had got halfway there through great efforts. As a result of his charitable work, Joe was recommended for an MBE which he accepted, quite unusually for Ballymurphy, and was very proud of.

He communicated by means of a stick and an alphabet board which he used to spell out his words, and an expressive range of guttural sounds. Once I asked a social worker to investigate the possibilities of using new technology to help Joe communicate. The department eventually discovered a small electronic keyboard which produced a visual message on a screen clamped to the arm of a wheelchair, and a typed-out message on a sort of ticker-tape. We got this for Joe, but he lost patience with it and soon went back to his old alphabet board, which he used much more quickly.

Joe told me that his speech defect, which he had had from birth, had resulted in his being put in Purdysburn mental hospital, and that his other injuries, which had put him in a wheelchair for life, had been caused by assaults by older patients.

Incidentally, Joe was one of the relatively few people, I thought, who actually deserved the honour they got. I have a deep aversion to the present honours system, an aversion that has nothing to do with constitutional politics. I think that a state should have a means of recognising those who have made a special contribution. There should be something like an Order of Merit for people who invent penicillin or things like that, or who create great works of art or literature. And there should be something to recognise bravery or voluntary unpaid effort for the community. What I object to are the honours that come up with the rations, honours that are distributed to civil servants just because they have reached a certain level, and irrespective of whether they have done more than just turn up for work regularly. Later, when I was involved in recommending people for honours, the general cynicism with which honours were offered, and in some cases received, only served to dissipate further my faith in the present honours system.

In the end, after much consultation, we produced a policy document which pointed the way towards normalisation, towards keeping mentally handicapped people in the community, towards allowing them to act as far as possible like other members of society, and towards getting mentally handicapped people out of the long-stay psychiatric hospitals, where a small number were still inappropriately placed.

My ideal was to keep the mentally handicapped person in the family for as long as family members could cope, and to provide sufficient support from the statutory services to enable them to do so. This might involve respite care, or holiday relief, or a guarantee that the responsibility would be lifted from them when it became a burden they could no longer manage, or reassuring parents that their mentally handicapped son or daughter would be cared for after their deaths. It also meant supporting the mentally handicapped in in-dependent or semi-independent living in the community, helping them into employment, or into activity in the arts or sport to the extent of their capability. There would, of course, be a need for short-term or medium-term hospital care, and some would need long-term care or asylum. The job of the carer was to find the ap-propriate mix for each case and to make almost an individual contract with each family.

An unsuspected by-product of normalisation was the reaction of both staff and parents who had become accustomed to cosseting. To take one small example, normalisation meant that mentally handi-capped pupils who were otherwise mobile should walk to school like other pupils and not be taken in special buses; it meant that they should not be lifted and laid as if they had no social competence whatsoever. Developing the policy involved countless visits and discussions in hospitals, schools and workshops. Selling it required another round of discussions with clinicians, with carers and with parents. In this respect Mencap was a wonderful body. Another important development I was glad to support was the Special Olym-pics. Both were steered by Evelyn Greer, who left a legacy in this field that generations of mentally handicapped people will be grateful for. At this time too, we started the movement, which I was glad to complete when I returned to the department, of transferring the schools to the Education and Library Boards and to the mainstream of education. I was always struck that the Catholic Church took very little interest in the special care schools, as if the children, never by their standards likely to come to the use of reason, were not likely to start a heresy either, and therefore need not be bothered with.

Another part of the battle, of course, was to get the programme included in the development plans of the department and the boards, and to secure the funds for this. This, I often thought, was where you really earned your corn, and where the network of relationships built up with many people in the system began to pay off.

As the policy developed and things began to happen, it was very rewarding to go round the new community facilities, the small hostels and shared houses, and see people who had been immured in hospital for years, forgotten and written out of life, finding themselves again with a degree of independence and beginning to function as contributing members of society. This, I think, is the real meaning of care in the community. It is not cheap care versus expensive care. It pains me to see community care used as a cost-saving slogan, employed simply to close institutions and to fling people out of care and on to the streets.

When I was under-secretary in the DHSS, Ken Shimeld called me in one day and asked me to accept appointment as a shadow regional commissioner to act in the event of a nuclear attack. There was to be a shadow administration of permanent secretaries, the RUC Chief Constable and the army GOC in a central headquarters outside the Belfast area, and four regional commands based roughly on the health board areas. At a given signal they were to retire to bomb-proof bunkers in predetermined locations and sit out the attack and the radioactive fallout and then emerge to begin to set up a civil administration and to pick up the pieces.

Each shadow controller was to pick a team drawn from the main agencies and prepare them in secret for action. Headquarters were to be selected, planned and built and the whole thing was to be in place in a couple of years. I was told that members of shadow teams could take their families with them to the bunkers and would be assured of survival.

I treated the whole idea with scepticism and a good degree of levity. Although advised to discuss the matter with my family, I did not do so, partly because I did not want to alarm them, partly no doubt from an inability to face the real issues of choice that would be involved, but mainly because it did not seem worth while to raise a volcano of anxiety and discussion about an event that seemed to me highly unlikely ever to take place. At best, it was a diversion from the problems of everyday life in Northern Ireland, where the threat was much more real and the likelihood of a violent death much more proximate. Incidentally, these were issues I did not raise much in the family circle either.

I was aware that any civil servant could be at risk, a Catholic civil servant doubly so. There were those on the republican side who could see me as a collaborator, as someone to be made an example of, as someone who had deserted the loyalties which should have commanded him. It only needed a stroke of a pen to change the policy and add civil servants to the list of acceptable targets which included police, judges, prison officers. Or some local hero might be looking for a target, or simply to fill a quota. On the other side there was the risk that loyalist paramilitaries would seek to remove a possible infiltrator, or Catholics who had got above themselves, or simply any Catholic, or seek a suitably prominent Catholic figure on whom to exact a symbolic revenge for murders committed by the IRA. I sometimes thought I might run the risk of being shot for a set of political beliefs I did not profess, or for adherence to a set of theological propositions which I found increasingly unsatisfactory. In the end, I suppose, it did not matter. I did not want to be shot, whether by mistake or otherwise. The thing I dreaded most was the fate of so many policemen and others of being murdered in the presence of their families and in the sight of their children. That would leave them with a legacy of hate and a potential desire for revenge which would be corrosive and destructive of their own lives.

However, I was fairly fatalistic about all this and tried to keep a sense of proportion. Above all, I did not want fear to invade the home or to distress the children by inducing the belief that they, or I, were at risk. I varied my route to work as much as was reasonable, I unobtrusively looked under the car when I could, I did not announce in advance my intention to visit strange places, I tried to be unpredictable in my movements (which suited my temperament quite well), but beyond that I avoided ostentatious displays or visible signs of security - special lighting, fencing, locks, surveillance cameras, or whatever. I reckoned that if you advertised to the world that you expected to be a target, somebody might actually make you one.

While I tried to protect my family from anxiety on these matters, it was inevitable I suppose that something would seep through from television and elsewhere. I remember once in the middle seventies driving my six-year-old daughter and a friend along the dual carriageway towards Stormont. When the building appeared high on the hill she said, 'That's Stormont. That's where my daddy works. I hope they don't blow it up.' To which her little friend replied, 'I hope they don't blow it up either. That's where my granda gets his old age pension from.'

But to get back to the fantasy world of civil defence. I assembled a team, all of whom shared my doubts. I would not like to have put much money on how many of us would actually have turned up on the day of doom – including myself. The whole thing quickly descended to the level of charade. At first we were told that money was available for the regional headquarters, which would be built as a matter of urgency. Then there was a progressive retreat by the Treasury. When the alternative was to drop services, civil defence was an easy target for cuts. The first major cut came when it was decreed that there would not be room in the bunkers for families (except maybe the families of regional controllers). I could see my little flock of intrepid pioneers melt away (as my own commitment did rapidly).

In the middle of all this, I was sent on a training course at a civil defence college run by the Home Office at a remote location in north Yorkshire. The college was straight out of *Dr Strangelove*. We were lectured by retired admirals and generals who were still in about year two of the Cold War, to whom the red menace was omnipresent and growing, and the destructive power of the Bomb getting bigger and bigger. They took a very poor view of levity and of anything less than total commitment to the cause of anticommunism. There was very little philosophical reflection, except on the importance of being more powerful than the next gang. There was a suggestion that once the safe period arrived, controllers should go out and commandeer all available cattle. I pointed out the likely response to such a demand in Crossmaglen. There was no thought about the effect of a land frontier in Northern Ireland, no real attempt at sociological analysis or projection, no reference to the fact that the survival teams were predominantly male. Noah had made a better fist of it.

I found the whole thing a turn-off, and this translated rapidly into the preparations we were making. We were told that there was no money for area headquarters, then to stop looking for one, then that there might be only one really secure and fortified place for the regional headquarters and the rest of us would have to fend for ourselves at a lower level of survivability. At this stage, my team and I and downed tools on the pretext that until a headquarters had been settled there was no point in bothering. Shortly after this, I became a permanent secretary and lost my high command and the promise of immortality. I never heard any more about it.

15
PEOPLE AND PROBLEMS

IN SEPTEMBER 1980, AFTER FOUR YEARS IN THE DHSS, I moved on promotion to deputy secretary to the Department of the Civil Service, DOCS. I had resisted some earlier proposals to move because I was very happy in what I was doing, and I was engaged in some interesting policy developments which I wished to carry through. (It is one of the weaknesses of the civil service that you tend to get moved around to meet the exigencies of the service, or because somebody retires or dies and starts a chain reaction of moves and promotions. You very rarely get the opportunity to see a project through.) I had previously been offered a post in the NIO which involved heading up the prison division. I declined on the grounds that I was more conditioned to letting people go than to locking them up. From time to time I have wondered whether this was not mere evasion, if not moral cowardice, whether I just did not want to get my hands dirtied, or whether subliminally I was worried about the heightened security risks and the constraints this posting would place on my family life. I have had some twinges of conscience too about whether I might not have been able to encourage a more humane prison regime (or at least one more sensitive to the peculiar nuances of the Northern Ireland situation), and perhaps to obviate the traumas of the dirty protest and the horrors of the hunger strikes and the political and social turmoil and the deaths and destruction that flowed from both.

I knew little or nothing about the technicalities of civil service establishment, or personnel management, work. I had no great desire to leave the interesting, and I thought valuable, work I was engaged in, but I could not be a no-man all the time, and I talked to Norman Dugdale who advised me that if I wished to progress, I should have experience in a central department such as Finance or the DOCS. So I went to talk to Ken Shimeld, who annoyed me by referring to my relative lack of experience. I pointed out that I had not sprung out of the ground when I came into the civil service, and that I had spent seventeen years before that in the trenches of local government. However, I agreed to go and the transfer was made.

It was typical of the civil service of the time that there was virtually no handover briefing, and no preparation for the new post. When I tried to read my way into it, I found that there were no books either, which reflected the lack of conceptual thinking, the lack of interest in theory or in developments in the wider world of personnel management which characterised DOCS at the time. In the end, I was reduced to asking one of my junior colleagues in the DHSS, who had been a trade union activist, to lend me a copy of a standard book on the Whitley system for industrial relations in the civil service.

In the Department of the Civil Service I had the great good fortune to work with Bobby Christie, a former colleague in the DHSS who had been one of my assistant secretaries on the Health and Personal Social Services (HPSS) personnel side. Christie was a man of great integrity and honesty, a highly respected former establishment officer dealing with personnel matters, and a rock of sense. As well as that, he was very good fun to be with, a gardener and a former athlete. We soon worked out a way to run the department despite the best efforts of Shimeld, who was a bit of a bluffer. He had a most annoying habit of insisting that we must hold the line firmly in negotiation with the staff side, and then giving away our positions, and more, in private conversations with senior trade union people behind our backs. He talked tough, but recoiled rapidly from any personal confrontation. He was nevertheless a personable man with an interest in the arts and cricket. It was sad that his career should have ended abruptly in 1984 after he found a bomb placed under his car outside his house on the Malone Road. It was hard to see why he had been a target because he was not in a high-profile job, and he was basically a man of liberal instincts who had done his best to open up the civil service to new influences and to promote anti-discriminatory practices. The experience shattered him and he took early retirement and returned to England, where he died soon afterwards. After this, Bob and I were on our own working directly to Ewart Bell, Head of the Northern Ireland Civil Service. We found out that Shimeld's last act had been to scuttle the ship he had himself commissioned, and to agree to the disbandment of the DOCS and its amalgamation with the Department of Finance.

Both the DOCS and the Department of Finance had suffered greatly from cronyism in the past. People were promoted there who would not have been advanced in other departments, most of them far beyond their competence. They were a small coterie on their own and they commanded little respect in other departments. The Whitley system which they operated was futile too, involving a ritualistic exchange between the chairman of the staff side and the chairman of the official side, each flanked by a dozen or so people who were silent all the time. Of course, preceding and following these elaborate minuets, private understandings and deals were done on the side, but they did not make the process any more sensible. Shimeld professed great openness, but he would not let us involve departmental assistant secretaries in the discussions. They were the people at the coalface with day-to-day experience of the real issues, but he treated them with contempt and we had to deal with them almost surreptitiously. Shimeld was also representative of another group, the administrative trainees who had joined the service straight from university through the 'fast stream' competition. They were nearly all English. They had not come high enough on the list for Whitehall or the diplomatic service and instead had got into the Northern Ireland Civil Service. They tended to look after each other, to push each other for promotions and for favourable postings. They looked upon themselves as more liberal, more sophisticated, more arty than their Northern Ireland fellows – but in the end they did little to leaven the lump of unionism, and there is little sign of their having fought any crusades to open up the higher reaches of the service to Catholics or to encourage diversification. By my time, most of them were passing out on retirement, but there was a simmering feeling of resentment among their colleagues. One interesting feature of this cadre of English-born officers is that they found the suspension of Stormont quite a shock, they did not take easily to direct rule, they were edgy in their dealings with the NIO, and most of them returned to live in England on their retirement.

After Shimeld's departure I began to represent the department at monthly Establishment Officers meetings in Whitehall and at conferences, and this was another welcome diversion. Many of the people I met were high-fliers who had served stints as personal secretaries to ministers. They had been very close to the political system and to the personalities who manned it, and they had fascinating insights into the personal performance of ministers and the working of democratic politics. At one conference at Sunningdale, early in 1981, we were addressed by James Prior, then Secretary of State for Employment. I sat beside him at dinner and we had a long discussion about Northern Ireland. Afterwards he spoke very frankly to the group about his disenchantment with the direction the Tory Party was taking, and his dislike of many of his colleagues. He regarded them as totally ignorant of the basic principles of man management and industrial relations, and told how he would dull their appetite for change by bringing in a boring green paper followed by a boring white paper in the hope that even the zealots would lose interest in the reforms they were proposing. I thought him a refreshingly open man, and one who would make a fine Secretary of State for Northern Ireland. A few months later, there he was in Stormont, his version of the Siberian salt mines, sent into internal exile by Mrs Thatcher as an alternative to the exterior darkness.

Prior brought along with him probably the best ministerial team to work in the NIO: Grey Gowrie, Nick Scott, and later Chris Patten. Gowrie was an interesting and flamboyant character. A poet and a student of literature, he was the first minister I had who could pick up a copy of *Finnegans Wake* from my desk and discuss it intelligently (or at all). He was disarmingly frank in his approach. 'When my friends heard I was going to Belfast, they said, "Ah! Stormont! The Avignon of the wets!"' I advised him to choose another metaphor, that some people in Belfast thought one Pope was enough, and any thought that there might have been two at the same time would be more than they could bear.

Prior and Gowrie between them had done much to lance the boil of the hunger strikes. Atkins had been a disaster, and Alison, his man on prisons, an essentially decent but weak man, had been far out of his depth. The NIO was in thrall to the Prison Officers' Association, the POA, who threatened to down tools and walk out at the first sign of compromise. What became clear was that if you lock two groups of people up together without respect, they brutalise each other. This was true both of prisoners and of prison officers, who were as much captives of the situation as those they were guarding. Indeed, they were even more at risk because even off-duty they were exposed to a campaign of murder and intimidation.

The stupid thing about government policy was that it allowed in-essentials to be elevated to the status of principle. It should have been possible, from an early stage, to say that any prisoner could wear his own clothes, that study was an acceptable alternative to prison work, and that association could be permitted at a level that did not allow the place to be run on the lines of a prisoner-of-war camp. The dirty protest that the policy induced resulted in a degree of collegiality that enabled the prisoners to carry through the greater sacrifice of the hunger strikes. Even when a compromise was reached after the first aborted hunger strike, it broke down over the petty bureaucracy that defined non-prison uniform as civilian clothes supplied by the prison authorities. The trouble was that no concession could be made that did not enrage the POA, and changes in the regime that would make sense in the Northern Ireland context were refused because of the fear of a read-across to English and Scottish prisons, which would bring objections from the Home Office. The hunger strikes, bringing with them heightened emotions in the community, were a severe trial for the civil service, yet here again, as in the Ulster Workers' Council strike, the centre held, people turned up for work, strike calls went unheeded, and the tensions of the outside world, by and large, did not enter the workplace. There were some particular difficulties in the Falls Road DHSS office, where the mother of one of the hunger strikers worked, and in other places in closed communities, but the general picture was of another crisis that the service had survived.

So in the end, when Prior and Gowrie after a decent interval pro-duced changes in the regime that met many if not all of the essential demands of the hunger strikers, and when one saw that the prison system did not fall into anarchy as a result, it made one wonder why ten men had to die to achieve them.

Strangely enough, I heard a senior colleague paying a glowing tribute to the prison administration at the time. I had to ask him by what criteria he measured excellence: the prisons budget was out of control, the prisons were run by the Prison Officers' Association, there had been a dirty protest, and ten men had died.

But most of the work in the Department of the Civil Service was less dramatic. First there was in April 1982 the merging of the department with the Department of Finance to produce the Department of Finance and Personnel. This was an attempt to achieve the best deployment of resources, both human and financial. It was to be a lean department, focused on essentials, stripped of the minor functions and agencies that both departments had assumed over the years. This was the opportunity for me to work closely with George Quigley, an opportunity that was to cement an old friendship and develop mutual respect. George had enormous cerebral horsepower, and produced enough ideas to keep the average government department going for years at a time. He read deeply and widely and was an interesting and pleasant companion on many a long stopover at airports as we travelled to and from London. By the departmental amalgamation, I became virtually head of personnel for the Northern Ireland Civil Service, with responsibilities for 18,000–20,000 civil servants, a far cry from the slender staff and humble resources of the council in Downpatrick. The position also brought me into fairly constant attendance at the Policy Co-ordinating Committee and involvement in senior promotions.

Between Bobby Christie and myself and along with the assistant secretaries in the main employing departments, now released to creative activity, we tried to develop systems for career development, for training and staff development, for planned transfers between departments, and for selection for the senior posts. We were trying to develop systems that would be fair and open, and that would be proof against ministerial interference or patronage in the event of a return to a local devolved administration. It was, however, a difficult time in which to maintain morale within the civil service, which in the Tory press was being assailed on all sides by Tory ministers, and especially by the prime minister, Margaret Thatcher, who represented all civil servants as barnacles on the ship of state, as parasites, as in no way comparable to their counterparts in the private sector.

There was indeed a job to be done in the public service to tighten up management, to get people to work to objectives, with some regard for the effective use of resources, to get middle management to reassert itself and regain the ground that had been surrendered to the unions, but it was difficult to preach this message, and harder still to get a hearing for it, while the members of your audience were being denigrated by their main employer, intent at all times on asserting their worthlessness and basic untrustworthiness. The task of mediating between Mrs Thatcher and her staff was not a particularly rewarding one, which I was glad to get out of when the opportunity came to return to the DHSS.

My relatively short stay in personnel exemplified for me other weaknesses of the civil service system: the commitment to generalism and the failure to develop specialist interests, and the tendency to rotate people through posts every couple of years or oftener. There is a perfectly sustainable approach to career development that suggests that people likely to get to senior positions should have experience in more than one department, and should have some knowledge of personnel and finance. But this is a relatively small cadre and it makes no sense for everybody to play musical chairs all the time. There is also the domino effect of changes through a system where one piece displaced requires the rearrangement of all the others. There was a tendency in senior management, even when convinced of the value of career plans for individuals, to sacrifice both the plan and the long-term needs of the organisation to block whatever particular hole in the dyke was letting in water at the time.

There was also the fallacy that anyone could do anything at this level if thrown in at the deep end. I had been projected into the personnel post with no knowledge whatsoever of civil service industrial relations and with no preparation. Whilst over the years I found changes in posting very refreshing, and the equivalent of a postgraduate degree in the amount of reading one had to do to master the brief, nevertheless the constant changes were not conducive to the continuing efficiency of the organisation. One by-product of this in the industrial relations field was that while the chairman of the trade union side had occupied his seat continuously for twelve years, there had been no fewer than five people in my seat on the official side. This left all the strength in negotiation with the trade unions.

It also made it very difficult to build and sustain the network of personal relationships on which any successful handling of industrial relations crucially depends. I was determined to make a change this time and I fought hard for the appointment of a real personnel man with a long track record in negotiation to take my place.

An abiding memory of the personnel job is the number of odd cases that arose. In a very large organisation you get all sorts, and what appeared as cases of inefficiency, insubordination, bad health or bad behaviour often disclosed the most bizarre domestic and personal situations which required a great deal of tact, patience and compassion to deal with as humanely as possible.

One aspect of the job that I found unusual was the responsibility for civil service security. On the one hand this involved inquiries into leaks of classified information, about which ministers tended to be inordinately sensitive. My experience led me to several broad conclusions: that leak inquiries are the supreme example of locking the stable door after the horse has bolted; that most information is over-classified anyhow and would create no stir if placed regularly in the public domain without the added glamour of a leak; that politicians find it hard to distinguish between information that really endangers public security and information that merely embarrasses the government; and that most leakages occur at the political level and over the dinner table rather than from officials. I am a firm believer in something like a Freedom of Information Act which would be a better protection of human rights and a better curb on the misuse of power, if linked with a strong and free press, than almost anything else.

Another aspect of security was the routine vetting of applicants for civil service jobs. I was anxious, having begun to establish norms of fair employment in the civil service, that the effects of these should not be negated by the application of criteria on grounds of security which ordained that it would be unsafe to employ people from this or that area, or from a particular political or social background. It is of course allowable to wish not to employ people who have been guilty of serious crimes, but exclusion should be on the basis of conviction, not suspicion, and it was important to remove the danger of guilt by association. So we devised a set of procedures which tried to ensure that criteria were objectively applied, that decisions were taken at a reasonably senior level, and that there was a means of appeal against an unfavourable decision.

Having been involved in the formation of the new Department of Finance and Personnel, in the exercise to combine the departments of Commerce and Manpower Services into the Department of Economic Development, and in setting up the Industrial Development Board, it was with some relief that I responded to Norman Dugdale's call in February 1983 to return to the DHSS as deputy secretary, and in the fairly sure hope of succeeding him as permanent secretary.

16
'THE CARING DEPARTMENT'

I RETURNED TO THE DHSS ON the hospital side, but with responsibility also for health services personnel. An oblique compliment that I enjoyed arose when one of the toughest of the trade union negotiators welcomed my return, saying, 'If Maurice isn't going to give you something he'll say so at the start and you don't waste time arguing about it.' There was indeed a difficult industrial relations problem arising out of the minister's refusal to give a guarantee of no compulsory redundancies in a case of restructuring some middle management grades. A strike was threatened. I asked the people in the department how many redundancies were likely. The pessimists said six, the optimists none at all. I went to the minister and pointed out that there were sixty thousand health service workers in Northern Ireland, that there were many and pressing personnel problems, and he was proposing to fight a bloody battle over six possible redundancies. He saw the point, and we were able to give the guarantee that satisfied the unions. In the end there were no compulsory redundancies. Later in the negotiations the minister asked me how things were going. As they were at quite a delicate stage, I simply said that the soufflé was in the oven. He took that as a hint not to open the door.

An early task on returning to the DHSS was to face the possibility of a public inquiry into what had become known as the Kincora scandal. This had surfaced during my previous period in the department when I was directly involved in social policy, especially child care. Kincora was a hostel for youths in care on the Newtownards

Road not far from the main gates of Stormont. The boys generally went out to work or to school each day and returned in the evening. They were looked after by a completely male staff. I remember at the time I had become concerned about the change in approach in social work practice that had downgraded the inspectorial role of the department's social work service to an advisory counselling role depending mainly on management in the Health and Social Services Boards to maintain standards and discipline. This was in line with developments generally at the time when management throughout the health service had become more diffused and less demanding, and when social work practice had tended to reflect concern rather than the hard-nosed application of standards.

Since the department had the residual responsibility for the well-being of children committed to its care – although delegated to its agents, the boards – I thought we should return to a more rigorous and regular inspection system to ensure that standards were being maintained and abuses checked. I was nudging the Social Work Service in this direction, and the chief social work adviser, Jimmy Wilde, and I began a series of visits to various homes and establishments to enable us to form a preliminary view of what was going on in the system. We began with what we thought the most likely places for problems to emerge: in large, oldfashioned, rather institutionalised children's homes in remote places in the country, generally in large old houses with extensive grounds. There we could see the dangers of children being isolated – especially if there was a school on the premises, so that children exposed to the danger of mistreatment might be cut off from contact with the wider world and unable to find anyone to complain to who would believe them, or even listen. Down at the bottom of our list of possible danger spots were hostels of the type of Kincora, not too large, on the edge of a busy street, with boys going out to work and school every day with lots of opportunities for contact with adults outside the home to whom complaints could be made or concerns addressed.

How wrong we were. The story broke on a Saturday morning in January 1980, a story by Peter McKenna in the *Irish Independent* quoting Gerry Fitt as a source and alleging sexual abuse of boys in the home by members of staff and others. I realised at once that it was serious, and knowing that I would have to brief Norman Dugdale and ministers on a course of action on the Monday, I phoned Gerry as the source of the story and went up to see him in his house on the Antrim Road. The house was like a fortress, with wire mesh on the front windows to deter loyalist attackers, and an elaborate locking system on the door. He took me out to the back to see the fortifications there, a cagework of iron mesh which had been erected to prevent stoning and invasion by his more aggressive republican neighbours. Gerry, even at this time, was under constant attack from Provo supporters from the New Lodge for his denunciations of IRA activity. Having spoken briefly to Anne, who supplied us with tea and toys for my young son, Dara, who had come with me, we went downstairs to the basement kitchen with Gerry. Over a couple of hours I had a typical Gerry performance, enlivened with anecdotes, with side issues, with biting but shrewd comment on all the main actors, and with yards and yards of unproven and unfounded allegations. I was not much further on. It was clear that Gerry had no more information than he had already given to the journalist, and that he had no direct personal knowledge of events. I suspected that he had been informed mainly by policemen from Donegall Pass barracks who were concerned about homosexual activity in the city centre, and that Kincora had been almost a peripheral issue, except that reports sent up to their superiors were not acted on, and the files sent up about it appeared to keep getting lost at headquarters.

What did strike me though, over the three hours or so that I was there, was the number of people who phoned up out of the blue to offer him more information about the home. In fairness to Gerry, he advised them all to take their information straight to the police. After one lengthy call he told me that it was from a bloody mad woman who alleged that some prominent politicians and churchmen knew all about it and had done nothing. Gerry could not decide whether she was paranoid or not, but he salivated at where he thought the story was leading.

I also went to see Jack Hermon, then RUC deputy chief constable, to tell him that the DHSS wished to have the matter thoroughly and effectively investigated. In the press stories, there had been allegations of a cover-up in the past, and I wanted to ensure that one did not happen again. I told him I was concerned on two points: that the investigating officers would carry out their job in a way that did not put pressure on children who were already disturbed and distressed, and that if it was discovered in the course of the investigation that there were reasonable grounds for suspecting that children were in continuing danger of abuse from either staff or others, the DHSS should be told immediately so that action could be taken to protect them. Hermon was most helpful and brought in Detective George Caskey who was in charge of the investigation and told him that he should report directly to me should such an eventuality arise.

I made another visit to find out some more information. Since rumours abounded, the place to find rumour was in the marketplace. There was, it seemed, a loyalist paramilitary connection with Kincora. I manufactured a reason for calling on an old acquaintance of mine from community relations days, who could best be described as being on the UDA reserve list. He was now involved in community work and I called to his house on the pretext of talking about this.

When we had finished our business, I broached the matter of Kincora and asked him if he had heard anything about it. He said he had. I said, 'There are a lot of strange rumours circulating about it.'

'I know,' he said. 'I spread them.'

When you allow for the Walter Mittyism of these characters and their tendency to exaggeration and self-glorification, the story he told me was still amazing. After Gusty Spence had been convicted and imprisoned for the Malvern Street murder, in the late sixties, the Ulster Volunteer force (UVF) had been in disarray and felt the need to regroup. They also needed a cover and they decided to shelter behind a zany Orange lodge called Ireland's Heritage. They were headed by a man called William McGrath who was a deputy housemaster at Kincora. After a while they got too big for their boots and had to be discredited. This was done by forged letters alleging sexual impropriety with the boys, written on a typewriter which was afterwards disposed of in the dam of the Edenderry Mill. (My source said they had done something similar to discredit a unionist politician whom they did not like.) When I asked him whether there was any truth in the rumours, he said, 'None at all! Decent man McGrath.' By this stage I had rather different information about Willie McGrath; but I held my peace.

A few weeks after this, I was at a wake in Ardglass on a Friday evening when I got a call from Detective Caskey. He said he was at the airport and wished to see me immediately. He came to my home in Downpatrick and told me the result of his inquiries. He had just returned from interviewing a former Kincora boy who was now a male prostitute in London, and the youth had given him enough information to justify the laying of charges against the three top people in Kincora. He told me that I could not use the information directly since he had not yet reported to his superiors.

The story he told was a chilling one in all its stark detail. It confirmed all our worst fears and the worst of the rumours that directly involved the home. I was in no doubt that urgent action was necessary, and I immediately phoned the Director of Social Services of the Eastern Board and asked him to meet me the next morning. He offered to come to Downpatrick and to bring with him the appropriate district officer. I told them both that on the basis of information I had been given in confidence, I had no doubt that the children were in danger and that they should take immediate steps to remove the top management of Kincora from access to the boys. I told them that a policeman had been sufficiently concerned to travel in his own time on a Friday evening to Downpatrick to tell me so that prompt action could be taken to protect the boys. I told them that there were several options open to them under the procedures, ranging from precautionary suspension (which would already have been justified by the stories in the paper) to sick leave, or study leave, or transfer to other duties not involving direct contact with children. They asked for full details, which I was not free to give them. I phoned Caskey eventually and asked him to get clearance from his superiors to speak more frankly, and to meet the others in my office at ten o'clock on the Monday morning.

On the Monday morning Caskey turned up with the chief of detectives, who left nobody in any doubt about the seriousness of the police view. He said that on the basis of the evidence available, a case was being prepared and the three men would be charged on the Wednesday. When I asked him directly whether he was saying that the people at present in charge at Kincora were a threat to the boys, he replied unequivocally, 'Yes.' I asked the board officers to contemplate what the position would be should the men appear in court and the judge, having heard what the police had to say, asked who was looking after the boys while all this was going on. I also said that if action was not taken by lunchtime, the minister would be advised to issue a directive to the board. The board officers went away to consult their chairman and just after one they phoned to say that the men had been suspended.

Pandora's box having been opened, cases started to fall out of the trees. There were allegations of abuse at Bawnmore, a Northern Board home which I had visited and been very impressed with. There Doug Smyth showed firm leadership and dealt with the situation without any prompting. Another example came from Rubane, a voluntary home in the Ards Peninsula run by the de la Salle Brothers. This Jimmy Wilde and I had visited; I had had an uneasy feeling about it because of the tendency to lock doors and the absence of a woman's touch – but nothing more than that.

The Rubane case emerged when a social worker heard some former Rubane boys at a hostel taunting one of their fellows as a cissy and linking him with a particular member of staff. In an example of competent work, she talked to the boy privately and got his story, of fondling and caressing by a brother of the order. This she reported to the board, who told the DHSS. It may have been the new climate, or it may just have been coincidence, but the Eastern Board was much quicker off the mark in reporting trouble in a voluntary home than in one of its own. As it turned out later, it had been aware for years of periodic complaints about Kincora and serious allegations against members of the Kincora staff which it had never told the department about.

I went to see Bishop Philbin, the chairman of the board of governors at Rubane, and told him of our concerns. The Eastern Board had already communicated officially with their secretary. I told the bishop that particularly in the light of the Kincora case it was important that the boy's allegations should be properly investigated and there should be no attempt to cover things up. I also told him of the experience of the board in relation to Kincora and I suggested that there should be at least a precautionary suspension. He was joined by Monsignor Mullally, his main adviser in these matters, and they promised to think about things and let me know.

I was a bit disappointed at what appeared to be a lack of response. Late that evening, however, the monsignor phoned me to say that the bishop had summoned the brother concerned, had told him to

270

remove himself from the home and to stay at a monastery in Belfast until sent for. Meanwhile they had made arrangements for the management of the home and the supervision of the boys.

I thanked God for hierarchy and firm government. There was no codding about with grievance procedures or natural justice or terms and conditions of employment. The welfare of the children came first.

I began to despair of the health of the child care system. I wondered whether we should have a wider inquiry into the role and utility of residential homes and whether we should not close them all and try finding some better way of providing for children who needed care. I still have my doubts.

All this had progressed while I had been away from the department. The three men involved in the Kincora scandal had been charged, convicted and sentenced to terms of imprisonment, as had a voluntary worker at Bawnmore. There had been questions in Parliament and allegations of involvement by the security forces and of widespread pandering and procurement to senior figures in the Northern Ireland Office. To fend off all this parliamentary interest, Prior had promised to hold a public inquiry when the criminal proceedings had been disposed of. Now came the time to deliver. He was being pressed to do so by the NIO, who would not, however, promote an inquiry under the 1922 Tribunals of Inquiry Act on the grounds that the issues were not far-reaching or of national importance. The NIO discovered a power in the 1972 Health and Social Services Order for the DHSS to order an inquiry, and this became the favoured vehicle.

It was vain for us to point out that the only matters that could be included in such an inquiry were those involving the powers and functions of the department and the operational responsibility of the boards as its agents. This was not what the media or the politicians were interested in. They wanted to know whether there had been a cover-up, whether the security forces had been involved, whether there were political ramifications. None of these matters could be dealt with adequately, if at all, by a DHSS inquiry, there would be cries of foul, and allegations of a further cover-up, no one would be satisfied, and we would have spent a million pounds on lawyers' fees that would have been better spent improving our services for

271

children. We thought too, after the court cases, that there was nothing significant left to find, and we were concerned at the damage that would be done to the child care service in the search for scape-goats, in social work being put on trial, and in individual workers becoming afraid to show the care and affection that the children really needed.

There was too much of a head of steam. Prior felt that he was com-mitted by his earlier statements and he was being pushed by the NIO which had nothing to lose in it. There was a ray of hope when it turned out that Robert Lowry would not release a Northern Ireland judge for the inquiry, and we began to think that it might not happen until Prior turned up with a Recorder of Norfolk, Judge Hughes, who was willing to act. We had to find him two assessors and a staff. I managed to persuade Paddy Patterson, who had just retired as chief officer of the Belfast Education and Library Board, to act by telling him that it would all be over in a couple of months. The other assessor was Paddy Whalley, just retired as director of social services in a London borough.

There had been an earlier attempt at an inquiry in 1982 headed by Stephen McGonagle, who had just retired as Ombudsman, with assessors Olive Scott, Professor of Social Administration at Keele, and Stanley Worrall, former headmaster of Methodist College. It had col-lapsed after a couple of days when the police refused to give an assurance that their investigations had finished and that there would be no more prosecutions.

By the time the inquiry opened in 1984, I was permanent secretary and first on the stand to explain the department's role and respon-sibilities. The inquiry was a harrowing experience for all concerned (except the lawyers for whom it was a lucrative cash crop). It lasted for months, and in the end turned up very little that was not already known. To the fury of the press it did not address any of the allega-tions about the security or wider ramifications and the cries of cover-up were renewed (as we had argued they would be). The main effect, apart from the cost, and the bonus to the legal profession, was to destroy the morale of child care workers and to make them terrified to show any affection to children, or to get into what might be regarded as compromising positions. As a result, children who had been starved of affection, and who needed a kind word or gesture more than anything else, did not get either; relationships became very stilted and artificial, and social workers, as a profession, felt themselves stigmatised and under attack.

One outcome that did surprise me was the failure of the board to take disciplinary action, except at the level of the lowliest of the three men who had been convicted, imprisoned, and lost their jobs and pensions. Nobody else in senior management was held to be in any way responsible, there were no resignations, no expressions of concern, no disciplinary proceedings.

One of the saddest stories that emerged from the inquiry involved not Kincora at all, but Bawnmore. A little boy of twelve from the Shankill Road, who was in Bawnmore, was an outstanding footballer who was selected to play for Belfast scouts against Dublin scouts. He came back from the match in Dublin to show the cup to his friends in Bawnmore, for whom he had bought presents. He had also bought presents for the housemother and father and for his own father. By some aberration, the present for his father was a statue of the Blessed Virgin. When he gave it to his father on his first home visit to the Shankill Road, his father took the effigy out to the backyard and methodically pulverised it with a hammer. The boy was shattered no less than the statue. He was consoled by the scoutmaster, an architect in the public service, who comforted and then seduced him. Years later, the boy was brought to give evidence to the inquiry, handcuffed to a policeman, from Magilligan prison where he was serving a sentence for rape and aggravated assault. I wondered how society could ever repair the damage it had done to that child while he was in its care. A similar case in Rubane, in which traveller children had been molested, made me wonder at the justification for a system of care that exposed children to greater moral danger and exploitation than if they had been left to scavenge on a rubbish tip.

I read every deposition that was made in relation to the cases. I read the transcript of every day's proceedings at the inquiry. I tried to find out as much as I could about the affair, and I think I know as much about it as anybody, except Detective Caskey – who, oddly enough, I thought, was not called to give evidence at the inquiry.

I have to say that I never found any evidence to sustain the wilder rumours or the allegations of widespread procurement or pandering or the involvement of senior community or political personages. I think some of these may have arisen from the coincidence of two sets of circumstances. One was the existence of a homosexual ring in Belfast that the police were investigating, and that irritated them, and the other was Kincora. The common factor was William McGrath.

In my view there were four elements to the Kincora affair. There was, first, undoubted abuse and exploitation of young boys by people who had been appointed and paid to take care of them. There was also gross bad management, mainly by the Belfast Corporation, which had been responsible for the home until 1973, a lack of adequate supervision, and failure, over a number of years, to respond to storm signals which had been raised on more than one occasion. Then there was a bitter internecine struggle between rival loyalist paramilitary groups, Tara and the UDA, and finally there was a British Army dirty tricks campaign to smear the DUP leader Ian Paisley by suggesting that some of his close followers were homosexual. I often thought that it was a case of nature imitating art: they told lies, and some of them turned out to be true.

A social worker colleague who had been working in Belfast at the time told me a story about the appointment of a deputy housemaster at Kincora. The selection board was chaired by a redoubtable lady of strong unionist convictions. There was one outstandingly suitable candidate who, unfortunately from the point of view of the panel and the hiring policy of the Belfast Corporation at the time, turned out to be a Catholic. Looking for a pretext to disqualify him, the chairperson scrutinised the small print of his application and discovered that he sometimes moonlighted on a Saturday afternoon as a clerk in a bookmaker's office. She brought this to the attention of the panel, who rapidly agreed that such a man would be a grave moral danger to the boys. So they appointed William McGrath instead.

One compensation for all this in returning to the DHSS was the new minister, Chris Patten, probably the best I ever worked with, with a Rolls-Royce mind, great political astuteness, and a very open and friendly manner. He sent before him a copy of his book *The Tory Case* which was an exposition of Disraeli's Toryism rather than Thatcher's. He was clearly uncomfortable with some of the more extreme expressions of Thatcherism, and he and Prior along with Nick Scott were a buffer against ideology. They were strong enough to follow their own course and we were ready enough to argue

274

that Northern Ireland was a special case and that maybe it would be sensible to wait and see how some of the changes worked in England before embracing them uncritically. It is a pity that some of the later ministers, eager to earn brownie points in the rush to catch the lady's eye, were not so resolute.

Once, when Chris Patten had gone on holiday to Brittany late in August 1985, there was a cabinet reshuffle. This used, traditionally, to take place at the beginning of July, when Parliament rose. Margaret Thatcher changed the date to late August, in order, so she said, not to spoil the holidays of her ministers. She probably ended up by spoiling them even more. Who could enjoy a month at the seaside with the threat of the sack or the hope of preferment hanging over them? At this stage, Patten was on the bottom rung of the ministerial ladder, parliamentary private secretary, having been held back unfairly for some considerable time because of Mrs Thatcher's antipathy to his perceived (and perceptible) wetness, and having watched lesser men who were his contemporaries outstrip him. He was hoping for an overdue and well-earned promotion to minister of state. The main cabinet changes took place, and the first round of junior ministerial posts was announced, and still no mention of Patten. His private secretary came in to me to say that Downing Street had rung several times trying to get in touch with the minister. After giving them the number of his holiday home the private secretary had tried to get through himself without success. I then suggested that he do what we would have done had the minister been in Cornwall, or west Cork: phone the local police and ask them to call round with a message to phone me. He did so, and half an hour later, Chris Patten was on the line. It appeared that he was in an annexe to a main residence and the phone had not been switched through. He had heard the cabinet changes on the radio, and the junior ministerial posts, with growing disappointment as he waited for the telephone to ring. I told him his boss was growing increasingly impatient and that he had better respond rapidly. When he did so, he got a rather chilly reception, but a promotion too. It was apparently the very last moment. So a glittering political career might have foundered.

I thought Mrs Thatcher was an awful person. She did great things, in the short term, for the British economy and for the public service. But she defeated inflation only at the cost of high unemployment, and, perhaps more serious, she left behind her the social legacy of a more divided and more selfish society, higher levels of crime, a retreat from the Franciscan values she parroted on her arrival, and a general grubbiness, meanness and lack of imagination.

Margaret Thatcher also personalised politics and policies to an unprecedented degree. The party of less government produced the most centralised system ever with health policies, education curricula and the level of local spending decided at the centre, local authorities emasculated and rate-capped, and matters such as the pay of individual civil servants requiring to be referred to the prime minister. The degree of personalisation was seen in her attitude to Europe and in her stance on the hunger strikes which became a battle of wills between Mrs Thatcher and the hunger strikers.

I first met Margaret Thatcher in 1975 during the Constitutional Convention when she visited as leader of the opposition, and before the image makers really got at her. The smile was less plastic, the hair less sculpted, the clothes more shapeless and the accent less deliberate. She was a dowdy, colourless woman with a handbag, standing in the middle of a roomful of men. She was not as dogmatic as she later turned out to be, but she seemed only to be interested in security and what she had seen with the army in south Armagh, and not at all with social conditions or politics. My fellow adviser to the Constitutional Convention John Oliver, in his courtly way, rushed to get her a chair from another room. She sat down on it with ill grace, surrounded by standing men, and she soon stood up again.

I met her a couple of times as prime minister and increasingly I found it unbearable to stay in a room with her. I usually circulated on the receiving line in order to avoid being presented.

Just before I retired from the DHSS in 1987, I got a phone call from Stormont Castle asking me to be at my desk at 9.30 the following morning to receive an important communication with a very high security classification. I was there on time, and was rung up by a cloak-and-dagger person from the Castle to tell me to present myself in Sir Kenneth Bloomfield's office at 10 a.m., whence I would be taken to a destination, he could not say where, to meet a person, he could not say whom. When I asked him what time the prime minister would arrive at, there was an explosion at the other end of the phone, and a strangulated voice said, 'Good God! How did you know that?' I told him the full programme was on the front page of the *News Letter*.

When I got to the Castle the other permanent secretaries were there, and after a period of desultory conversation we were pushed into two police cars and driven at high speed in cavalcade around the back streets of east Belfast until we arrived, appropriately enough, at the Castlereagh Holding Centre, notorious for Red Cross and Amnesty International reports, and allegations by almost every terrorist on trial of ill-treatment of suspects while under interrogation by police there. I felt like an about-to-be-deposed member of the Politburo being driven past Lenin's tomb for the last time on his way to the Lubyanka jail. There was another long wait until the prime minister was helicoptered into the yard outside. She rushed into the room, asked three questions which she answered herself, and then departed, fortified by the rightness of the views with which she had arrived. Prompted by Robert Andrew, the permanent under-secretary, whom she obviously despised (which made him a decent man by definition), to say something about the performance of the health service, I began to make the point that the health services represented a meeting point in a divided society where people worked together in harmony and with a sense of common purpose. 'Yes,' she snapped. 'And then they go home and vote for Sinn Féin.' And marched off.

Patten was followed by Richard Needham, who became the longest-serving minister in the NIO. He had not assumed his title as Sixth Earl of Kilmorey, but his family links with Newry and Mourne gave him a sense of belonging and a great commitment to Northern Ireland. He could be flashy and volatile and did not have the intellectual horsepower of Patten, but he had an acute political nose, he was a shrewd negotiator, and his heart was in all the right places.

The DHSS was really a great conglomerate. There were three main groups of businesses: health and personal social services, operated through the boards as agents, the social welfare system, paying out benefits on direct drive through a network of local offices in every sizeable town, and an odd ragbag of functions which sat oddly with the rest of the department, and included liquor licensing legislation, betting, gaming and lotteries legislation, the Registrar-General responsible for registration of deaths, marriages and births, and for the

Census of Population. Between them they were responsible for half of all Northern Ireland public expenditure; the health service was by far the largest employer in Northern Ireland.

The DHSS was a fascinating job. There was, first, the size of the management task, which was made easy by the quality of the people who were there or whom I was able to attract in on promotion. There was a great sense of identification with the department and its tasks. There was a feeling that its staff were there to help people, expressed in Norman Dugdale's phrase, 'the caring department'. This was particularly true in the social security division, both at the local office level, where staff met the public in all its moods and demands, and in the slogging, humdrum work of the great processing factories of the central benefits units.

At this time the health service was heading for crisis. The National Health Service is, I believe, one of the great social artefacts, a noble vision sustained for the best part of four decades: that no one should be ill because they could not afford care, that no one should fear sickness because they had not the means to pay for it, that no one should fear the onset of old age because of the fear of disability and the workhouse. Norman Dugdale had grown up with the system and helped to build it, as had most people in the department. He defined it as the right care in the right place at the right time – free at the point of delivery. There was never any reference to cost. The same attitude permeated the whole service: we were doing a noble thing, we were doing it well, the demand was endless, we would have to meet it, the money would have to be found. I remember when I joined the department first, in the mid-seventies, being sent out to talk to a seminar of senior health service managers. It was the chore given to the latest arrival, but I took it seriously and did a bit of work on it. I told them about comparative health costs in a range of developed countries, how the affordability of health care was increasingly being questioned in all such countries and how fundamental questions were being asked about the system. These senior people laughed, looking on me as an innocent who had strayed into their game. There had always been enough money for health care, they said. There had been scares in the past and talk of cuts. There had been previous cries of 'Wolf!', but in the end the money had always been there.

There were two main concerns in the health service: to sharpen up management and to help people to live within their budgets. As to the first, I was more concerned to give people time to settle down than to shake them up yet again. At a political level there was a constant obsession with NHS reorganisation. Somehow, it was felt, if the structure could be got right, all else would follow. This ignored the fact that they were the same people all the time who had got to be persuaded to deliver. All this was extremely upsetting to staff: no sooner had they begun to accept one change than somebody would throw all the bits in the air and ask them to start all over again.

17

HARD CHOICES

T HE MAIN CHALLENGE TO THE HEALTH care system was how to cope with an ever-increasing demand with resources that were constrained if not actually reducing. These problems were not confined to Northern Ireland, they were worldwide in the developed countries. Health care systems were under pressure of demand for two main reasons, technological and demographic. The technological pressure was that modern medicine was able to do more and more things that had only been dreamed of a generation before. New equipment, new techniques, new diagnostic tests, new drugs, new diseases even were being discovered, to say nothing of spare parts surgery. Most of them were extremely expensive. To quote one example: by the miracle of microsurgery it was possible in many cases to reattach a limb severed in a farm or factory accident. Formerly there would have been a fairly routine surgical procedure, amputation, and the one-off fitting of a prosthesis: relatively simple – and inexpensive. The new technique involved teams of highly skilled and dedicated people working for hours to rejoin severed veins, muscles and nerve ends, it involved protracted physiotherapy and rehabilitation, and could boast a high degree of success. That was a very satisfactory outcome for the patient – but at a cost.

Advances in medicine were having a double effect; in extending the range of possible treatments and in reducing the time people needed to stay in hospital. The possibilities of noninvasive surgery and the potential for day surgery were just beginning to be recognised, and would slash the need for hospital beds. Apart from which, Northern Ireland, like Scotland and the Republic, was oversupplied with acute hospital beds, the legacy of a pattern of small hospitals, most of them dating from the nineteenth century. There was also a historic (at least since the 1950s) overexpenditure on health in Northern Ireland compared with England. Given a UK mean of 100, Northern Ireland expenditure per head ran at 125–130 compared to an English level of 94. In one way it was unfair to compare Northern Ireland with England as a unit, since that figure was skewed by the prosperous South-east. It would have been more reasonable to compare it with an area like the North-east with a similar population profile, and similar levels of poverty and unemployment. You could also, of course, argue that the health services in England were under-funded, and that we did not need to descend to their level. Although I was prepared to argue resolutely for Northern Ireland's need for a higher level of expenditure, and while some premium was un-doubtedly justified, it was hard to sustain an argument for an expen-diture 25–30 per cent above the mean. We used to pursue a circular argument in our attempts to satisfy the Treasury. Why is the level of prescribing higher in Northern Ireland? Because there is more ill health. How do you know there is more ill health in Northern Ireland? Because of the higher level of prescribing! Allowing for social conditions and poverty, I could, without much difficulty, argue for expenditure in Northern Ireland on health services that would be 9 or 10 per cent above the mean. Arguing remoteness and the need to sustain expensive specialisms for a population of 1.5 million could earn Northern Ireland another couple of percentage points, but after that the sums became very difficult indeed.

A more basic question, of course, was whether the National Health Service as a whole was adequately funded and properly managed. The answer on both counts is, I think, no.

So it was necessary to nudge the system in three directions at once: towards prevention, towards long-term care of the elderly and chronic sick, and towards the more efficient use of hospital beds. I took the view that we were in a transitional stage, that new tech-nology and the application of developments in computerisation and information technology would profoundly change the practice of medicine. It seemed to me quite possible that diagnosis could become decentralised as treatment, especially highly specialised treatment, concentrated on one or two sites. I thought the Northern Ireland hospitals could be run as a single system with the Belfast hospitals supplying regional specialisms and acting as intensive care wards while diagnosis, pre-treatment, recovery and day surgery could increasingly be dealt with at the local hospital. It was clear too that a need did not exist for more than one major trauma centre, that in an emergency the important thing was to get the patient to the right hospital as quickly as possible. This postulated the need for a greatly improved ambulance service which would get to the scene quickly, ensure that the patient was stabilised in care, and would get him to the right hospital quickly.

If you wanted to be really heroic about it you could have argued that one large hospital could serve a population of 1.5 million; compared with other countries and given the geographic compactness of Northern Ireland and improvements in the ambulance service, nobody would be too far away from the service. Modern medicine and surgery required dedicated and experienced teams of people, and these, and their attendant equipment, required a constant throughput of cases, not only for economic running, but to maintain the level of skill and competence. This the smaller hospitals could not provide. On the other hand, at any time fewer than 10 per cent of the population required hospital care, and probably less than 10 per cent of those required the services of a high-tech hospital. So there was a tension, as there always will be, between ease of access and the level of specialisation. Local hospitals were all too often a sort of virility symbol for a small town and a useful vehicle for local politicians to drive round on (but not to be sick in) without thinking too much of the real needs of the local population not only for local services but also for the really complex and expensive treatments.

The question was, of course, who was to make these decisions. Health economics was a new discipline anywhere, and almost unheard of in Northern Ireland. In the end I believe that what the US health economist Calabresi called 'tragic choices' need to be made, and by doctors rather than by economists. For this reason I engaged in a lengthy dialogue with the doctors on the basis of medical ethics, arguing that the use of scarce resources was an ethical issue too which could not be shuffled off to the accountant or the administrator; that money wasted on unnecessary treatment for patient A deprived patient B of the treatment he or she required; and that in electing to treat either, the doctor made a decision with ethical consequences that required to be faced. If the doctors did not do it, somebody else would do it for them, and they would not like the outcome. Neither would such an outcome necessarily benefit the health service or the general public.

This, in a sense, is what has happened. The accountants have taken over at the expense of the doctors. And while some of the changes in the health service, including the realisation that it was not sinful to keep to a budget, were long overdue, health is not a commodity, patients are more than customers, and there is a component of care and compassion that cannot be measured, and that, because it is invaluable, cannot be priced. Moreover, it is important to recognise that, despite its failings, the NHS was the envy of most developed countries. By the main indicators of health – life expectancy, infant and child mortality – the UK was better than a lot of countries that spent considerably more of their resources on health care. All this was achieved at an expenditure of 5.6 per cent of gross domestic product (GDP). It is ironic that at a time when other countries are looking to the NHS as a model for controlling expenditure on health, Britain, with ostensibly the same aims and in pursuit of free-market ideology, should be heading in quite the opposite direction. In particular, it seems perverse to attempt to import from the United States the market-led approach to health that has brought their expenditure to 12.5 per cent of GDP with the promise of rising to 15 per cent by the end of the century, which has produced an unstoppable spiral of health costs, which has promoted self-serving and defensive medicine, and which has provided a very poor service indeed to the lowest quartile of the population. Just when Britain is intent on embracing uncritically the untested glories of the health maintenance organisation and the purchaser/provider split, the USA, faced with a crisis in health care, has been groping towards something that might in the end bear an uncanny resemblance to the NHS.

Whatever about the rest of the UK, Northern Ireland in recent years has embraced these new departures rather too enthusiastically. There was an opportunity to allow these theoretical and not very well worked out proposals to be tested in England before implementing them in Northern Ireland. Apart from which, the new approach is essentially about running hospitals more efficiently, and not about health. Northern Ireland had a unique model integrating health and social services which was worthy of preservation if not development. But the result of change has been fragmentation rather than universality, a concentration on conditions amenable to correction or cure, and a weakening of services for the chronically ill, for the elderly, for the mentally ill and for the mentally handicapped. So you get the large psychiatric hospitals run down (as they should have been) without the facilities being provided in the community for those who need support and care. Care in the community is not a cheap option – but it is being used as such – to get the patient off the hospital balance sheet and into the oblivion of the 'community': the hard-pressed family, the dosshouse or the gutter.

The worst feature of the past few years has been their effect on the morale of people working in the health services. What they needed badly was a period of consolidation, a period in which to absorb the changes in medical practice and in patient needs and demands, a time to digest the organisational changes that these required, a time to absorb a new culture, a time to adapt, to develop and to draw on the strength of a long tradition of care. Instead they saw change piled on arbitrary change, all the old landmarks removed at the same time, new ones put up and also removed, lack of purpose, lack of direction, abandonment of a common purpose for individual and group self-interest, and widespread demoralisation as staff feared what additional threats the morrow might bring.

During my own time at the DHSS, the distribution of hospital beds was at once the most technically difficult and the most political of the policy decisions that had to be taken. On the one hand the system was gridlocked by the historic pattern of small local hospitals and by the expense and long lead-in time required to provide a new hospital, and on the other it was threatened by the fluidity imposed by new demands, new techniques, and population growth and movement.

The lead-in time required for new hospitals is well exemplified by the Belfast City Hospital tower block. This was conceived in the 1950s, planned in the 1960s, built in the 1970s, and opened in the 1980s. It was out of date before the concrete was poured, and was probably not needed in the first place – the outcome of rivalry in the early days of the health service between the Royal Victoria Hospital, the main regional centre, and the old Workhouse hospital, which felt itself the poor relation of the Royal and needed to assert itself. By the time it was built, half a mile away from the RVH, the population of the inner city had all but vanished. The addiction to the workhouse site meant building upwards, expensively in the middle of a working hospital. A move to Musgrave Park would have had the merit of being near the new areas of population growth and permitting a low-rise building. Apart from which, the tower block was the trendy architectural thing at the time, and Northern Ireland, in the high tide of O'Neillism, had to have one of these too, along with Divis Flats, a motorway or two, a new city and a new university. Then it had to be designed by Northern Ireland architects whose previous experience had been local authority housing and schools and for whom this was a quantum leap. It was designed, furthermore, before the oil crises of the 1970s, in the belief that oil was something which oozed out of the sands past the noses of unsuspecting Bedouin. The building was fully air-conditioned and fully oil-fired. Added to that, the building work took place during the worst troubles of the 1970s, workers were shot on site or *en route*, work stopped through intimidation, and there were huge additional costs in security and in inducements to get the workers to turn up at all. As if this were not enough, progress was halted to allow an additional two storeys to be planned and erected after the original steelwork had been erected. This was done at the behest of the University Grants Committee which required lecture rooms and other student facilities to be 'embedded' in the building, despite the fact that the main medical school teaching block was less than 200 yards away. This had the effect of letting every subcontractor off the hook, so that time penalties could not be imposed, apart from which most of the delays were occasioned by the clients' failure to make up their minds about details and by changes in requirements as new consultants arrived with different needs and expectations, and the practice of medicine changed. In the later stages, plans had to be revised substantially, and expensively, as a result of disasters elsewhere. The fires at Maysfield Leisure Centre and at the Hillsborough football stadium, in Sheffield, caused huge extra expenditure as fire precautions requirements were revised. The final blow was the discovery, during the commissioning period, that the building was taking in damp at certain vital spots.

I remember doing a sum on the back of an envelope which convinced me that the hospital would be so expensive to run in terms of heating and staffing costs, without actually being necessary, that it would be cheaper to turn the key in the lock and walk away at that stage without opening it. This of course was not the sort of decision that politicians could take. I lived in the vain hope that some benighted bomber would take the view that the tower was an economic target, or a symbol of oppression and deal with it in that way – but no such luck. In the event, a building that it had been estimated in the 1960s would cost £7 million finished off at £74 million and gave me a couple of trying days at the Public Accounts Committee at Westminster explaining why.

As I saw it, the job of the permanent secretary was to create the environment in which the staff teams could work, to secure the resources in public expenditure and manpower to enable them to do so, and to provide liaison with ministers and with the political process.

This meant that a good deal of my work was done outside the department. The bit that I enjoyed most was the Policy Co-ordinating Committee, the PCC – a group composed of the Northern Ireland permanent secretaries and a deputy secretary from the NIO chaired by the Head of the Northern Ireland Civil Service. This group generally met weekly and considered broad policy issues that crossed departmental boundaries. It was a group of interesting, committed people, all of whom worked very hard, in which there were some outstanding figures.

Ewart Bell was the first Head of the Northern Ireland Civil Service, the NICS, to make his mark fully in the NIO. He introduced a businesslike approach to the work of the PCC, he encouraged it to address issues, and he took more of a leadership role than any of his predecessors. He was also the first Head of the NICS to be recognised as second secretary in the NIO, which gave him both a role that ranged more widely than Northern Ireland departmental responsibilities, and access to the Whitehall permanent secretary network.

The intellectual giants were Quigley and Bloomfield, either of whom might have become head of the service. Both were scholars at heart, both were widely read men whose interests ranged far beyond any departmental responsibilities, and each was a personality in his own right. Both were entertaining and witty speakers, although Ken had the lighter touch. George Quigley had the most total command of a subject of anybody I know. With a good degree in medieval history, he had come up through the old Ministry of Labour and then the DHSS and he had almost singlehandedly hewn out the industrial relations policies and machinery that had served Northern Ireland well for years. He had been in the forefront of developing policy and legislation on fair employment and equal opportunities, and he had set up the Department of Manpower Services. He had been released to prepare a report on developing the Northern Ireland economy in which his carefully nurtured and seminally Keynesian judgements fell on the stony ground of latter-day monetarist theory. He had a spell in charge of industrial development in the heady days of DeLorean, and he was now in charge of Finance. This gave him a scope, which he embraced, of ranging widely over the whole field of social and economic policy.

Ken Bloomfield, also a historian, had had less departmental exposure, but he had been central to the political process in Northern Ireland for three decades, as deputy secretary to the cabinet in Stormont days, and as secretary to the power-sharing Executive. He had subsequently been head of the Department of Economic Development and of the Department of the Environment.

The great thing I found about the PCC was the sense of collegiality and the openness of discussions. You knew where people were from, and that was part of the value. You knew, for example, that Jimmy Young, a patriarchal figure who had held sway in Agriculture for years, was strongly unionist from a rural farming background in Tyrone, and was very well in tune with the hopes and aspirations of the Protestant small farmers. That was an important voice, needing to be heard. Nevertheless I never saw him look at an issue in political terms and other than rationally and independently. I don't remember a discussion at the PCC at which I was not happy to take part, or which was determined by political or sectarian considerations.

Even the discussions on the 1985 Anglo-Irish Agreement fell into that category. I used to get hints from time to time from Chris Patten who would remark that 'the Sherpas had been over to Dublin again'. One day at a meeting in London, Nick Scott told me that they were worried whether Mrs T. would buy it, whether Douglas had been able to sell it to her, or whether Enoch Powell would get in there first (or the ghost of Airey Neave), or whether in the end Robert Armstrong would manage it. When we were told officially about it in the PCC by Ken Bloomfield at a late stage, I had no sense of any strong reaction. There were differing ideas about the practicality of what was being proposed, and varying degrees of scepticism about the likelihood of it bringing an end to violence. As I remember, the strong arguments advanced officially to support the agreement were the need to improve the international standing of the United Kingdom with the United States and the European partners by appearing to do something, to end the alienation and disaffection of the Catholic community, and to strengthen the SDLP as the voice of constitutional nationalism against Sinn Féin, and to end the violence by withdrawing support from the IRA by involving the Irish government in the process, both to close off a bolthole to the South and to legitimise the actions of the police in the North. These were generally seen as desirable objectives and I am conscious of no spirit of animosity to them, or any desire on anyone's part to resign, or to do anything to make the system unworkable. There were worries, which we all shared, about unionist reaction, but it was felt that they had made gains too by the agreement, in the recognition by the Irish government of the constitutional position and the principle of consent.

The second main function of the PCC was to act as an advisory panel for senior appointments to posts at assistant secretary level and above. This took up a great deal of time and was done with painstaking care. I had reservations about methodology and outcome, but I never had any doubts about the fair-mindedness of those engaged in the process. I never saw any attempt deliberately to disadvantage any person or group, or any evidence that religion or background were in any way a factor. Indeed, I can be categorical and say that they were not. A big problem at this time was a lack of Catholics and women among the groups from which promotees were drawn. I would have preferred some more radical approach to broadening the field by drawing on the wider public service, or by opening up recruitment at different levels to public competition. However, this would have meant taking on the civil service unions which, while vocal about equal opportunities for everybody else, were not particularly receptive to programmes that would reduce promotion prospects for their own members.

I believe that it is important that the public service in a place like Northern Ireland should be as broadly based as possible, and that the debate inside the system at the policy-making level should be in tune with what is going on outside; all voices should be heard and a wide range of views should be articulated, or at least recognised. This argument is strengthened by what happened in the UK civil service in the wake of Mrs Thatcher and fifteen years of unbroken Tory rule. This had the result of negating the beneficial effects of periodic changes of government which had reinvigorated the system and enabled the civil service to maintain that it could serve governments of any political complexion. The fact that even some senior people knew nothing but a Tory administration created a danger that the UK civil service would replicate the position of Stormont under the unionists. This danger was exacerbated by Mrs T.'s determination to appoint only those who met the 'one of us' test. One came across excellent people in Whitehall whose promotion had been blocked in this way.

All of which raises important questions about the relationships between senior officers and ministers. No one would argue that civil servants should not work under the direction of a minister, or that the bureaucracy, an unelected and unrepresentative body, should have the power to frustrate the wishes of an elected government. On the other hand, they should be more than eunuchs unquestioningly carrying out the instructions of the government of the day (a role that becomes even more questionable if the government of the day is the government of yesterday and of tomorrow too). It is difficult to express this in terms of constitutional law and theory: there is not, in fact, a neat dividing line between policy and executive action, roles and relationships are rarely clear-cut, and much depends on the personal chemistry of the participants. I would argue that the permanent officials are an important element in the system of checks and balances that is inherent in democratic politics. The framers of the Constitution of the United States were explicit about this, and the system of checks and balances and the dispersal of power is better developed there. In this spirit, I believe that, although unstated, the true role of the senior civil servant is to exercise a challenge function, to have the courage to remind the emperor that he has no clothes.

One of the difficulties of the British system is the lack of any court of appeal, the lack of any means of ventilating professional worries, perhaps even the lack of any well-developed code of professional ethics for civil servants. Clive Ponting, not otherwise the most charming of people, found this out when he had concerns about the *Belgrano* affair and took his problem to an opposition MP, Tam Dalyell. The subsequent advice of Robin Butler, permanent secretary to the Treasury and the senior UK civil servant, that a civil servant in these circumstances should share his worries with his permanent secretary was limp to the point of inefficacy. My own preference would be for something like the 'three wise men' system which comes into play in hospitals in cases where professionals have serious doubts about the competence of a colleague. On this model, there could be a few designated Privy Councillors, senior statesmen or judges from different parties who could be asked to adjudicate on such matters in private.

Another aspect of the permanent secretary job was developing relationships with colleagues in Dublin. This would involve a general get-together over a couple of days in which a group of people drawn from both services would discuss matters of common concern under the aegis of the Public Service Training Council of the Institute of Public Administration. These were largely related to management: an exchange of views on how the public business might be handled, on the impact of new technology, on problems of economic development, or health or unemployment, which were common to both jurisdictions. Those present did not get involved in political matters and there was no attendance by politicians. They were, however, an important means of getting to know colleagues who shared a similar range of responsibilities and concerns. They were valuable for us, too, because of the generally wider experience the Dublin civil servants had of international organisations and the European Community, and the better insights they had, because of the direct access they had as officials of a member state, on the possibilities of drawing information and assistance from Europe on a wide range of practical issues.

I was struck in these encounters by the quality of the Irish public service, by the added dimension given by their access to Europe and the United Nations, and by the confidence engendered in having been involved during the Irish presidency of the EC in chairing or servicing a wide range of EC committees and subcommittees. On the other hand they were, at this time, much more segmented by departmental divisions than we were, and slightly less likely to take action without specific ministerial sanction.

Health was a particularly good example of an issue that transcended departmental boundaries and of the value of a body like the PCC which could take a wider view. While we were beavering away in the DHSS at hospitals and health care, the factors that really determined the health status of the population lay elsewhere – in heredity, in the environment, in personal behaviour, and in economic conditions. For this reason, it was important to have a concerted approach to tackling the problems. Because housing was an important factor in public health, I was happy to support the prioritisation of housing expenditure above health care for a number of years. And because health was so clearly related to economic status, it was more important to tackle poverty than to build hospitals. Environmental matters were only beginning to be appreciated at this time: it is significant that the medical officer from the DHSS who was advising the Department of Agriculture on the impact of Chernobyl did not think to inform his own permanent secretary until he asked for information, and was in any case more concerned with the presence of a load of timber in the docks and with the effects on sheep than with public concern about radiation borne on the winds and in rain. It was in these cross-departmental cases that tensions between government policies and objectives appeared. Every year, before the budget, the secretary of state for Northern Ireland would receive two submissions, one from the DHSS strongly advising him, in the interests of health, to urge the Chancellor of the Exchequer to increase excise duties on tobacco, and the other, from Commerce, strongly advising him, in the interests of employment in cigarette factories, to urge the Chancellor to do nothing of the sort. Similarly, it was difficult to get wholehearted support for a campaign to reduce cholesterol levels in the diet in a country where agriculture and especially dairy farming and beef production were the backbone of the rural economy. In this regard, the EC's Common Agricultural Policy was a disaster in more ways than one: it subsidised the production of high-fat products with its butter and beef mountains and it fortified the Northern Ireland farmer in a high-input-cost, high-productivity form of agriculture which was more vulnerable than any other to the new appreciation of organically produced food and the new care for what went into the food chain. A signal opportunity was lost in the 1970s and 1980s to re-create a food industry in Northern Ireland based on cleanliness and purity and the lack of additives and chemical fertilisers, an industry that would be labour-intensive in an area of high unemployment and that would be more firmly based on the natural products of the area with as much value added locally as possible.

Another vexing issue was Sellafield. There was concern at what appeared to be a relatively high incidence of cancer along a stretch of the County Down coast. We were anxious to mount a small epidemiological study, in order to allay public concern, based on an anaylsis of death certificates in the district council area. In the event, the incidence of cancer was so low that the results were of no statistical significance and no useful conclusions could be drawn. One observation suggested that there was more radiation occurring naturally in the soil, or from a granite gatepost, than was likely to be blown across the Irish Sea. Nevertheless, public worry remained unresolved. What was noticeable was the vicious resistance of Whitehall departments (led by the Department of Energy) to any suggestion that there should be even the most modest sort of inquiry, or that any doubts at all should be thrown on the operation of Sellafield. Only the intervention of Chris Patten as minister enabled us to carry our study through.

Another case where health became highly political was in relation to AIDS, which was seen, in the West at least, as a disease associated with lifestyle: with casual sex, with a lack of moral standards, and particularly with male homosexual promiscuity or with intravenous injection of drugs by addicts. All of which had been 'legitimate targets' for the Pecksniffian morality of Thatcher's Britain, which made it very hard to develop a constituency in which the dangers to public health could be discussed rationally, never mind one in which they could be countered.

That they were at all was the work, almost singlehandedly, of Donald Acheson as the UK's Chief Medical Officer. One of the first appointments to that post from a university department of public health rather than from within the system, he was a persistent man of independent mind and great moral courage. Mrs Thatcher was most difficult when a public information campaign was designed to warn the public in very specific terms of the danger of certain forms of sexual activity. Her refusal to allow it to be broadcast on the grounds that it amounted to an obscene publication delayed the programme for almost a year, resulting in God knows how many additional cases in the interim. Generally, it was only on the hint of what would happen if AIDS transferred to the heterosexual transmission scale that the penny began to drop.

My work at the DHSS brought other interests too. Oddly enough, as I have mentioned, the department was responsible for legislation dealing with liquor licensing and betting and gambling, as well as hare coursing and greyhound racing. When Chris Patten came to the department, he declared a wish to see the reform of liquor licensing laws and the control of betting and lotteries. The two subjects were linked in an odd way. Both had been on the long finger for a long time: liquor licensing since the mid-seventies and betting and gaming for almost as long. Now both had a security significance since paramilitaries on both sides were thought to be extracting large sums of money from illegal (and now legal, in some cases) drinking clubs and from levies on gaming machines in places of entertainment. The police were very anxious to be given additional powers to control the business and to squeeze the flow and funds to illegal organisations. This was the first sign of an increased sophistication on the part of illegal organisations: at one level there was a mafia-type operation, at another a complex system to launder money, provide employment for unemployed gunmen and support for the families. It was a time when the authorities were beginning to realise that a good accountant was more likely to frustrate the terrorists than additional armaments. After all, Al Capone had been finally brought to book for tax evasion rather than for mass murder. In order to push ahead with both the liquor licensing and the gambling programmes we set up a task force headed by the amazing Zelma Davies. Zelma was a most unusual civil servant. She looked the epitome of the puritan maid. She was honest, hard-working, no-nonsense, and possessed of unassailable integrity. She turned out to have had childhood experience of dog racing, and she took her duties so seriously that she brought her team around to bingo halls, race meetings and coursing matches the better to understand what they were being asked to legislate for.

I got more involved in liquor licensing which was more political, with the licensed trade pressing for Sunday opening and the Protestant churches pressing for a more restricitive regime. I suggested to Richard Needham, who had by this time replaced Patten as minister, that he deal with the clerics while I received the representations of the trade. I took some satisfaction from being able to tell one irate trader, who was complaining that nobody in the department knew what the business was about, that I had often bottled a hogshead of stout before going to school in the morning, and that I was the only person there who had bottled from the wood. In one sense the legislation was closing the stable door: the early proposals contained in the Blackburn Report of the mid-seventies had been designed to control pubs. Now pubs were not the problem, in fact you could not give pubs away, and the trade had passed to licensed clubs and to off-licences and carry-outs where young people could buy cider and wine in bulk and drink in the park. In one way I would have liked to see the liberalisation going further, in making pubs into centres for family entertainment and allowing food to be served to children.

In the end, we managed to legislate for Sunday opening without outcry or controversy and the police were given a lever on the activities of clubs, who now had to file financial returns.

In July 1987, I had to retire. The age of retirement in the civil services had been reduced to sixty and I was forced to go. I would have liked a couple more years to complete the changes I had initiated and to carry through the redirection of the health service. In retrospect too, I would have liked to withstand the rush to follow experiments in England which were to throw the service into disarray over the next couple of years; and I would have liked to hold together the team of young and committed people I had built up. Neither was I willing or able just to stop. I had four children at university or near it at the time, and another beginning grammar school. I was active and full of energy with no desire to go into retirement. I was considering an offer to join a consultancy practice which wished to expand its activities on a European basis in health service management, when I was recommended by my colleagues for the post of Ombudsman which was just then falling vacant. This was a great honour, and it also indicated to me that I was not yet ready to leave the public sector entirely, that there was an interesting job to be done, and that I should have a go at it.

The greatest danger I faced in the health service was in eating my way out of it. A succession of convivial colleagues and professional groups insisted on dining me out, which was very pleasurable and much appreciated. Some events gave me particular pleasure. The first was when Joan and I were invited to a private house in Belfast to find a gathering of people from voluntary community groups from all over Northern Ireland and from all religious and political backgrounds. They thanked me for having made the administration accessible to them, for having been ready to listen, and to help where I could. Another special event was when Liam St John Devlin, the chairman of a review body on departmental administration in the Republic, assembled a group of my friends in the public service there and asked me down to dine with them. The third was when Richard Needham, my last minister, invited all the ministers I had worked directly with in health and social services to a dinner at his house. The fourth was when the secretary of state, Tom King, allowed me to invite my friends and valued colleagues to a dinner which he hosted at Hillsborough. I suppose, in the manner of diplomatic and bureaucratic memoirs, I should be able to set down the menus and list the wines, but the people and the conversation were much more interesting.

I was happy to hand the department over to Alan Elliot, a classicist (an Instonian, indeed), who had been a good colleague in many hard battles over the years, a protégé of Norman Dugdale and Ronnie Green who would maintain the apostolic succession that had been so briefly interrupted.

To be an Ombudsman was something else.

18
OMBUDSMAN

STRICTLY SPEAKING THERE WAS NO SUCH thing as an ombudsman in Northern Ireland. I was appointed to hold two offices with the cumbersome titles of Northern Ireland Parliamentary Commissioner for Administration and Northern Ireland Commissioner for Complaints. As a rough rule of thumb, wearing the first hat, I received complaints through members of Parliament about the actions of Northern Ireland government departments (but not the Northern Ireland Office), while in the other role I investigated complaints received directly from members of the public against local authorities, health boards, and most of the publicly funded agencies in Northern Ireland.

I was anxious to promote the use of the term 'Ombudsman' which had by now come into common parlance, and gained international currency. I was also anxious to promote the idea of the office as a single entity, and to increase our accessibility. So we became the Office of the Ombudsman. At first it was 'The Parliamentary Commissioner for Administration – the Ombudsman'. Gradually, the typeface changed, the 'Ombudsman' became bigger and bigger and the official title smaller and smaller until it disappeared altogether except on the frontispiece of the official report to Parliament. We worked towards producing a composite report, which seemed to go down quite well. I also thought it anomalous that the office should rely for legal advice on the government legal service whose members, though excellent in every way, were nevertheless also the people who advised the departments we were dealing with. I therefore decided to appoint as my legal advisers a local firm of solicitors with an interest in administrative law and a good track record on human rights.

My main concern was to make the office even more accessible and more readily understood. To this end I began to conduct a series of visits to country towns where I held clinics. I would put a notice in the local paper saying that the Ombudsman would be in the public library or other such meeting place on a certain date, and inviting people who had problems with a public authority to come along. On the previous evening I would hold a reception to meet local councillors, representatives of government offices, officials of public boards and representatives from voluntary organisations. There I would explain the nature and scope of the office. I encouraged them to think about how they delivered services and about the expectation of the citizens that they would be treated fairly, with civility and a reasonable standard of service. This was before the days of the Citizen's Charter, but my office was heading in the same direction. We wanted to make the office less inspectorial, less threatening to the local official, and to stress a common interest in a better standard of administration and a common purpose to achieve it. My thesis was that any body dealing with the public, if it was worth a damn, should be able to sort out the problems of its own consumers. I cited the customer services department of Marks and Spencer as an ideal. I looked forward to the time when a main function of the Ombudsman would be to carry out a systems audit on the internal complaints procedures of the larger organisations. This was, in a way, the application of a preventive health philosophy to public administration. If we could be assured of the continued good health and performance of the administrative system, the Ombudsman would have worked himself out of a job.

An important element of these visits was the access they gave to the local papers and to local radio programmes, both of which are important means of communicating with large numbers of people in Northern Ireland. In most cases advice on the spot was helpful, and obviated a more formal complaint, or a phone call to a local office would break the logjam.

We also began a freephone and a freepost service to the

Ombudsman and maintained an open door to the office in downtown Belfast. In general these were not abused, but the open door meant that we did get our share of paranoids, oddballs, chancers and chronic complainers who would not be satisfied by any investigation, however thorough, or any adjudication, however fair-minded, that did not give them the outcome they desired. I remember one case, of a man who had been fighting with a government department for twenty years over a very small patch of land. It was very doubtful if he had any title to it, or if he had suffered any injustice, and in any case the matter should have been capable of resolution by the courts or by the lands tribunal. If the department had simply repudiated liability, or advised him to take his case to the courts, I would not have entertained the complaint. However, at one stage, a sensible under-secretary, concerned at the mountain of paper that the rood of land was generating, and the cost, set out the basis for a compromise to which the complainant had agreed in principle. Unfortunately, before the transfer of the land could be effected, this officer had retired and his successor, on legal advice, decided to repudiate the bargain. All this happened, despite the man having had a letter from a minister stating that the case was being settled. However, if the department had shifted the goal posts, they had also provided the grounds for intervention by the Ombudsman. Whether or not there had been maladministration in the original decision, there certainly had been in the way in which it was subsequently handled. I took the view that an under-secretary should be able to bind a department. If a citizen could not make a bargain in good faith with a very senior civil servant without some confidence that it would be honoured, then nobody could really do business with the government. I persuaded the permanent secretary that he should accept this view, that the land should be transferred to the complainant, that his reasonable legal and other costs (amounting to some thousands of pounds) should be paid, along with some monetary compensation for his trouble. The permanent secretary said that it would be easier for him, for accounting purposes, if there could be some consideration, however small, that the land should not be given away free. I fixed the consideration at one pound and went, with some satisfaction, to report success to the complainant. He turned it down flat. 'It's my land. Why should I pay a pound for it?' I gave him three weeks to make up his mind, but he still refused to compromise and lost everything.

Another, contrasting, case, which gave me great satisfaction, was that of a woman who had lost a ring in an operating theatre. Everybody agreed that she had gone into the theatre wearing four rings and had come out with only three. No one suggested theft, but the fourth ring was not in her or on her or under her, or anywhere in the hospital. The health authority repudiated liability and the case came to me. There were some defects in procedure which the hospital agreed to rectify. However, on the advice of their lawyers, they refused compensation on the grounds that 'the ring was at all times in the possession of and under the control of the owner'. I pointed out that the owner was a lady in her eighties who had been subjected by the hospital to a total anaesthetic, and could not reasonably be said to be in control of anything while in that state. I eventually found maladministration, and the health board agreed to compensate the lady for the loss of her ring. Later, her son telephoned me to say: 'It was not the money, but you were the first to believe my mother.'

With less time needed for run-of-the-mill cases, I was able to spend rather more time on those cases that involved some substantial issue of principle, or that broke new ground. In particular I became interested in complaints that seemed to be capable of introducing some of the concepts which were beginning to emerge from the European Court, such as subsidiarity, proportionality and legitimate expectations. There had always been the concept of reasonableness, and that any decision which was manifestly unreasonable must involve an element of maladministration. However, we had become slaves, I thought, to procedures. It seemed that so long as the rules were followed slavishly, no fault could be found with the outcome, however bizarre. The effect was, especially in fair employment and equal opportunities tribunals, that people were in effect forced to pay huge amounts in compensation for what were no more than clerical errors, while blatant injustices went uncorrected just because somebody had been smart enough to follow procedures.

I tended not to want to take a legalistic view of complaints. To my mind the Ombudsman was one fair person, in possession of the facts, making a reasonable judgement. It was not a question of trying to second-guess people, especially with the benefit of hindsight, and I tried to be aware of the pressures under which people had to work and the time available to them, sometimes, to make decisions. Very often there was no right answer and I was likely to get it wrong from time to time too. But whatever the judgement, it would be mine, I could justify it to myself, and I hoped to others. The important thing was to be consistent with oneself – although even here one was always learning, and there were cases dismissed or rejected in the early days which I would have looked at more closely later.

One interesting case involving proportionality (and several other interesting issues too) arose when a taxi-driver who was suspected of picking up passengers where he should not have done so, complained of harassment by the licensing department. The specific instance arose from a brief altercation with the officer in charge which resulted in his licence being impounded with no reason given. He took the case to court for judicial review and had his licence restored. He was not however compensated for the six weeks he had been off the road as a result and he came to me. I normally could not investigate a complaint where there was access to redress through a court or tribunal, but I had devised a rough and ready rule of thumb for myself: if the complaint involved some important principle of law, or great amounts of money, or if it turned on the conflicting evidence of witnesses, or the complainant was a great corporation with the resources to hire lawyers, then I would defer to the courts, but if it was a small case with no great problems of legal interpretation, brought by old Mrs Jones who had never been in a court in her life, and would have been terrified to do so, then I should take the complaint and investigate it.

In this case, I asked the complainant why he should not go back to the courts. He said he had been advised that to do so he would have to prove malice, which he thought he could not do. On this basis I investigated the case. It turned out to be even worse than the courts had discovered. Not only was there a complete lack of natural justice in not informing him of the reasons for the withdrawal of his licence, every time he had been served with a notice requiring repairs it had been erroneous in some way, the wrong form used or the wrong regulation quoted.

I eventually interviewed the officer who, using words of not more than one syllable, had confiscated the licence and asked him why he had done so. He said that the driver was not a fit person to hold a licence. I asked him on what he based this conclusion. He pulled out a grubby sheet of paper and pointed triumphantly to one line: 'There,' he said. 'He was rude.'

On inspection, the paper turned out to be a series of admonitions to drivers not to overcharge, not to take circuitous routes, to be helpful to passengers and not to be rude. I took some satisfaction in pointing out that the injunction, if that was what it was, concerned the treatment of passengers. There was not a word in it about being impertinent to civil servants.

I found maladministration on the grounds that it was entirely disproportionate to fine a man, in effect, an amount of several thousands of pounds (which he would have earned in the run up to Christmas) for the comparatively minor offence for speaking rudely to a civil servant.

Another concept raised the issue of legitimate expectations, which I took to mean that in its dealings with the public a department should act consistently, and a citizen, having dealt with a department in a particular mode over a period, or seeing it act in a certain way, could reasonably expect it to continue to do so until it gave notice to the contrary. Change should not take place at a whim, and the effect on people already committed to the system should be taken into account.

In this case, a farmer had submitted proposals to reclaim an area of mountain in the Mournes, and was told that he might begin the work although 'approval' was specifically reserved. When he was well into the scheme, and had spent £70,000 or £80,000, leaving a huge and unsightly gash across the mountainside, he was told that he must stop, and that approval would be withheld. I can only assume that a complaint (to my mind justified) from an influential member of the environmental lobby, or a minister or a senior official out for a Sunday drive in the Mournes, appalled by the despoliation of the countryside, had alerted headquarters to the scheme and caused panic in the department.

Not only was the farmer being prevented from finishing the work as a grant-earning scheme, but he was told that no grant would be forthcoming for work already done (for which he had employed a contractor in the belief that 75 per cent of the cost would be refunded from some European Community scheme).

I was glad that I was not required to give a view on the general utility of the programme; that was a policy area, quite outside my remit. It did seem quite mad to be paying farmers thousands of pounds to reclaim poor mountain land which would be worth a few hundred when the job was done, and which resulted in the destruction of acres of the small area of wild mountain landscape which we had. At the same time farmers on rich land in the valleys were being paid large sums to take land out of production.

The department relied on the footnote stating that its letter of acknowledgement did not constitute 'approval' although it did permit the farmer to begin work. I took the view that it was unfair to expect a citizen to enter into commitments of up to £100,000 in contracts while the department reserved up to the last minute the right to say yes or no. I established that farmers had generally regarded the letter of acceptance as approval, that bank managers were prepared to accept it as a basis for an overdraft, that the department had itself on occasion paid money directly to the banks on foot of it. I therefore concluded that it was reasonable for the farmer to expect that the department would continue to do so and entirely unreasonable for them to pull the rug out from under him. I am glad to say that the department came to this view too and paid the grant. Just as important, they amended their procedures and the letter of approval.

Another of the rewards of being Ombudsman was *ex officio* membership of the Standing Advisory Commission on Human Rights, SACHR. This body had been set up under the 1973 Constitution Act, and for a number of years it had coasted along under a succession of undistinguished chairmen, doing nothing in particular. Under the forceful chairmanship of Seamas O'Hara, however, it had now developed a cutting edge and had dedicated itself to a review of the law relating to discrimination in employment. Seamas O'Hara was a solicitor in practice in Belfast with a long record of public service, and he had long taken a constructive interest in issues of discrimination, especially in employment, and especially as they had impinged on the Catholic community. He knew the system well and he had a healthy scepticism of the ability of any bureaucratic or governmental system to reform itself without constant prodding.

The SACHR Report on fair employment was, conceptually at least, strongly influenced by the advocacy of Chris McCrudden, an outstanding lawyer, of a more forward-looking model which would move far beyond redressing individual wrongs and towards a more complex and intrusive concept of equality of opportunity. In this analysis, the group became more important than the individual; there was, by implication, a particular preferred distribution of jobs between groups, and increasingly, equality of opportunity would be measured by equality of outcome.

The report was an important catalytic document in changing public perceptions of the nature of the problem, in conveying a sense of urgency, and in helping government to develop and refine policies to meet the need, notably expressed in the 1989 Fair Employment Act. The report recommended, as a general principle, that the reduction of inequality in employment should be a main aim of government policy. But the report recognised that the task of reducing inequality went far beyond legislation and involved economic planning, the distribution of public services, the location of industry, housing, education and social policy. There was too a recognition of the fact that indirect discrimination could be more pervasive, more damaging and much more difficult to detect and eliminate than direct discrimination against an individual.

The SACHR Report recognised that legislation on its own was not enough and that a wide range of policies and programmes had an influence in reducing discrimination, or in fortifying it. For this reason, and in order to be able to measure whether the complex mix of policies was working, the commission recommended that the government should set itself a target of reducing the differential between Catholic and Protestant unemployment rates from 2.5 to 1 to 1.5 to 1 over five years. This recommendation was not accepted by the secretary of state.

Indeed the fate of this particular recommendation underlies much of the tension that exists between government and advisory bodies – even those it sets up itself under statute. I had been as guilty as anybody else when on the other side of the fence, particularly in relation to the recommendations of the Assembly in the mid-1980s. There is a tendency to select those recommendations that support the line that policy already dictates, or along which government wishes to progress. Recommendations which do not fit in with the departmental view of things are quietly ignored.

The SACHR Report came at a most opportune time for government. The 1981 census had highlighted the employment imbalance between the two communities and several subsequent reviews had reinforced the message of inequality. There was a growing concern at the electoral rise of Sinn Féin and the increase in what was imprecisely called the 'alienation' in Catholic areas, especially in Belfast, where there was endemically high unemployment. 'Alienation' was generally a misnomer for political disaffection rather than a denial of government in the classic sense. Catholics were not anomic or apathetic or uninterested in government – quite the reverse – it was just that they did not like the Thatcherite government they had and rejected its policies as being oppressive, divisive and socially unjust. As well as that there was an increasing overseas interest in Northern Ireland affairs, heightened in the USA by the campaign for the MacBride Principles on fair employment which was beginning to affect inward investment by making Northern Ireland a less attractive place for companies seeking to set up the factories which would provide jobs. So there was a need for a policy, government was receptive, and the SACHR Report was a welcome explication and endorsement of the policies which government was on the whole ready to accept.

SACHR was interested in a lot of other issues which government was less enthusiastic in responding to. Any human rights body would have to be concerned at the encroachment on individual liberties that arose in the security system in Northern Ireland, and at the continual invocation of the public interest and national security to prevent these being thoroughly investigated. In a situation of civil conflict the problem is how to preserve the greatest extent of due process when ruthless men and women who do not play by the rules are trying to pull the edifice down and the state is trying to protect itself. The difficulty is that the public conscience becomes callused, that standards are incrementally lowered, that temporary measures become permanent, that the abnormal becomes the norm. In Northern Ireland this progression had manifested itself in extreme form in internment, but more insidiously, and more dangerously, in the suspension of trial by jury, in the use of questionable methods of interrogation, in unduly long periods of detention and remand, in the use of the law of conspiracy and in an increasing lack of openness with which these procedures were carried out. Time and again the commission made recommendations on the treatment of prisoners and the handling of people under interrogation. One case in point was the authorities' consistent refusal to record on video police interrogations of suspects. This would not only ensure that the police complied with prescribed standards of behaviour, but it would also obviate challenges on the admissibility of statements obtained under interrogation, it would protect the majority of police from the misdeeds of a few, it would avoid the collapse of trials as cases were thrown out by judges, and it would help to preserve respect for the law and the police. Sadly, few of these recommendations in the security field were accepted. It was as if human rights were all right where they were least needed to protect the individual, but security was a matter for the big boys who were not to be bothered with trivialities.

The work of the Ombudsman was not all serious. One day I received a letter in Irish from a man who complained that the education authorities would not answer him when he wrote to them in Irish. He was, I think, surprised when I replied in Irish, although I did take the precaution of attaching the English version too so that other people in the office could deal with the file. I was able to establish that government departments had a policy, when someone wrote to them in Irish, of having the letter translated and the matter dealt with and a reply sent in English. Which I suppose, at the time, was better than ignoring it, as the education board had done. The substance of the complaint also intrigued me. The complainant had withdrawn his children from school so that he could educate them at home through the medium of Irish. He was not asking for the earth – simply for some help with equipment and some of the time of a French *assistant* to help with conversation. The board seemed not to have been too assiduous in pursuing its statutory duty to see that the children were being adequately educated at home, and it seemed to have taken fright at the political and linguistic challenges of the case. I was able to establish the average amount the board would spend on providing the services requested to children in their own schools, and in the end it agreed to make the complainant a grant which would enable him to buy them for himself.

As the case dragged on, with lengthy discussions with the board and bilingual correspondence with the complainant (who became so enthused by his treatment that he began to bombard me with complaints against other bodies too), we all took a great interest in the progress of the children. I was very pleased to read, years later, that each in turn had gone to university and secured a first-class honours degree.

A sadder note was hearing that Ken Bloomfield had been the subject of a murderous bombing attack which had destroyed his house and nearly killed himself and his family. This was all the more galling given his efforts to promote fair employment in the civil service and the drive he had spearheaded to direct policies and resources at the social and economic problems of west Belfast. What was even more disappointing was the tardiness of the public service unions in condemning this attack, as if attacks on senior management were any less an affront to the dignity of labour and the right to work than attacks on junior officers. Ken, it is true, was attacked as a symbol rather than as a person. It was probably the tone of the IRA statement claiming responsibility, and the remarks of Sinn Féin spokesmen which finally tipped the balance in convincing ministers that such people should not be allowed to be heard on television or radio.

Prior to this, Douglas Hurd as secretary of state had introduced a system of politically vetting bodies that applied for grant support from public funds. I regarded this vetting as wrong, impolitic and counterproductive. Of course no one would fault the state for trying to stem the flow of funds to those involved in violence, but it went further than that. The fear was, in government circles, that paramilitary organisations would infiltrate ostensibly peaceful voluntary bodies and use them as a front, or would use them to build up their own image as disinterested helpers of the community.

There was a difficult judgement to be made at times between the official paranoia that every voluntary organisation in Northern Ireland was a front for some God-awful paramilitary organisation, and the fact that some of them actually were. But the effect of vetting was to make it extremely hard in some of the more deprived areas for voluntary bodies to get support. If they were in any way representative of the local community they were almost bound to have somebody on the committee who was, or had been, or might be thought to be an active paramilitary, or even to support them politically. This had the effect of penalising the people who most needed help, on both sides, of alienating them even further and driving them into the hands of the paramilitaries. It also resulted in an unholy alliance between church and state, since government departments, anxious for social improvement, preferred to work through the politically safer channels of the Catholic parish. This had the effect of stultifying community development, of building leadership through priests (often excellent and energetic men) who then moved on leaving a leadership vacuum, and of reinforcing the power of a paternalistic and male-dominated parochial system.

In the end, enjoyable and all as the job was, I resigned before completing my term as Ombudsman. I would have had to go on age grounds in the summer of 1992, and in fact I resigned at the end of January 1991. The job was interesting and I still had a lot of energy and zest, but government policy on privatisation and contracting-out was removing more and more functions from the jurisdiction of the Ombudsman. The changes in social security legislation were deliberately framed to do so. On the other hand, the development of the Citizen's Charter pre-empted much of the work, and newly devolved executive functions seemed to have been designed to have their own complaints mechanisms. Apart from which, the office was in good shape and ticking over, there was a good deal less pressure, and I was beginning to get the itch to move on to other things. I had become increasingly involved in the voluntary work of the Ireland Fund, a charitable foundation to raise money in the USA and other countries and to use it to assist community groups and others working for peace and reconciliation in Ireland. I had become chairman of the Advisory Committee which involved a good deal of travel. I was also acting as director of Leadership Challenge, a developmental programme for senior managers in the public service. I was anxious to be free to write, to comment on public affairs, to take part in discussions and seminars, and to travel. I was also becoming increasingly interested in business, and Tony O'Reilly had been pressing me for years to join the board of Independent Newspapers as a voice from Northern Ireland and from the public sector. I eventually agreed to do so at the end of 1990.

I stayed on until the end of 1991 in order to induct my successor,

Jill McIvor, the first female Ombudsman, to clear up outstanding cases, and to prepare and publish the annual reports for 1990. I was not, however, to be allowed completely to leave the public service. After I had announced my retirement, I was approached by the Department of the Environment, which had the responsibility for arranging for a review of local government electoral boundaries in time for an election to be held in 1993. It was having difficulty in finding someone who would be broadly acceptable to the political parties, and the job needed to be done in a hurry. The financial arrangements they proposed were incidentally much more favourable than those I had enjoyed as Ombudsman in not involving the curtailment of my civil service pension.

I was not anxious to get involved in another commitment, but this was not entirely full-time, within limits I could regulate it to suit myself and, while not totally free, I would have more liberty than in my previous posts to do other things. So I acquired, temporarily at least, the sonorous title of Local Government Electoral Boundary Commissioner for Northern Ireland. Eventually, after two years' work involving hearings and meetings with local councillors in which I became familiar with every district council boundary and every townland in Northern Ireland, I made my report in December 1993. This was accepted by the secretary of state and endorsed by Parliament. At which stage I was what the administrative law textbooks describe as *functus officii*, out of a job. I laid down my staff of office and retired from the public service.

19
MINORITY VERDICT

*It is a settled rule with me to make the most of my
actual situation and not to refuse to do a proper thing
because there is something else more proper which
I am not able to do.*
EDMUND BURKE

'VERDICT' HAS A RING OF FINALITY ABOUT IT, perhaps ill-suited to an interim statement, a working hypothesis, a memoir, an echo, a collection of disconnected if not quite idle thoughts. A verdict should be judgemental, or at least judicious, as if after weighing all the evidence a conclusion had been drawn by some dispassionate, objective independent authority. Such is not the case here. What I have done is to bring some episodes, and some individuals, up briefly to the surface of memory, before letting them slide back into history. Other people will have remembered differently, others will have viewed the same unfolding events from a different perspective and drawn quite different inferences from them. An actor is not usually a very reliable judge of the play in which he himself has a role, although an extra in some of the crowd scenes may be thought to have rather more time than those who play the leading parts to reflect on the discontinuities in the plot, or the performance of the principal players, or the backstage gossip.

As to 'minority', I suppose most readers will assume that I am speaking as a member of 'the Minority' in Northern Ireland, traditionally so classified, a Roman Catholic from a nationalistic background holding more or less nationalist views. This is undoubtedly true, but it is not the whole truth. In the first place I do not presume to speak for anybody but myself. Furthermore, I have always resisted being lumped into a group that is expected, both by outsiders and insiders, to behave in a predictable way. I have generally thought of myself, for a variety of reasons, as a minority within a minority within a minority. My contention would be that there is more than one minority group. Indeed, I would argue, the more minorities the better, in order to provide the richness of variety, and to avoid the oppressiveness of an overweening and unchallenged majority. I would argue too that a person can inhabit more than one cultural space at the same time, can move in more than one cultural milieu. It is the overlapping of these existences, the possibility of providing linkages through the interaction of personalities, the ability to use and comprehend a variety of accents and idiom, that provide the real excitement in life.

Nevertheless, in a deeply divided society like Northern Ireland, identification with one or other group is almost unavoidable. Membership is by attribution rather than by conviction. One group lays a claim, the other by reflex rejects. There is little room for the maverick, the less than totally committed. And yet peace in the long run may depend on the mavericks, or at least on those who, while not forgetting or denigrating the values of the group, are prepared to assert some degree of individuality in order to reach out to other individuals as fellow human beings. The great danger in these situations is stereotyping, the treating of opponents as cardboard cut-out figures, as robots programmed to perform in a certain way, or as puppets controlled by some ignorant if not malevolent Gepetto. The even greater hazard is of living up to one's own stereotype, of acting as the tribe, or as the force of tradition, or as simple bigotry would have one behave.

For we are all, in these situations, bigots to a greater or lesser degree. This is the classic case of the need to remove the beam from one's own eye before attempting to purge the mote in another's. The person in Northern Ireland who claims to be free from prejudice is either a saint, of whom there are few, or simply self-deluding. The best we can do is to recognise our disability, and to begin to peel away, like the skins of an onion, layer after layer of acquired prejudice. And, like peeling an onion, this can be a tearful process. At least it helps to clear the mind of cant and to begin to see other people as individuals with the same range of needs, with the same desires and fears and dreams, as ourselves rather than as part of a menacing and oppressive majority or as a subversive and threatening minority.

310

Minorities, too, tend to close in on themselves in self-defence, and to develop a culture of victimhood in which they become relatively secure and perversely happy. I was lucky enough to be brought up in a society, in Lecale, where people had been accustomed to mix and even (up to *Ne Temere*) to intermarry for generations, where there was some degree of openness and communication, where people had the self-confidence to deal with their neighbours, and where the duties and responsibilities of hospitality and neighbourliness transcended religious divisions. It was only when we came to deal with the organs of the state and of local government that there was any sense of needing to know one's place. My disposition therefore was not to regard myself as excluded from anything, not to disbar myself, but to join in.

There was a slogan in Belfast in the 1950s, designed to encourage people to participate in a lottery: 'If you're not in, you can't win.' The lottery was run to provide funds for the Mater Infirmorum Hospital, founded and run by the Sisters of Mercy, which had been excluded from the newly formed National Health Service and from financial support from public funds. Indeed the Mater might serve as a paradigm for the Catholic community in Northern Ireland at the time. One of the main teaching hospitals in Belfast, with decades of devoted service to all sections of the community behind it, it was not able to join the new Northern Ireland Hospitals Service on terms that would preserve its character and ethos as a Catholic teaching hospital. Despite the fact that comparable hospitals in Britain had been accommodated without difficulty in the new arrangements, the Stormont government refused to make the adjustments that would allow the Mater to come in. This was interpreted as an act of hostility to the Catholic community and of deliberate exclusion. The hospital issue became a *cause célèbre* in the relationship between the government and the Catholic community until it was resolved on acceptable terms as almost the last act of the unionist administration in 1972. In the meantime the Mater survived through the voluntary support of the community (and by no means only from Catholics), a system within the system – and also outside the system – serving, as did other hospitals, the whole community without regard to creed or class.

It was, of course, more complex than that, because alongside the official exclusion there were the networks on personal and professional lines and through the medical school that maintained the hospital as a functioning (if unpaid) part of the health care system in Belfast. Which prompts the reflection that individuality and personal friendships will breach most divisions if they are given the opportunity to develop, and underlines the importance of creating as many bridges as possible on a variety of functional and non-threatening levels across the rifts in a divided society.

My own instinct has been to join in things, to work from the inside to change systems or attitudes rather than to lecture or hector from without, not to take umbrage or to imagine slights or rebuffs, and to try to effect change incrementally over time. My experience is that most people respond to a personal approach, to an honest effort to understand them and their motivation; they want to be taken on trust, and they want to appear reasonable. If you can get behind the rhetoric, remove the pressure of emotion and the drive towards uniformity, if you can get them to relax, then communication may take place, and in addition some approach to mutual understanding, if not necessarily to agreement.

Even large organisations are rarely monolithic. However regular and uniform they may look from the outside, there are generally fissures and cracks. Inside there is rarely unanimity. Organisations are run by people, and most people, thank God, are not yet automata. The greatest offences committed against human decency in the present century were committed when people allowed themselves to be persuaded, by whatever means, to subordinate themselves, their judgement and their ethical and moral standards to the interests of the state and the organisation, and to treat other people as less than human, as counters on a board, as nonpersons. The safeguard against depersonalisation is to treat people as individual human beings, to search out their individuality and their idiosyncrasy, to force them to recognise and cherish it, even against their will. I remember being struck by the experience of Brian Keenan and his fellow hostages, that for each of them there was a critical moment when the guards recognised them as fellow human beings, and they for their part recognised the essential humanity of their captors – a fleeting moment perhaps, and one from which there were numerous regressions, but dramatic in the way in which it changed the nature and quality of the relationship.

In the course of my career, I have frequently been in places or posts where there had been very few Catholics before; I was often the first Catholic to hold a particular post, generally in a minority, often of one. It is not something that I had a complex about. My upbringing had disposed me to do my best in any job I had, and I was lucky to hold posts that provided considerable intellectual stimulation and that involved both responsibility and commitment. They were interesting jobs, and I was interested in them. They also, I believe, contributed to the general good of society and to the alleviation of individual distress. I did not feel myself under any particular pressure in being a Catholic. I was, at times, conscious of the desirability of not making such a mess of things that people would confirm their stereotypes and say that Catholics could not cut it, or could not accept responsibility. I did not want to queer the pitch for succeeding generations of young Catholics in the public service. But these were private and fleeting thoughts. It was not something to brood over in the press of day-to-day activity, and while I may have had an array of chips on my shoulder, being a Catholic was not one of them. I did feel part of the Northern Ireland Catholic community, I wanted to see its members engaged as equal partners in the society and to contribute my own administrative and managerial skills and experience. For this reason, I think, I found it difficult to accept tempting offers from time to time of jobs elsewhere. I saw my role as, in a modest way, opening up society, having a foot in the door which enabled me to express concerns and aspirations that would remain unsaid, or at least unheard, if I were not there.

I came into the public service doubly or trebly from the outside, from teaching into local government, from local to central administration, and from a community that had previously been excluded from the corridors of power (or impotence). I never felt in any sense excluded. The senior civil service may be a club to which it is difficult to secure admittance, but once you are in there is a degree of collegiality that I found to be both accepting and acceptable. I never felt excluded from any business in which I might have expected to be involved. I was aware of no cabals or caucuses or sinister interest groups – and I do not believe there were such. I found that my comments on subjects and issues outside my particular frame of responsibility were both sought and welcomed. I felt at times that my main function was to represent the thoughts and dreams of the hitherto unrepresented, to provide a linkage into government for the inarticulate and the voiceless.

From that, I came to the conclusion that it was important for a public service to be as representative as possible, to give a voice to all the disparate minority groups in society, so that the debate that goes on outside is reflected inside the policy-making framework. In this way, I believe, better decisions would be taken, and people would take them better, aware both of their need and of their impact.

I am a strong believer too in a public service ethos, one that really is based on a sense of serving the public, and on honesty, integrity and fairness. I do not believe that these values can be translated into items on a balance sheet – neither can they be costed. That they are invaluable does not mean that they are valueless. To my mind, whatever good Margaret Thatcher did (and it was considerable) was badly discounted by her denigration and debasement of the idea of public service, by the sort of people she attracted into politics and administration, by her insistence on unswerving loyalty to a poorly understood ideology, by the reduction of everything to the supposed values of the marketplace, by the demand that civil servants be 'one of us'. Of course the public services should be efficient, of course management should have a proper regard to objectives and the effective use of resources, yes the public sector trade unions had become arrogant and obstructive, counterproductive and stifling of initiative, yes there had to be some form of stimulus that equated to the bottom line, the profit motive – but the answer was not to destroy the morale of a service, to throw the baby out with the bath water, to reduce all to a figure in brackets in the profit-and-loss account.

I do not, for example, believe that it is possible to treat health as a commodity, or education, and whilst it is important to get the best return possible on the available resources, this is not necessarily best achieved by consigning both to the competitive rigours of the marketplace. Indeed I do not know how what the economists call 'externalities', the benefits that services like public health, or clean air or environmental services bring to the public in general, can be expressed in terms that make them attractive to entrepreneurs who cannot gain personally and who do not have a clientele to purchase the product. There must always be a residuum of services that will not

314

be provided at all (or at least not in the risky stage of development) if not by the public sector, and there must be a range of activities that depend on a sense of service and a degree of personal commitment and loyalty that it is difficult to command on a purely materialistic agenda.

I became interested in the public service early on, partly through my father and his work. At school I was lucky to have teachers who encouraged a questioning attitude, and especially to have zany and quite mad headmaster, a de la Salle brother, who made us test every linguistic and logical theory to destruction. Catholic social teaching, at school level, was in its corporatist phase, but we were brought into contact with ideas about the labour market and the use of capital through the papal encyclicals *Rerum Novarum* and *Quadrigesimo Anno*, with the principle of subsidiarity of function and the elegant simplicities of Occam's Razor. Communism was anathema, taboo, godless Marxism was worse, and Freud was not to be mentioned in decent society. Later, at university, I had the great good fortune to be lectured in philosophy by Monsignor Arthur Ryan, a monument to the continuing failure of the Irish Church to promote intellectually distinguished and critical men to the higher levels of the episcopacy. He was a proto-European for whom the sun had risen on Christmas Day in the year 800 when Charlemagne was crowned in Cologne as Holy Roman Emperor, and set in the effete splendour of Ravenna six centuries later. He induced a way of looking at things that was European, that eschewed narrow nationalism, and that was probably forty years before its time.

In the course of my life, I have been fortunate to have worked with first-class people, with Paddy O'Keeffe in the GAA, subsequently in the civil service with people like Paddy Shea and John Oliver, John Benn and Norman Dugdale, Bob Weir, George Quigley and Ken Bloomfield, Robert Lowry in the Constitutional Convention, and later Tony O'Reilly in business and philanthropy. There have been outstanding political figures too: Brian Faulkner and Terence O'Neill, John Hume, Willie Whitelaw, Jim Prior, Chris Patten and Peter Melchett. From all of them I have learned a great deal, and all of them remained good friends and colleagues throughout my career.

I believe that learning is a lifetime occupation, as is teaching. Any manager is essentially a teacher, a communicator imparting a vision (or even only a clearer view of what lies ahead), helping people to grow and to combine to achieve a common purpose, unlocking potential and focusing energy. Any senior executive is a custodian of the values of an organisation, helping to conserve and develop, redefining, articulating anew and adapting to changed conditions the traditional verities and assumptions. It is dangerous when only one person holds the vision or when people become so morally and intellectually cowed and so subservient that only a single orthodoxy prevails. Better, I believe, to have a ferment, an interaction of ideas and a common shared vision forged out of an amalgam of personal experiences and values.

Despite the popularly accepted belief and the caricature so brilliantly captured in the television comedy series *Yes Minister*, most civil servants in my experience prefer a strong minister to a weak one. At least then you know what the policy is, you don't have to wait for it to be made up on the wing or enunciated in after-dinner speeches, you don't wonder whether it will change from day to day, or at a whim. A good minister too will deal with the policy issues and will not wish to be a managing director as well, still less will he wish to spend time in the engineroom immersed in the minutiae of day-to-day administration. He will give clear and firm direction and will let people get on with it. What you need a minister for is for direction, for political judgement, for the public presentation of the policies, to argue the departmental case in cabinet and with other ministers, and to secure the resources necessary to carry out the programmes.

I have, over the years, maintained a high regard for most of the politicians I have worked with. For one thing, they had all done something I could not do, offered themselves to the public and been elected. That gave them a legitimacy I and my colleagues could not aspire to, and which it was wise not to forget. Some of them have been brilliant, some extremely stupid, and some merely misguided, but I have met none who was not motivated by some even partial or imperfectly understood concept of the public good. It has been fashionable to denigrate Northern Ireland politicians most of all and to denigrate them for the mess that we are in, or at least for not getting us out of it. Which is to underestimate the deep-seated nature of the conflict and the intractability of deeply held values and the difficulty of securing a meeting of minds where a fundamental change in attitudes is required, and where positions are historically determined and reinforced and fortified by a race memory that recalls only the hurts received and not the wounds inflicted.

If I have a complaint about politics in Northern Ireland it is about the middle-class professional and business people who wash their hands of politics as a dirty business, who withdraw into their commercial and cultural ghettos, who play no part in public life and castigate as bunglers or pygmies those who do make the effort. They are no less bigoted or obscurantist than those they purport to despise. It is, if you like, *le trahison du moyen gens*.

Meantime, those who are elected are expected to solve one of the most difficult problems on the political agenda, one that has baffled statesmen from Gladstone on. For some years the Northern Ireland conflict has been seen as some sort of aberration, a hangover from the Hundred Years War or the sectarian squabbles of the sixteenth and seventeenth centuries. Modern societies, materialistic, rational, humanistic, did not behave in that way, whether in a market or a planned economy, whether democratic or socialist, whether of the right or the left. And then came the fiasco of former Yugoslavia, the disintegration of the Soviet Union, the rise of militant Islam, and suddenly Northern Ireland was seen to be not such an odd place after all – it was no more comfortable, perhaps, but slightly more fashionable. Indeed, one might argue that the people of Northern Ireland have made not such a bad job of containing their conflict short of the point of societal meltdown, or in maintaining a simulacrum of normal social and business life despite being apparently brought to the brink time and time again as atrocity piled on outrage and murder followed mayhem.

What more than anything is needed in Northern Ireland as a precursor to political activity is a build-up of trust. Too much energy is squandered in a search for great and complete constitutional constructs that will solve all problems at once, and for all time. At every possible occasion, negotiators tackle the most difficult and divisive issues first. They head off for the North Face of the Eiger, without first traversing the foothills of trust. They eschew the easy climbs and head for the peaks. Not surprisingly they either fall off or get stuck halfway up. There does need to be a framework of laws, a mechanism for securing and protecting human rights, some basic and minimalist agreement on where the society is heading and what the priorities should be. But after that most of what is required is a process to build trust, to throw small bridges across the rifts in a deeply divided society where fissures run from top to bottom of the class structure. It is a mistake to think of Northern Ireland as a society where sectarianism and bigotry are found only in working-class areas. Division and prejudice permeate the whole society. Conflict is endemic. The only difference is that at some levels people are less able to cope, whether by social conditioning, or by not having the means or the money to insulate themselves by residential segregation, and it is in these areas that they seek resolution by violence. What is needed in this society is not some great constitutional initiative, but thousands of small initiatives at a personal and community level that will help people to open up to each other, to overcome historical suspicion and animosity, and that promote self-respect and respect for the views of others, toleration and mutual understanding. Love thy neighbour is a hard precept, but it is not necessary to like him in order to do so. Paradoxically, the less likeable he is, the greater the merit in loving him.

During my working life, I have seen remarkable changes in society, in people's expectations and in the response to them. Employment has opened up, there is greater equality of opportunity and, ironically, fewer jobs to be shared around. There was the apathy of frozen attitudes in the sixties, the incipient *perestroika* of Terence O'Neill (a much underrated man, especially by Catholics), the heady excitement of the civil rights movement and the descent into the hell of violence and murder. I believe that the civil rights movement, and people like the McCluskeys, did more to change society in two years than anybody else in the previous fifty. I think the movement did effect real change, and would have achieved more and produced a new society at ease with itself over a decade or so. It is a big question, of course, whether those who traditionally held power or their supporters would have conceded change without themselves resorting to violence. The signs were that a substantial segment would not, despite the moral high ground being occupied by the agents and advocates of change. However, the question must remain hypothetical because of pre-emption by the men of violence, and because the issues became indelibly associated with a campaign of violence that forced those who were timidly emerging from the trenches back into the armed camps to which history had assigned them. Since then it has been mainly downhill, and the cause of mutual understanding and a real resolution of our problems has been put back by a couple of generations.

The first half-century in Northern Ireland was not so much an era of unionist misrule as the slogan writers have it, as fifty years of lost opportunities – on both sides, but mostly by the unionist majority who as the government could have shown more generosity had they not been dominated by a laager mentality, had they been less motivated by petty spite, less dominated by the most raucous and populist elements of sectarian animosity. The last twenty-five years have seen the society groping for the light, uncertainly, buffeted by events, and with much backsliding. There was, however, in all that time, or in the earlier period, no injustice, no unfairness, no degree of discrimination that was worth the sacrifice of a single life. And the conflict, which has cost three thousand, and ten times that number maimed and injured, and tens of thousands traumatised and embittered, has only driven the communities farther apart and left gaping wounds that will take generations to heal, and much sorrow to individuals and families.

During this time, I believe the public service has been the cement that has held a fissionable society together. Services were maintained, the basic life-support systems were maintained. Indeed it could be argued that it was counterproductive to maintain the illusion of normality in that it permitted extremists on both sides to indulge in terror, and permitted politicians the luxury of continuing intransigence in the knowledge that somebody somewhere would keep the wheels turning and the transfusions of money from the Treasury would not be cut off. The public service survived attacks on personnel, murder, intimidation and riot, it weathered the internal tensions caused by external events such as the hunger strikes, internment, the UWC stoppages, the fall of the Executive, the Anglo-Irish Agreement, the ebb and flow of political passions, and atrocity after atrocity that seemed destined to drive society into the arms of the ultras. And it demonstrated the ability of people in the various services to work together in harmony despite being exposed by upbringing or by kinship or residence to all the emotions, the traditional loyalties of their own communities.

I have been privileged to work with some very fine and dedicated people, not all likeable and not all liking me, some stupid, some short-sighted, some merely ignorant, but on average they were very good and the best were exceptionally talented people. What held them together and gave sense to their activities was a shared desire to improve social conditions, to lessen the effects of conflict and, if possible, to lay the foundations for a peaceful society. They did not, oddly enough, see this as a political activity, and most of them would have run a mile from politics. But the best of them did believe in the possibility of changing society for the better, in the need to be constantly trying, pushing forward, stretching the elastic as far as it would go. Most of them would fall into the ranks of Koestler's 'active fraternity of pessimists whose chief aim will be to create oases in the interregnum desert'.

> will not aim at immediately radical solutions because they know this cannot be achieved in the hollow of the historical wave; they will not brandish the surgeon's knife at the social body, because they know their own instruments are polluted. They will watch with open eyes and without sectarian blinkers for the first sign of the new horizontal movement; when it comes they will assist at its birth, but if it does not come in their lifetime, they will not despair.

There is a fond and commonly held belief to which people cling in modern society that every problem must have a solution, and that there must be somebody somewhere who has the answer if only we could find him. A belief that failure to resolve a problem reflects badly on the participants, who must be stupid or irrational or just bloody-minded, or on the government who should be able to manage things better, or on the politicians who could do it if they only had the will, or on the churches or on the media or on outside agitators or whatever. There are, however, problems that are not amenable to solution. These are the conflicts that Richard Rose characterised as being about the 'great unbargainables' of religion and allegiance. In most such cases it is a matter of conflict management rather than of conflict resolution. It is not enough to say, 'The problem is, there's no solution.' The challenge of politics and to government is to help people to live with the conflict, to massage it for long enough for time and other circumstances to provide a new context which may enable the issues to be reformulated in terms in which they are perhaps resolvable.

I do not believe that there can be victories in these situations, except the victory of rationality and decency in which all can share, in which all are winners and there are no losers, and which is the opposite of a zero sum game. Oppression is not an answer, neither is assimilation. There is little point in an outcome that merely sows the dragon's teeth of truculence in a defeated and depressed minority group. In a way the Northern Ireland problem is the original endgame: there is no way by which either side can win without creating an even bigger problem. There is no point in replacing one minority with another, or of substituting for one conflict another that is even more bloody.

Northern Ireland has been characterised (by Keith Kyle) as the 'overlap of nationality', where Britishness and Irishness overlap in a series of distorting lenses and filters, or (by Harold Jackson) as the double minority problem: Catholics seeing themselves as a minority in Northern Ireland and part of a majority on the whole island, Protestants – a majority in Northern Ireland – fearful of becoming a submerged minority in a united Ireland. And so both groups exhibit simultaneously the worst traits of both categories, the arrogance and insensitivity of a majority and the insecurity and lack of self-confidence of a minority.

What this does mean is that the complexity of the situation and the *mélange* of conflicting allegiances and identities must be accommodated in whatever constitutional envelope is designed to provide a framework for government. It is unlikely to be neat and tidy, or to be found ready made in any of the textbooks. There will be anomalies and eccentricities – but if it confines the outward expression of conflict to rhetorical flourishes, then so much the better. And if the process goes on for years, then so much the better. People are more important, ultimately, than lines on a map, and lines themselves lose significance when there is free movement of labour and capital within the European Union. In a new context, perhaps political arrangements will reflect the realities of the marketplace, and will accommodate too the richness of relationships and interactions within these islands, which share not only a common language but a common legal and administrative system, and will reflect too the intermingling of peoples and traditions that have resulted in movements in both directions across the narrow sea over the centuries. The nation-state concept has outlived its usefulness. To argue that only one set of values can be contained within a single polity is to argue for Balkanisation, for the politics of Bosnia and Rwanda, for ethnic cleansing and population movements and for apartheid in a world that is turning its back on militarism and on force as an arbiter of political disputes. It is the role of politicians to help people through this transitional period by redefining concepts, by revising the language and the terminology of debate, and by adapting old values to new and changing contexts.

As I write, at long last there is a ray of hope. For the first time in a quarter of a century the guns are silent, the bombs unblasted, the streets free from riots, and from soldiers. For the first time almost, people know the value of peace. They appear also to be ahead of the politicians in their demand that peace be pursued through discussion and negotiation. It may take years to work out an accommodation, but perhaps the signs are there.

I draw from the Ulster Cycle two stories that might stand as metaphors for our predicament. In the first, from the *Táin*, Cuchulain, the epic hero, the prototype of the dour and uncompromising Ulsterman, refuses all offers of peace and rejects all compromises out of hand. When asked if there is anything that will satisfy him, he replies, 'There is, but I will not tell you what it is. When you find someone who knows what it is, I'll agree to it.'

In the other story Macha, the wife of Cruinniuc macAgnomain, lost a child in premature labour because although pregnant she was forced to enter a race against horses because, in pursuit of a stupid conflict, the men of Ulster had lost all sense of proportion, all decency and compassion, all human feeling. She cursed them so that for nine generations the men of Ulster, in their hour of greatest need, would be debilitated by the pains of childbirth. It did not happen after nine, but maybe after nine times nine generations, the pangs of Ulster are indeed coming to an end.

INDEX

Friers, Rowel, 111
Fulton Report, 234

Gaelic Athletic Association (GAA), 16, 17,
   46, 48–57, 75, 78, 79, 88, 315
   'foreign games', 56–7
   and RUC, 119–20
Gallagher, Dermot, 155
Gallagher, Reverend Eric, 102, 119
Garda Síochána, 119, 210
Gibson, Norman, 155
Gillespie, Tony, 136
Gillies, Reverend Donald, 69
Girvan, Sam, 241
Goldaber, Irving, 130
Good, Harold, 73
Goodman, Arnold, 213
Goulding, Cathal, 106
Government Information Office, 68, 105,
   111, 135
Government of Ireland Act, 144
Gowrie, Grey, 259
Greally, Andrew, 149
Green, Ronald, 61–2, 295
Greer, Evelyn, 251
Grey, Lord, 99, 100
Grey, Mike, 106
Griffiths, Hywel, 92, 133, 148

Haines, Joe, 246
Haire, Jimmy, 118
Halloran, Professor Jim, 110
Hammond, David, 67, 111
Hanna, George, 46–7
Harland and Wolff, 104, 116, 178, 185,
   206, 208, 225, 234–5
Haughton, Ron, 149
Hayes, Joan, 16, 100, 226
Hayes, Maurice
   childhood, 10–13
   university, 14–15, 17
   teaching career, 15–16
   town clerk, 18–32, 40–6, 78–9
   GAA County Board, 50–6
   environmental interests, 63–7
   public administration, 69–72
   experience of troubles, 72–5
   community relations, 76–98, 99–131
   and internment, 132–48
   dream, 149–50
   assistant secretary, 153–60
   and Executive, 161–84, 185–204
   Belfast survey, 207–9
   and Convention, 212–29
   in DMS, 230–1

in DHSS, 231, 232–5, 232–55, 265–95
   and civil defence, 252–5
   personal safety of, 253–4
   in DOCS, 256–64
   retirement, 294–5
   Ombudsman, 295, 296–308
Health and Local Government, Ministry of,
   61
Health and Social Services, Department of,
   61, 165, 170, 173–4, 190, 197, 231,
   232, 260, 262
   Hayes in, 236–55, 264, 265–95
   Kincora inquiry, 271–4
   functions of, 277–8, 291–4
Heaney, Seamus, 111
Heath, Edward, 103–4, 146, 149, 166, 175,
   176, 202
Heenan, Cardinal, 121
Henderson, Brum, 111
Henderson, Dill, 80
Hendriks, Dr, 91
Hermon, Jack, 121–2, 267–8
Hezlet, Colonel, 222–3
Higgins, Ian, 78
Hoey, Caldwell, 155
Holden, Sir David, 201
Home Affairs, Department of, 100, 135
homosexuality, 248–9, 274
housing, 23–4, 33–40, 61–2, 70, 72, 291
   effects of riots, 135–42
Housing, Department of, 165
Huey, Scott, 223
Hughes, Joe, 249–50
Hughes, Judge, 272
Hume, John, 88, 145, 315
   and power-sharing Executive, 164, 165,
      168, 171, 176–8, 182, 185, 201
   UWC strike, 192, 193–5, 200
   and Convention, 223, 225–6
hunger strikes, 256, 259–61, 276, 319
Hunt Report, 119
Hurd, Douglas, 146, 288, 306
Hurley, Michael, SJ, 97
Hutchinson, Dougie, 219

Independent Newspapers, 307
Industrial Development Board (IDB), 264
industrial relations, 232–5, 257, 261–4, 265, 287
Information, Minister for, 165
Institute for the Study of Conflict, 97
Institute of Public Administration (IPA),
   221, 290
International Fund for Ireland, 174
internment, 42, 82, 106, 112, 122–3,
   132–41, 146, 150, 202, 304–5, 319

326

Paisley, Ian, 30, 97–8, 142–3, 164, 166, 219, 225, 227, 228–9, 274
Parker, Dame Dehra, 83
Parkin, Ken, 64
Parliamentary Clerks, 220
Patten, Chris, 259, 274–5, 277, 287–8, 292, 293, 315
Patterson, Hugo, 190–1, 200
Patterson, Paddy, 272
Peacock, Dr, Bishop of Derry, 118
PEN International, 113
People's Democracy, 112–13, 114, 135
Philbin, William, Bishop of Down and Connor, 102, 116–17, 270
Pinder, John, 214
Policy Co-ordinating Committee, 240, 286–90
Ponting, Clive, 290
Powell, Enoch, 58, 225, 288
Presbyterian Church, 118, 119, 219
Prior, James, 259, 271, 274–5, 315
Prison Officers' Association, 260
Protestant and Catholic Encounter, 96
Provisional IRA, 122, 147, 166, 167, 171, 176, 202, 203, 227, 235, 246, 253, 306
  growth of, 87–8, 94, 104, 107
  internment, 136, 139
  Kingsmills, 229
Public Accounts Committee, 13, 51, 286
public administration, 69–72
Public Health Act (1878), 42
Public Record Office (NI), 229–30
Pym, Francis, 175

Quakers, 118–19
Queen's University Belfast, 14–15, 17, 71, 82, 85, 232
Quigley, George, 84, 109, 112, 169, 170, 230, 261, 286–7, 315
Quigley, Gerry, 71
Quinn, George, Bishop of Down, 118

Ramsey, Dr Michael, Archbishop of Canterbury, 29–30
Ramsey, Robert, 112, 181, 184, 195, 237
Rankin, Brian, 148
Red Cross, 134, 138
Rees, Merlyn, 176, 192, 201, 206, 207, 209, 235
  Convention, 212–29
refugees, 72–3
Reid, Max, 239
Rent Restriction Acts, 38
Rhodes, Ted, 69, 91
Robb, John, 136

Roberts, Tommy, 162–3
Robinson, Mary, 155
Rogan, Father Sean, 117
Rose, Richard, 129–30, 230, 320
Rowlands, David, 148
Royal Belfast Academical Institution, 214
Royal Ulster Constabulary (RUC), 74, 86, 121–2, 143, 203, 207, 210
  and GAA, 119–20
  and internment, 133, 134, 141
  UWC strike, 186–7
  and Kincora scandal, 267–8
Royal Victoria Hospital (Belfast), 136, 285
Rubane home, 270, 273
Runnymede Lecture, 155
Ryan, Monsignor Arthur, 315

St Malachy's College (Belfast), 14, 117, 123
St Patrick's School (Downpatrick), 12, 14
Salzburg Seminar for American Studies, 66–7, 68
Sands, Bobby, 142
Scarman Tribunal, 78
Scott, Nick, 259, 274, 288
Scott, Olive, 272
sectarianism, 23, 36–8, 44–5, 318
Sellafield, 292
Shawcross, Neil, 239
Shea, Paddy, 105, 109, 315
Shimeld, Ken, 230, 252, 257–8
Shuttleworth, Joseph E., 20
Silent Valley reservoir, 71, 137
Simms, G.O., Archbishop of Armagh, 118
Simpson, Robert, 76–7, 79, 84, 108, 111, 113
Sinn Féin, 86, 106, 277, 288, 304, 306
Slinger, Bill, 77, 79, 84, 134, 136
Smith, Howard, 108, 144, 148, 150
Smith, T. Dan, 69–70
Smith, Ted, 155
Smyth, Doug, 270
Smyth, Hugh, 225
Social Democratic and Labour Party (SDLP), 51, 71, 126, 144, 159, 162, 212, 288
  emergence of, 115, 125, 157–8
  in Assembly, 180
  and CRC, 180–1
  UWC strike, 191–2, 200
  Convention, 215, 221, 222, 223–4, 226–8
social policy, 240
Social Work Service, 266
Society of Friends, 118–19
Spence, Gusty, 268
Spender, Sir Wilfrid, 101